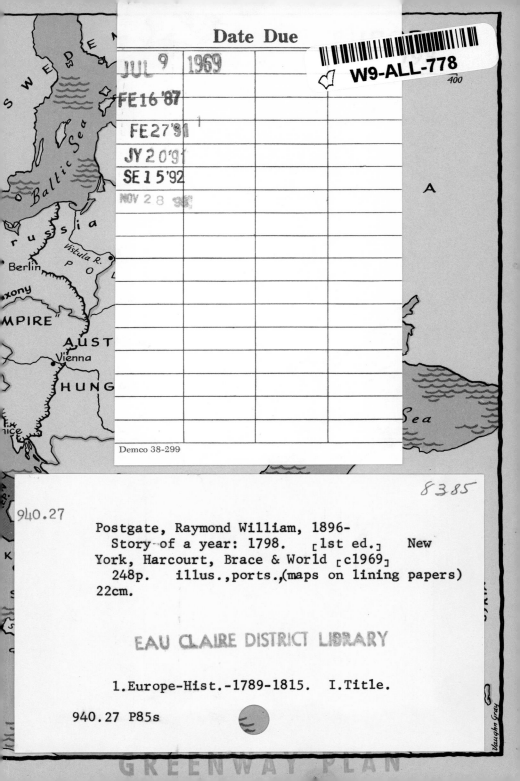

W9-ALL-778

400

8385

GREENWAY PLAN

STORY OF A YEAR:
1798

Raymond Postgate

STORY OF A YEAR:
1798

HARCOURT, BRACE & WORLD, INC.

New York

FOREWORD

This book, though complete in itself, is also a sequel to an earlier book, called *Story of a Year: 1848*. That was received very kindly but with a certain amount of perplexity. "Who wants to read about one year, anyway?" demanded a Dublin paper. That inquiry was a fair one, though coming oddly from a country so preoccupied with single years (1690, 1798, 1916, for example); and the appearance of this book is an answer to it. It is my plan to present reasonably detailed, truthful and interesting pictures of the civilized world as it was every fifty years, which will bear to the orthodox continuous history something of the relation of a painting to a moving picture. Or perhaps it would be more exact to say that I am trying to stop the film of history and study on each occasion one separate frame. At the end I may have offered up to a half-dozen of these stills, which will make a series of abrupt panoramas spanning two hundred years or more. They should have a sequence and significance. This is the second of them. Whether I complete the series depends upon my industry, the length of my life, and the forbearance of my publishers. On none of these are any promises made.

I have incorporated some passages, rewritten or altered, from the introductory part of my life of Robert Emmet written forty years ago.

R.W.P.

CONTENTS

III. *Winter*

LIST OF ILLUSTRATIONS

(*Between pages* 120 *and* 121)

The Adelphi Terrace

"A Sailor's Prayer before Battle"

Napoleon Bonaparte accepting the surrender of Malta

Interior of the Temple of Apollinopolis at Edfou

View of Rosetta

The British and French fleets at the beginning of the Battle of Aboukir

Napper Tandy

Wolfe Tone

The United Irish Patriots

Lord Edward Fitzgerald

The last full parade of the Irish Volunteers

Ferdinand, King of Naples

King Ferdinand, Sir William Hamilton, and Lady Hamilton

Roger Griswold and Matthew Lyon dueling in Congress

An assignat

Touissant L'Ouverture

WINTER AND SPRING

I

I

THE PEACE CONFERENCE
ASSEMBLES

RASTATT is a middle-sized town in southern Germany, not far from the Rhine. It lies in the northern part of the old grand duchy of Baden, and a little to the south of the right-angled corner at the northern end of French Alsace. It is a dull town, with (according to *Varta*, the German equivalent of the Michelin Guide) a "see-worthy" (*sehenswert*) castle and a church, and one good restaurant. It has no important place in history, but in the year 1798, when it had no more amenities than now (and not even the good restaurant) it very nearly became famous. Throughout the early days of that year there converged on it delegates from a large number of European powers. They might have given peace to the world, for they were supposed to draft a treaty to end a war which had involved nearly all the major powers, and shaken, in most people's opinion, the founda-

3

tions of society everywhere. One side consisted of a single power only, the French Republic. It was obviously the victorious side; only one of its many antagonists, Great Britain, was continuing to fight it. The other side consisted of a large number of different-sized states with different policies, complicated and confused, of which the most important was Austria. Great Britain was not attending the conference; some other states had separately made their peace with the French. This conference was to regularize existing arrangements and settle all outstanding questions; nothing then would be left to the victorious French (they may well have thought) but to finish off their last antagonists, the English.

The world which was represented at Rastatt—and also that part of it which was not—was very different from that of our own day. It was at once smaller and much larger. It was larger in the sense that immense time was needed to travel around it; parts indeed of the world no man could reach at all. Months were required for an Englishman to reach his most important dependency, India; weeks to reach the capital of any foreign country except France and the Lowlands. If a man averaged more than five miles an hour, he was traveling fast. It was to be twenty years before London stockbrokers could regularly make their favorite journey, the fifty miles to Brighton, in a single day. But though the world around him seemed to the man of 1798 almost limitless in its distances, nevertheless the area that was known and was of importance was quite small, and its population far less than today. With certain exceptions, to be recorded presently, the effective center of the world was Western Europe. Here there happened the events that settled the history of the world; here was civilization. The other continents lay, comparatively, in obscurity. Nothing of importance happened in them, or at least nothing was recorded; if it was recorded, it was not known.

Of Africa, the outline had been discovered, but little more. An exception was a hundred-year-old settlement of Dutch at the Cape of Good Hope, recently taken over by the British. The north coast of Africa, the modern Morocco, Algeria, Tunisia and Libya, was also fairly well known; it was called Barbary, and was occupied by Moslem pirates, nominally subject to Turkey. Everywhere else there was little but trading posts and fortresses, situated on bays or at river mouths, whose most profitable merchandise was slaves brought down from the interior by the local chiefs, often as a result of wars deliberately provoked for the purpose. Most of the African coast was claimed by the Portuguese, though they no longer had the lion's share of the trade. At the outbreak of the French Revolution there had been forty European "factories," as they were called, on the Guinea coast, the best source of slaves. Of these, 15 were Dutch, 14 British, 4 Portuguese, 4 Danish and 3 French. The annual shipments of slaves were perhaps more significant: the figures were: British, 40,000; French, 20,000; Portuguese, 10,000; Dutch, 4,000; Danish, 3,000.[1] The interior of Africa was darkness, illuminated only by thin lines of light where reckless travelers had journeyed. 1798, however, was a year of great intellectual activity, and some of the darkness seemed to be lifted. It was found possible to deduce from these journeys, and from the stories of traders, the main outlines of internal African geography. Mr. James Rennell, a Fellow of the Royal Society, summarized and co-ordinated the evidence. He laid the results, which seemed incontrovertible, in a paper before the members of the African Association.[2] The basic structure of Africa consisted (he explained) of a "vast belt of elevated land of great breadth often swelling into lofty mountains" running from east to west, starting with the mountains of Abyssinia and ending at Cape Verde. This feature was complemented by "a ridge stretching to the south through the middle of South Africa, and forming an impenetrable barrier between the two coasts." Its existence was confirmed by evidence from the Portuguese in Angola and the Congo, who had never succeeded in getting through to the Indian Ocean. Another great geographical fact could be deduced from the huge flow of waters in the rivers. "In order to produce this effect, there must necessarily be a vast hollow in the interior of Africa, between the high land of Nubia on the east and Manding on the west."

Nothing so preposterous, no vast T-shaped mountain range, no giant unknown internal lakes, were postulated in Asia; but knowledge of that continent was nevertheless very inadequate. The cen-

[1] For references see pages 232–237.

ter was known to consist mainly of a confusion of decaying but
fanatical emirates and khanates. Little was known about them;
but what was, was not extravagantly wrong. The great subconti-
nent of India was well known and thoroughly explored, it is true;
the French and English had fought each other over it for years.
There were some settlements, mainly Dutch, in what is now Indo-
nesia, and a few British convicts in Australia; Spain had a languid
control over the Philippines. The world knew, indeed, that there
was a rich and enormous empire in the Far East, but foreigners
were not allowed even to see it. China, like the small adjacent
islands of Japan, cut itself off from the world, not from fear but
from an illimitable conviction of its own superiority. This year it
was reported that the emperor Ch'ien Lung, at the age of 87, had
become paralyzed, and Chia Ch'ing (whose name means "High
Felicity") had taken his place; the Western world had no idea
what this might mean. The sole contact Europeans were allowed
with China was in a small area in the city of Canton, where they
were allowed to stay part of the year to trade with an association
formed for that purpose, called the Co-hong, but with no one else.
They had made attempts to penetrate farther; the most recent was
an embassy sent by the restless British in 1793, headed by Lord
Macartney. It had been received with apparently exquisite courtesy,[3] allowed to reach Peking, and even to see Ch'ien Lung, because it was convenient to the Emperor that an embassy bearing
tribute from barbarians should be seen to arrive. It presented
George III's letter suggesting that a British ambassador should be
accredited to the Chinese court, and received as answer an imperial mandate "bound on the back of a mandarin and conducted
by a bodyguard of sixteen other mandarins."[4] It ran, in part, as
follows:

"We have perused your memorial; the earnest terms in which it
is framed reveal a decent humility which we find commendable.
In consideration of the long journey undertaken by your envoy
We have shown him special favour, even allowing him to be introduced into Our presence. Your entreaty however that one of your
nationals should be accredited to Our Court of Heaven cannot be
entertained. . . . Even if your reverence for Our Celestial Dy-
nasty has filled you with the desire to adopt our civilization, We

must protest that our ways have no resemblance to yours and that even if your envoy were competent to acquire some rudiments of them he could not transplant them to your barbarous land. If we have commanded that your tribute offerings are to be accepted it was not because We have any interest in outlandish objects but solely in consideration for the proper spirit which prompted you to despatch men from the remote island where you live. As your envoy will have seen for himself, We are in need of nothing, We possess all things. We have expounded Our wishes and it is now your duty, King, to respect them. . . . Reverently receive our presents and note the tenderness of Our regard. A special Mandate."

With that, the curtain fell again.

Most of inland America was little more accessible than Africa. A papal bull of 1493, translated into a treaty in 1494, had divided the new round world between Spain and Portugal—Africa and most of Asia going to Portugal (plus the shoulder of Brazil because the line was drawn straight southward from the point of Greenland); all the rest of America and the far end of Asia to Spain. Spain had left the interior and greater part of South America unoccupied and even partly unexplored. Except where there were gold or silver mines, or other obvious sources of wealth, the Spanish and Portuguese settlements were on or near the coast, rarely more than fifty or a hundred miles inland, with the considerable exception of "New Spain," which is now called Mexico. The West Indian islands, immensely more valuable commercially and strategically, were thoroughly explored and exploited; they had been half a century ago the strongholds of pirates, and were still intermittently fought over by the French, the English and the Spaniards; minor contenders were the Dutch and the Danes. None of these areas, naturally, could be directly represented at Rastatt; nor were the vast and sparsely settled areas of Louisiana (the whole Mississippi basin; French) and Canada (British, but with many French-Canadian *habitants*). The only strong indigenous community was on the north Atlantic coast, from Georgia to Maine, where there was a thick belt, like the smear of a great thumbmark, which was totally different from the rest of the continent. It had no reason not to call itself "the united states of Amer-

ica," for there were no other states in America. It consisted of
thirteen states, originally the British colonies of New Hampshire,
Massachusetts Bay, Rhode Island, Connecticut, New York, New
Jersey, Pennsylvania, Delaware, Maryland, Virginia, North Carolina, South Carolina and Georgia, each of which had a settled,
prosperous and civilized English-speaking population, democrati-
cally governed by assemblies elected by the people (a word which
in this year of course did not include women or slaves), and it
was an ideological discomfort to every other government except
the French. But the discomfort was ideological only; the United
States had no wish whatever to interfere in the affairs of other
powers, nor did those powers seem likely to interfere wantonly
with them. Few Americans were even aware of the assembling of
the conference at Rastatt, and even those who were had only the
mildest interest in it.

Of those powers which were interested, the three most important were the French Republic, the Kingdom of Great Britain and
the disorganized mass usually called the German Empire and
whose head was the Austrian Emperor Leopold II. Beyond this
center, were, to the north, the Scandinavian powers, which (as
they were to do even more in later centuries) had avoided close
entanglement in the European conflict—the King of Sweden did
send a delegate but that was because he was also Duke of Pomer-
ania in east Germany. To the west were Spain and Portugal,
whose boundaries were the same as they are today, and whose
empires have already been referred to. They were rich, they had
the appearance but not the reality of strength. To the east there
were two vast and sloppy empires; their exact boundaries were
not certainly known by the Western world and, it may be, not
always even to the despots who ruled them. One was the Russian
Empire, one the Ottoman or Turkish Empire. They had long been
at enmity with each other; of recent years the Turks had usually
been defeated. They had lost the Crimea to Russia and the port of
Azov on the Black Sea in 1774, and in 1787 a great slice of what
is now the southern Ukraine, including the strong point of Ocza-
kov. Both empires had been effectively almost untouched by the
principles of the French Revolution. There had been some slight
sympathy initially in Russian noble and court circles; in Turkey

none whatever. There had been little permeation in Spain and Portugal either.

All European states outside the French sphere of influence had basically a common structure, they were hierarchical. There were at least three layers in the hierarchy. The monarch oppressed the nobles, the nobles oppressed the peasants. The differences between the countries lay in how much these oppressions were restrained, by custom or by law, and in the variations of rank and privilege recognized within the divisions. These were often of considerable complexity and, as is always the case in hierarchies, were guarded with passion. Nor was it impossible sometimes to play one rank against another; it was far from unknown even for the monarch to pose as, or even in fact to be, the aider of the lowest classes in society against the nobility. All the states, in addition, were almost completely rustic. Three-quarters of the population in Italy and Germany were rural, nineteen-twentieths in Russia. The town population, disproportionately active and important though it was, was still trivial outside France and England. In 1780 Vienna had about 200,000 inhabitants, Madrid 150,000, and the two chief cities of northern Italy, Milan and Venice, 130,000 each. At that time London had 850,000 and Paris 650,000.[5] Within them, there was far from a united population; there would be relatively small groups of rich merchants, doctors, clergymen, lawyers and large employers of labor (fifty being "large") and below them master craftsmen, small traders, journeymen, laborers, servants and apprentices—these last six groups being what was usually described as "the people," "the lower orders" or "the mob," according to the politics of the speaker.

The most easily seen variation between the states was in the amount of power retained by the aristocracy against the king. In Russia, Prussia, Denmark and Naples (controlling Sicily as well as all south Italy) the crown was almost all-powerful. The aristocracy could do as it pleased with its peasants or serfs, but it could offer no resistance to the throne; the nobles had become either the servants of the state or politically powerless. In Spain, Hungary and Sweden, on the other hand, the great landowners retained considerable powers, personally or in their assemblies;

the monarch might have to alter his policy to meet their wishes or
even to admit that whole areas (as in Spain) could be governed
by their own laws. But these liberties were of no benefit to the
"people" despite the occasional use of Whiggish and even radical
phrases by individual nobles, and the chief weakness of an aristocracy had been underlined by the recent fate of a great power in
which the nobles had had almost total control. On March 12 of
this year there died in the Russian capital, St. Petersburg, where
he had lived half a dozen melancholy years, a short man (five foot
seven inches) with a "majestic aspect" and very sharp eyes; he
had been king of Poland and grand duke of Lithuania; his name
was Stanislaus Augustus Poniatowski.[6] With him passed away, to
all appearance, the last trace of his country. The extinction of
Poland was no fault of his (he was personally a brave man) but
wholly the fault of the great landlords, whom the smaller gentry,
the *szlachta,* had followed unquestioningly. They elected the king
and controlled the Diet, in which any one of them, by what was
called the *liberum veto,* could forbid any action which displeased
him. But a multiplicity of selfishnesses was not only less tolerable
but also weaker than the single selfishness of a king; the three
greedy neighbors of Poland—Prussia, Russia and Austria—in
1772 by a first partition cut off nearly a quarter of the country
without resistance. In May 1791, taking advantage of the absence
of some of the greatest landlords, King Stanislaus in a passionate
speech which brought tears to the members' eyes, persuaded the
Diet to introduce widespread reforms, including the abolition of
the *liberum veto,* legal protection for the peasant, a splendid educational system, and a reform of the judiciary. But even then the
Diet could not bring itself to grant democracy to the people; and
there was no popular revolt when the tricked landlords called in
the Russian army and canceled the constitution. A second partition followed, reducing Poland to one-third of its old size. This
time Russia and Prussia only took part. In 1794, when the famous Kosciuszko based his government upon the freeing of the
workers in the town and the peasants in the country, there was
some stern fighting; but it was then too late. The Poles were
crushed; the third partition among the three original ravishers followed in 1796, and Poland existed no more.

The third party to this assassination (which troubled the conscience of none of them) was the ruler of Austria, Leopold II. But he was not only ruler of Austria; he was also "the Emperor"; his delegation to Rastatt was called the imperial delegation and his troops the imperial armies. He was the heir of Charlemagne, and the ruler, so far as there was one, of what had been called the Holy Roman Empire, including Germany, Austria, northern Italy and Bohemia. It was now hardly an empire at all. Leopold was not only hampered by his arrogant Hungarian magnates; the German princes, kings, electors, dukes, and bishops who were theoretically subordinate to him and still frequently paid him subsidies, were no longer subject to his orders. They acted as if they were—as the larger of them were in fact—independent.

The task of Leopold's chief delegate at Rastatt, Count von Metternich, would not have been easy even if they had been more amenable. The French delegation was arrogant and from the beginning behaved more like conquerors than negotiators. They had some reason for this. Half a dozen years earlier, their country had been torn by civil war, its navy ruined, its armies defeated, and invaders from a powerful coalition were marching on its soil. That coalition had consisted of seven powers: Britain, Spain, Portugal, Sardinia (which included Piedmont), Holland, Austria and Prussia, to whom was later added Russia. It now had ceased to exist. Spain and Prussia had withdrawn from it. Holland had been revolutionized and was now the "Batavian Republic." Portugal had ceased any activity; Russia had never begun any—in fact, the new tsar had negotiated a peace treaty, and it was the French who had not ratified it. The King of Sardinia was trapped by the French occupation of Piedmont.

Leopold had suffered worst of all. His armies had been defeated repeatedly in northern Italy by the French, led by a young general, Bonaparte, and he had lost the whole country with the small compensation of annexing the ancient Republic of Venice. He had been driven out of the Austrian Netherlands (the area which today is called Belgium), and the whole of Germany up to the banks of the Rhine was now in French hands. The chief business of the Rastatt conference, indeed, seemed likely to be arranging compensation in the rest of Germany for the electors, dukes or bishops who had lost their dominions in the west; it was likely to be complicated.

The French delegation to begin with had been headed by the same General Bonaparte, who immediately made clear his opinion of where the real power lay in the conference. The King of Sweden had sent as his representative Count Axel Fersen. This was both stupid and rude, for Count Fersen had been the intimate friend of Queen Marie Antoinette and had organized and paid for her unsuccessful flight with Louis XVI; he had himself driven the coach half the way to Varennes. But neither the King nor anyone else expected the way this insult to the French Republic would be resented. Bonaparte simply interviewed the Count and ordered him to go. He went, too; a harmless Baron de Bildt took his place. The ownership of the city of Mainz was contested; Bonaparte arranged for its occupation in a noticeably ostentatious manner "with a band of Turkish music, consisting of eighty able musicians." He had a Tree of Liberty planted there in front of a great crowd of soldiers and civilians; it is one of the oddities of history that the two citizens who delivered the correct speeches of rejoicing were named Hatry and Metternich.[7]

Bonaparte soon went home; he was needed to advise on and if possible supervise and direct the destruction of France's last enemy by a force which was beginning to assemble around Boulogne and was called the Army of England. His successors, however, were equally domineering. The fact that they did not immediately enforce their wishes on their opponents was not due to any weakness in their position, or even to their own lack of haste (they did not, to begin with at least, see any reason for hurry) but to the disorderliness of the delegations with whom they were dealing. Leopold's representatives were wholly unable to discipline or direct their nominal inferiors, and hardly any question could secure a definite answer within a reasonable time. The King of Prussia, through his delegation, was almost openly obstructive to the imperial delegates, and rallied around him the rulers of Brunswick, Hesse-Cassel, Mecklenburg, Württemberg and Zweibrücken. The Elector of Saxony (an "elector" was one of those entitled to "elect" an emperor) refused to co-operate either with Austria or with Prussia, even when rearrangements were suggested which enlarged his territories; the gossip in Rastatt was that he was interested in nothing but the education of a daughter on whom he doted, and was simply refusing to attend to business at all.[8] The aged Elector of Bavaria had just married a young Austrian archduchess, and was single-mindedly occupied in spiting the Duke of Zweibrücken, whom he disliked and who looked like being his successor.

In such a conference delay and controversy could be almost unlimited, and they were. The retrocession by the French of Kehl and Cassel, the building of bridges across the Rhine, the suppression of tolls on the Weser River, the operation of the laws on *émigrés* in the ceded areas, the freeing of navigation on the Rhine, the independence of Hamburg and Frankfurt (or their annexation)—these and many other problems were debated to exhaustion; what hopes existed of their settlement were further damaged by the unspoken but ceaselessly watchful hostility between Lutheran and Catholic princes throughout Germany.

It was not unnatural, as the months passed, that the French should begin to suspect that the other side was stalling, and had no intention of making peace at all. The former chief delegate, Bonaparte, had no doubt of this and no doubt either of who was the right man to deal with it. The Directory, the government of France, ignored him and selected two other envoys to plod along as before. He stormed in upon a meeting of the Directors; they were betraying the republic, he said, and undoing all the effects of his famous campaign in northern Italy. They must send him back to Rastatt as a plenipotentiary, or else he would send in his resignation. But the time had not come yet when generals could bully the government of the republic. "Here is a pen," replied Reubell, one of the Directors. "You need a rest." [9] Bonaparte stamped out again; afterward there were those who claimed they had heard him say, "The pear is not ripe," but this is probably only part of the Napoleonic legend.

2

THE GREAT ANTAGONISTS:
BRITAIN

THE ENGLISH are not myth-makers about themselves on the German scale, but they created and still believe a myth about themselves during the French wars, and especially about themselves in 1798. It is a myth of a confident, powerful, united nation, of whose victory there was at no time any serious doubt, led by a prime minister who was a paragon of competence, courage and eloquence. It was a myth which, in one form or another, was to serve the state again very well in the future. But the reality in 1798 was different. The outcome of the war was not certain, it was seriously doubtful. The nation was in graver danger than it had been since 1588, and the discouragement of those qualified to judge was deep. Colonel John Drinkwater, bringing in 1797 the news of a badly needed victory off Cape Saint Vincent, had met with gloom and even disbelief:

14

"Nothing but England's disgrace and downfall was foretold and talked of throughout the kingdom." [1] Lord Cornwallis, one of the most levelheaded of British generals, asked: "Torn as we are by faction, without an army, without trusting entirely to a navy whom we may not be able to pay and on whose loyalty no firm reliance can be placed, how are we to get out of this cursed war without a revolution?" Canning himself had put and answered the essential question: "If peace is to be had, we must have it. When Windham says we must not, I ask him 'Can we have war?' It is out of the question; we have not the means. We have not what is of all means the most essential—the mind." As late as July the *London Chronicle,* not an official journal indeed, but authoritative and sober, was still writing: "On a careful reperusal of the last French papers, we find that fortune continues to promote the ambitious projects and the plan of universal disorganisation which form the basis of the French system." [2] The position could be summed up quite bleakly.[3] The allies of England had vanished or been defeated, her antagonist (as in 1941) had twice her population (which was now around eight and a half million).[4] The heaven-born leader, as flatterers called him, was himself in poor condition. William Pitt was ill, his sharp nose now poking out of a swollen face; his energy seemed to have failed during the past year; he had abandoned his attempt to marry the woman of his choice (Eleanor Eden) and lost his reputation as the "restorer of the national credit." [5] Strangely enough, to us, it was this last failure which was most vocally condemned. The "fear of invasion of Ireland" had been blamed for a suppression of payments in specie in Newcastle last year; this had swiftly spread about the country, and at the end of February the Bank of England itself had suspended payments in coin. Late in October its Court of Directors had adopted an equivocally phrased resolution which passed across to Parliament the question of resuming payment; it thus, in effect, had abandoned gold. The currency (it was feared) had collapsed, money was disappearing, notes would become as valueless as French *assignats*—there was no end to the alarming prophecies.[6] Pitt attempted to counter these by a measure which seemed to some rather to show desperation—an income tax. Previous taxation, he told the Commons in a speech of great length and bitterness, had been frustrated by "shameful evasions" and "scandalous frauds"—these vague but obviously genuinely furious words recur again and again. Violent though the new impost admittedly was, he claimed in a calmer passage that it would raise ten million pounds annually (it only raised £823,286 this year, but in one year—1801—it did in fact bring in six millions[7]). Previously, his proposals had been for five shillings a bushel tax on salt, five per cent on tea sold at or over half a crown a pound, and duties of between half a guinea and two guineas on armorial bearings; the Commons debate on these trivial taxes had turned mainly upon whether the salt tax was a burden on the laboring class or not; Tierney changed the subject to the last item, which (he said) explained to him why Pitt, whom he disliked, had created such an inordinate number of peers.[8]

In one thing the myth was not false, in its account of the vehemence of the reaction of a large part of the British nation, once the danger was realized. Urgent steps were taken to protect the coast from invasion. Sir John Moore, as yet only a colonel, surveyed the defense of London; he came to the unexpected conclusion that the stretch of coast from the Thames mouth to Harwich was the most vulnerable. The country to the northeast of London was "so very much enclosed that it is supposed the enemy would penetrate only by the great roads . . . the enclosures are strong, and to observe anything you must get on top of the churches." [9] Plans were made, and in part carried out, for blockhouses in city squares, alarm bells in each street, and grenades to be stored in corner houses. The lords lieutenant of the counties were given instructions for what was later to be called a "scorched-earth" policy. Wherever a landing took place, the cattle would be driven off, mills and ovens would be dismantled, and parties of civilian pioneers would break down bridges and wreck the roads.[10] Another anticipation of the future was what were in effect "commando raids"; one on Bruges in May was particularly dramatic— though most of the landing party was captured, the locks were destroyed, the canals and basin drained dry, buildings blown up, and the movement of the invasion flotillas badly dislocated. As for money, a subscription—not a loan—opened in the City of London for defense purposes in mid-February was subscribed at the rate of £400 a minute.[11] As for men, as soon as a call was made, there was an inrush of volunteers comparable to the million Home Guards of 1941, forty thousand enrolling in London alone. "I am well aware," said Dundas, the War Secretary, "of the danger of entrusting arms to the whole population without distinction" but the risk had to be taken.[12] The volunteers' uniforms were picturesque and varied, and their armament haphazard, but their enthusiasm was intense, and their military value far from negligible.

They would, by themselves, have thwarted an essential part of the plans of the French invaders. These plans were well conceived, and had had lightning success on the Continent; they are outlined in the instructions to the general who was to invade Devon and Cornwall, which were captured and printed in a white paper for the House of Commons.[13] They go into great, and practical, detail, about crossing rivers, night marches, firing the outskirts of towns to confuse the defenders, and other things common in the military manuals; parts, however, were new to the War Office, as (for example) the paragraph saying: "The class of people most easily to be moved to insurrection, as in all countries, is the poorest class. This may be effected by distributing money or drink among them; by ascribing to Government the public wretchedness; by instigating them and facilitating their means to revolt, to pillage the public granaries, and to plunder the property of the rich, whom they always regard with the eye of envy." Adaptations of this general policy had been carefully made to allow for English prejudices. The estates of the "lords who belong to the Opposition party, whenever they are known," were to be spared from pillage, and note should be taken that although the English people were "regardless of morality, they are attached to their laws and respect their magistrates," so the property of magistrates also should be respected. The insurrectionary English should be organized separately from the army, but given French officers.

There is no need to continue; the expectations of the French were quite logical and totally unrealistic. Dundas and his class had reason enough to fear the English people, but even the most profound and justified resentments were swept away in the surge of emotion caused by the possibility of an invasion. He found it almost alarmingly great; "the secretary at war," says the Commons report of March 29, asked everyone to "guard against several of the vulgar prejudices relative to foreigners." It was thought "that every foreigner must be a Frenchman, and every Frenchman must be an emigrant." The rest of his speech shows oddly enough that *émigrés* were disliked by the ordinary Englishman rather more than other Frenchmen. However, this was a fine distinction; most men would have agreed with Sydney Smith, who wrote from Edinburgh: "I now consider the war between France and England no longer as an occasional quarrel or temporary dispute, but as an antipathy and national horror, after the same kind as subsists between the kite and the crow, or the churchwarden and the pauper, or the weasel and the rat." [14]

Dundas's disquiet, shared to begin with by most of his associates, might well have arisen from an uneasy conscience, though it probably did not. For the government, and the landed class to which it overwhelmingly belonged, had been occupied for years, and was still occupied, in ruining the livelihood of a great part of the population of Great Britain. The kingdom was still mainly a rural country; what happened to the farm workers was of more importance, numerically at least, than the fate of any other single section of the community, and what was happening to them was misery, hunger, and loss of independence. A fluent and learned historian, of impeccable conservative principles, has drawn a vivid picture of the English village before the French wars began.

"Arthur Young, writing in 1789, enumerated in a Norfolk parish of 231 families 38 husbandmen, 26 spinners, 12 farmers, 12 publicans, 8 carpenters, with a total of 57 different classes of employment . . . such employments were intricately interwoven. The farrier, the miller and the maltster generally also held or rented farms, each village craftsman had his garden and, in an unenclosed village, his holding in the common fields. . . . Like other local crafts it [weaving] afforded domestic occupation and employment not only to men but to women and children, endowing every member of the family with a measure of independence. The wealth thus acquired and diffused, as Wilberforce said, was not obtained at the expense of domestic happiness but in the employment of it." [15]

As Sir Arthur Bryant's enthusiasm rises, he continues: "In many counties a gallon of beer a day was not thought an excessive allowance for a working man. Men still lived on the fresh fruits of the earth they tilled; the germ of the wheat remained in the bread, the waste of man and beast went back into the soil and the healthy cycle of nature was unbroken. Every substantial cottage had its flitches of home-cured bacon hanging from the smoky beam and its copper for brewing ale. Eggs, geese, poultry and rabbits abounded." [16]

Now this is undoubtedly too glorious a picture—there were certainly areas of wretchedness—but it is far from being wholly untrue. It was now being replaced by one almost as unrelievedly sordid, a study in blackness. The governing class of England was and had been destroying English rural life, at its very base. The means used were enclosure acts; the motivating impulses were selfishness, a total absence of imagination, and in certain cases malice against the common man. The more humane aristocrats and farmers regretted what was happening, the more intelligent sought for a remedy, though vainly and without perseverance; but they were a small minority. Enclosures of the common land meant money in the pockets of landlords and farmers, and the acts succeeded each other steadily. It was not possible to stop them. The plea of public good was often heard, and it was true that the enclosures which made Colonel Moore realize he could not spot immediately the movements of invaders had, in general, greatly increased either the yield of crops or the quality and weight of beasts. In counties as far separated as Northumberland, Lincoln and Norfolk what was effectively totally waste land was brought into cultivation; the improvement was even more striking in Scotland.[17] But such advantages could have been secured by a fair distribution of the common land. The time was right for its utilization. There was a great demand for farm produce during the French wars, as there always is during wars. But this excellent market made it only the more sure that the newly available lands would not go to the laborers. The great landowners profited greatly, the clergy and tithe owners did fairly well, the big farmers very well, the small farmers not well, and the cottagers profited not at all.

In France, there had been one type of agricultural revolution; it turned a servile nation into a society of small proprietors. In Britain there was another; it was what is quite properly called a capitalist revolution. The unit became a big farm, when it was not a great estate; its owner had to be a man of capital. The number and the importance to the community of the agricultural workers were not sufficient to protect them; their isolation and ignorance made them weaker than the townsmen.[18]

The Members of Parliament who passed the acts could not have pleaded ignorance. Petitions poured in on them, some of them spelling out in detail the result; here is one which is particularly clear, from Raunds in Northamptonshire. "The petitioners beg leave to represent to the House that under pretence of improving lands the cottagers and other persons entitled to right of common on the lands now intended to be enclosed will be deprived of an inestimable privilege which they now enjoy, of turning a certain number of their cows, calves and sheep, on and over the said lands; a privilege that enables them not only to maintain themselves and their families in the depth of winter, when they cannot, even for money, obtain from the occupiers of other lands the smallest portion of milk or whey, but in addition to this they can now supply the grazier with young or lean stock at a reasonable price, to fatten and bring to market at a more moderate rate for general consumption, which they conceive to be the most rational and effectual way of establishing public plenty and cheapness of provision; and they further conceive, that a more ruinous effect of this enclosure will be the almost total depopulation of their town, now filled with bold and hardy husbandmen from among whom and the inhabitants of other open parishes the nation has hitherto derived its greatest strength and glory in the supply of its fleets and armies. . . ." [19]

There is much more of it, equally patient and reasonable, directed to the presumable thoughts of what the petitioners believed to be "the House, the constitutional patron and protector of the poor." Such protests were vain; a report by the Surveyor of the Board of Agriculture for Somerset in 1798, a Mr. J. Billingsley, shows why, in speaking plainly the beliefs of both the great landlords and the medium farmers. "Moral effects of an injurious tendency accrue to the cottager from a reliance on the imaginary benefits of stocking a common. The possession of a cow or two, with a hog, and a few geese, naturally exalts the peasant in his own conception above his brothers in the same rank of society. In sauntering after his cattle, he acquires a habit of indolence. Quarter, half and whole days are imperceptibly lost. Day labour becomes disgusting; the aversion increases by indulgence; and at length the sale of a half-fed calf or hog furnishes the means of adding intemperance to idleness. The sale of a cow frequently succeeds, and its wretched and disappointed possessor, unwilling to resume the daily and regular course of labour from whence he drew his former subsistence, by various modes of artifice and imposition exacts from the poor's rate the relief to which he is no longer entitled." [20]

The last words are the most sinister. The "poor's rate" was becoming the Englishman's refuge. When the cottager lost his beasts and his rights, by decisions of "commissioners" appointed by the landowners,[21] he was dependent on the wages paid him by the farmers; he no longer had any reserve and therefore no bargaining power. Some of the more humane Members of Parliament were aghast at the results, and another Dundas, Member for Berkshire, had called a meeting of the justices of the peace in the Pelican Inn at Speenhamland (now part of Newbury) on May 6, 1795, for the purpose of increasing the wages of the poor. They debated seriously, and decided not to apply the Elizabethan statutes enabling them to fix wages, but rather in their capacity as justices of the parishes to allow from the rates to each laborer enough extra to his wages to enable him to live, calculated according to the changes in the price of bread. The intention was excellent, the results inevitable. The laborers became paupers dependent upon the Poor Law for their living. They reached the lowest level, both in conditions and in spirit, that a man can reach. The system was called "the Speenhamland system"—unfairly, because impoverished laborers had been farmed out from the workhouses for years[22]—and it spread rapidly over the south of England and the Midlands. There was now no reason for a farmer to pay his workers a living wage (the parish would make it up), nor any chance for the workers to resist effectively. They might, it is true, riot and burn ricks, barns, and butcher shops;

when they did, wages rose for the moment, prices temporarily fell, and their leaders were hanged or deported.

Another section of the population, not so numerous but equally important, had been treated almost as badly. But it was not equally invisible and inaudible to its rulers.

The Royal Navy was both the pride of Britain and its distress; it was praised and loved, ill-treated and mistrusted. The British sailor was at once proud, skilled, and passionately patriotic; oppressed, miserable and even mutinous. Upon the navy depended the continuance of Great Britain as an independent state, and the very lives of its inhabitants; yet in the past year this vital defense had vanished for weeks on end. The navy had mutinied; the fleets at Spithead, the Nore, and Yarmouth (in that order) had gone on what was not then called a strike at a time of great danger. The red flag had flown at their masts; disliked officers had been put by force on the quaysides, white with fear or purple with rage and with their baggage beside them; the House of Commons committee reported that the fleets were called "The Floating Republic." The evidence for this last, however, was trivial, and the committee which believed it was nearly hysterical.[23]

If the Commons had examined closely the documents attached to the committee's report they could have seen that with one exception (and that from Spithead, the most loyal and least dangerous mutiny) all the evidences of revolutionary sentiment referred to Irishmen who had been pressed into the navy. If there was any naval conspiracy at all, it had been a plot of the United Irishmen. The state of mind of the British tar, as he liked to be called, was summarized perfectly by one mutineer:

> *For the Lords Commissioners of the Board of Admiralty*
> Dam my eyes if I understand your lingo or long proclamations, but, in short, give us our due at once, and no more of it, till we go in search of the rascals the enemys of our country.
>
> HENREY LONG
> *Nore, of June 1797. On board his Magesty ship Champion.*

The truth was not only that the seamen were intensely loyal, but that the mutinies of 1797 were the most salutary things that had happened to the navy in a hundred years. Though neither the thunderstruck officers nor the government would ever realize this fact, they had already in 1798 begun to reap the benefit. Greed, evasiveness, unimaginativeness, the peculiar slovenly incompetence of the eighteenth-century governing class, and not any conscious wish of the guilty administrators and legislators, had made life in the navy intolerable for the sailors. In personal liberty and in money wages a merchant seaman was almost immeasurably better off; the navy could only be manned by forcible recruitment. The press gang was a terror of the ports; it was so hated that Wilkes, as sheriff and as lord mayor of London, had actually been able to forbid it operating. The wages of the sailors had not been raised since the reign of Charles II; merchant seamen earned roughly four times as much. The food provided was unnecessarily bad—rotten, weevily, and insufficient—and pursers had a tolerated habit of withholding one-eighth for their own use or resale, which in some cases was said to make their job worth £1,000 a year. The captain's rule was autocratic; if he was a brute or bully, life on a ship could be a hell. "Rome had her Neros and Caligulas, but how many characters of their description might we not mention in the British Fleet?" asked the Nore mutineers.[24] Petitions having been met by evasions the sailors had decided that force must be used. The result had been that wages had been raised, peculation in food had been largely prevented, and the most unpopular officers had been induced to ask for transfers.[25] Discipline remained harsh; brutality did not end; still, this was a brutal century. The belief that flogging and other torture were inadmissible barbarity was but one of the ideas put about by the French Revolution, and had scarcely reached England. Certainly, the sailors thought their officers far too free with the lash. In the words of one of their songs, of which the tune is unknown:

> Good Providence long looked with pity at last
> For to see Honest Jack so shamefully thrashed . . .
> 'Your brothers' said Neptune, 'his all firmly resolved
> To banish all tyrants that long did uphold
> Their crewel intentions to scourge when they please;
> Sutch a set of bace villains you must instantly seize.' [26]

But they cared less than we would; sailors were men who had a professional pride in being rough and tough; they could be as

brutal to each other as their officers were to them; a number of
them were criminals collected from the jails who perhaps could be
restrained in no other way. And their profession was sweetened
for them by two very English sweeteners, it was a gamble, and it
brought them personal glory. Commander J. A. Gardner in his
Recollections recorded a song sung by the women of Gosport
which neatly epitomizes both (though once again the tune is
lost):

> Don't you see the ships a-coming?
> Don't you see them in full sail?
> Don't you see the ships a-coming
> With the prizes at their tail?

>> Oh, my little rolling sailor,
>> Oh, my little rolling he!
>> I do love a jolly sailor
>> Blithe and merry may he be.

> Sailors they get all the money
> Soldiers they get none but brass
> I do love a jolly sailor
> Soldiers they may kiss my a——

>> Oh, my little rolling sailor,
>> Oh, my little rolling he!
>> I do love a jolly sailor,
>> Soldiers may be damned for me.[27]

The women "catching hold of the lieutenant and midshipmen,
began to hug and kiss them, and it was some time before they
could get out of their clutches." The occasion was a gamble that
came off, a resounding success under Admiral Kempenfelt.
Months and years might pass fruitlessly, but good luck (and luck
could often be good in wartime) brought sudden rewards. The
value of a captured ship, a prize, would be divided among officers
and men. A good one might well mean a thousand or more
guineas for the commander, and twenty-five guineas each for the
common seamen. Multiply these figures by ten or twenty to reach
modern values; they provide one good reason for the delirious
welcome by the women of Gosport. Another, more valid for
staider citizens, was that the navy had never been defeated. It was
the army that had lost the American war. It was because of the

crews of Rodney, Howe, Duncan, Hood, Anson and Keppel that the citizens of Britain, from Plymouth to Inverness, could walk about in safety. The gnarled, tarry, cursing figures rolling around the port areas deserved gratitude and admiration. Did they drink too much? It was a common failing, shared by their betters. They fought and brawled when ashore? Certainly, because they were fighting men, and they rarely made trouble in respectable quarters. They swore horribly? All of them. "Blister my tripes, where the hell did you come from?" was Gardner's welcome when he joined his first ship.[28] Their oaths were extensive, but only the rising evangelicals were deeply shocked; most citizens were no more distressed than we would be. They fornicated freely on shore, and loose women thronged the ships in port? Regrettable, but they hardly ever bothered respectable women, and a father who let his womenfolk visit dockland unescorted was an incomparable fool. The sailors in short were Hearts of Oak, like their ships; they deserved admiration; it would have been unjust, and perhaps even unwise, to withhold it.

It was fear that had compelled the governors of Britain to right the sailors' wrongs. But it would be unfair to suggest that when that stimulus was absent they were utterly indifferent. Many of them were exercised about the misery they saw around them, and discussed remedies; but their remedies were ill-conceived and were rarely ever applied.

The most serious attention which Parliament had given to the "condition of the industrious poor" had been two years before, 1796, in discussing a minimum-wage bill presented by Samuel Whitbread, the famous brewer and reformer, and a man far superior to his fellow members in penetration of thought as well as nobility of character. (Like another M.P. of whom the same might be said, Sir Samuel Romilly, he ultimately put an end to his own life in despair.) His bill was to repeal the Elizabethan and earlier statutes which empowered justices to fix maximum wages, and to give them powers to fix minimum wages. Its reception illuminated the thoughts of both parties in the House of Commons. Leaders of both spoke. Fox, the Whig, in a speech which was brief and clear, supported Whitbread. The House, he remarked, was proposing to form an association to use only a particular sort of bread because of the present scarcity, should it not also form itself into an association to raise the price of labor proportionately to the rise in the cost of subsistence? The truth was that "the great mass of the labouring part of the community" was being forced to apply to the Poor Law; apart altogether from the extensive wretchedness this implied, this meant that by existing law every such man was deprived of the franchise (which was then the case, with only trivial exceptions), and thus "every poor man was compelled into dependence and then reduced to servitude." Pitt, the Tory, in a long and rambling reply, began by explaining that he had given the question prolonged study, and went on to offer as results a series of platitudinous considerations such as prime ministers often did, and do, when wishing to avoid action, even urging the House to rely upon "the beneficence never surpassed at any period in history" which was being shown by the rich to the poor. "Would it not be better for the House to consider the operation of general principles and rely upon the effects of their unconfined exercise?" True, he agreed, there were unwise statutes, which should be amended, in particular the law of settlement, by which those who had recourse to the Poor Law could be sent back to their original parishes. "Three great points, of granting relief according to the number of children, of preventing removals at the caprice of the parish officer, and of making them" (the pauperized laborers, apparently) "subscribe to friendly societies, would tend in a very great degree to remove every complaint." [29] The three great points were hardly likely to have achieved this, but that was no matter; Pitt had not carried them on to the statute book.

What was the explanation of the inactivity of Parliament? Laziness, greed, heartlessness are not adequate reasons; they are universal faults, and of every age. Nor was the cause ignorance of the facts—most of the members were countrymen, and could see with their own eyes the ravages. In the towns the signs were equally clear; the report presented by Dr. Perceval on the conditions in the mills in Manchester, for example, showed how the children working in them were dying of "fever" which they spread around the city, while their parents were unemployed, lived off their labor and "subsisted by the oppression of their offspring."

Even in London "the fine London watchmakers were becoming hands in sweat-shops. The learned societies of the Spitalfields silk weavers were rioting for bread. The small owners were losing their place and their skilled workers were losing their livelihood." [30]

One reason was the universal belief that the distress was temporary. It was due to the war; when the war was over "the operation of general principles" would mysteriously restore to the ordinary Englishman his old happy life. Hardly one politician knew how far worse things would in fact be when the war ended and, in Robert Owen's words, "the great customer died." Procrastination was easier than offending the farmers, landlords, factory owners, and City men who were making such excellent profits.

Another reason was that the House of Commons was no longer the House of Commons. Everyone knew, and the textbooks all announced, that the British constitution was a mixed constitution. The elements in the mixture were King, Lords, and Commons. There were certain accepted checks on the first two—accepted since the days of Pym and Hampden. The curious might have reflected on the fact that they were never used; but no Parliamentary statesman of eminence questioned the fundamental truth of the description. Fox, the most intelligent of the Whigs, had epitomized it in a thoughtful statement of policy in 1791. "He laid it down as a principle never to be departed from, that every part of the British dominions ought to possess a Government, in the constitution of which monarchy, aristocracy and democracy were mutually blended and united; nor could any Government be a fit one for British subjects to live under, which did not contain its due weight of aristocracy, because that he considered to be the proper poise of the constitution, the balance that equalised and meliorated the powers of the two other extreme branches." [31]

What was not clear to contemporaries, and even to later writers, was that this mixture did indeed exist, but where it was now to be found was inside the House of Commons itself. This was why the debates in the Commons excited so much interest and were printed at length in, for example, the *Annual Register* while those of the Lords were abbreviated; this was why names like Burke, Pitt, Fox, Tierney, and other commoners bulked dispro-

portionately large in so aristocratical a society. The Commons
mirrored the structure of power, the Lords did not. Some proportion of their members was returned by the people; there were
seats such as Westminster of Preston where by a "scot and lot" or
similar franchise what would now be called the working class had
a majority of votes. The county members, the "knights of the
shires," were mostly returned by forty-shilling freeholders, and
they carried more weight than their fifty-odd number would indi-
cate, because of the "respectability" of their origin as well as their
character. But neither of these categories, which alone historically
or grammatically deserved to be called the Commons of England,
controlled the House. The Society of the Friends of the People, a
reforming association, had had the House investigated by a committee five years earlier, in 1793, whose conclusions remained
exactly true this year:

"Such a proportion of the 513 representatives of England and
Wales is returned by a few as renders it of little consequence by
how many the remainder is elected. Your Committee find that
256 members, being a *majority* of the Commons of England, are
elected by 11,075 voters, or in other words by little more than the
170th part of the people to be represented, even supposing them
to be only two millions." [32]

The persons whose votes elected these two hundred and fifty-
six members were selected in odd enough ways, but of who in fact
chose the members there was no doubt:

"The numbers of electors in the boroughs concerned varied
from 230 in Bridgwater to 9 in Winchelsea and seven in Old Sa-
rum. They were electors by right of being burgage holders, inhabitants at large, potwallopers or other strange qualifications, or by
birth, servitude, redemption, commonalty and otherwise. One
third or more of these freemen did not live in their boroughs and
it would have cost them usually several days and several pounds
to vote. Seventeen dukes, seven marquesses, forty earls, five vis-
counts, and thirty-six barons owned or effectively influenced 217
seats in 1797, and 144 more were controlled by rich commoners,
about half of whom were knights or baronets." [33]

Twenty years or so earlier there had been at least a partial
separation between the two nondemocratic elements in the consti-

tution, the lords and the king. There had been an identifiable group of "king's friends" in the House, and much warmhearted rhetoric has been spent upon the Whig resentment of its existence, and of George III himself. The King was obstinate, stupid, garrulous, narrow, a good man indeed but a bad king and a bad father (for his sons mostly turned out louts, fools, or knaves, hideous embarrassments to all loyalists—the "damnedest millstones," Wellington called them), but by losing the American colonies he had done the most damage that he could, and now was content to put all his power and patronage behind the young premier he had chosen, William Pitt. Whether in so choosing he had collected a servant or a master is no matter now; the two elements were no longer divided.

Outside the House, aristocracy retained its "due weight," even more, perhaps, than Fox would have wished. Out of a cornucopia of examples let us take the case of Lord Camelford, who killed Mr. Charles Peterson early this year at English Harbour in Antigua. English Harbour was an important base for the navy in the West Indies. It slowly decayed when sail was abandoned; until a year or two ago it was almost unchanged, and the scene of the crime could have been inspected by anyone. Lord Camelford was in command of H.M.S. *Favorite,* and Peterson of H.M.S. *Perdrix,* Peterson was a lieutenant, temporarily replacing his superior, Captain Fahie, who was away for some reason. Both men, Camelford and Peterson, considered themselves meanwhile to be the ranking officer in command at English Harbour, Camelford because (apparently) Peterson had once served under him, Peterson because he represented Fahie, who was admittedly the superior of both of them, and perhaps also because Camelford did not hold a commission, but only a "warrant" from the Admiral, Harvey. Both men were young; both issued orders to each other, which they both ignored.

As the two ships "were hauled together alongside the dock yard," there was ample opportunity for conflict. On one day there was an open altercation between the two men on the quay, with the crews of the two ships lined up against each other, and listening.

"His lordship then quitted the place for about two minutes and

returned with a pistol in his hand. Mr Peterson was standing at
the head of his men as before, with his sword drawn, the point of
it resting on the ground. In this position Lord Camelford went up
to him with his pistol in his hand and said:

" 'Do you still persist in refusing to obey my orders?'

"To which the lieutenant answered:

" 'Yes, I do refuse'.

"On which Lord Camelford instantly clapped the pistol to his
right breast and fired."

Peterson, shot through the heart, died instantly; he was little
more than a youth and "of a very respectable family." Lord Camelford went to the guardhouse and informed whoever was there of
what he had done; a court of five captains found no difficulty in
acquitting him of what appears to have been a wholly deliberate
murder. The report is brief, but there seems to have been little
other reason for acquittal than that he was a lord, and had been
provoked by a commoner.[34]

A less gruesome instance of the same partiality is provided by
the action of the House of Lords on the second reading of the
divorce bill presented on behalf of Mr. Esten in February. Mr.
Esten had signed articles of separation from his wife a year or two
before and had then been appointed to a ship in the West Indies.
On his return from there he had found his wife living in adultery.
Unfortunately, her seducer and keeper was the Duke of Hamilton,
and though Mr. Esten's counsel protested that in similar cases
divorces had habitually been granted, the House was not willing
to do anything to vex so eminent a fellow member. However, that
was not the reason given in debate. "Lord Auckland said that the
practice" (of obtaining divorces, or of committing adultery; it is
not clear which), "among others imported from France, had become more frequent since the rejection of all virtue, religion and
morality in that country. The Bishop of Durham considered it a
consequence of the gross immoralities imported of late years into
this kingdom from France, the Directory of which country finding
that they were not able to subdue us by their arms were determined to gain their ends by destroying our morals. They had sent
over persons to this country who made the most indecent exhibi-
tions on our theatres, which would not have been allowed even in
France. It was his intention to move an Address beseeching his

Majesty to remove all such persons out of the kingdom." Mr.
Esten's divorce was refused him *"nem. diss."* [35]

The successful intervention by the Bishop was not an evidence
of the power of the church to enforce Christian behavior upon the
governing class. There was a more powerful intervention made
this year by one of the most respected supporters of the church
and endorsed by politicians of eminence, which failed despite the
pledged word of Parliament, its eminently Christian character,
and its much greater importance. William Wilberforce on April 3
called on the House of Commons "to be faithful to its own resolution of May 1st, 1792 'that from and after the first of May 1796
the slave trade should be abolished.'" [36] His own speech, and
those of Fox, Canning, Pitt and Thornton, even in the summaries
now available show in their logic and warmth why the eighteenth-
century House of Commons held the respect and admiration of
other nations and sometimes of its own; even the speech of the
spokesman of the West India planters, Bryan Edwards,[37] has its
interest as exposing the economic sources of the opposition. The
figures of the voting show why the House's reputation was in the
end undeserved; Wilberforce's motion was rejected by eighty-
seven to eighty-three and an act regulating the size of slave ships
substituted—the fate of even this having been put in doubt by
massive deputations of slave-traders from Liverpool and Bristol.

The primary cause of Wilberforce's failure may not have been
Mr. Edwards's economic arguments; Lord Ellenborough, a
thoughtful judge and not a brute like Lord Eldon, offered Wilberforce a little later another excuse, one commonly accepted in wartime.

"I have always," he wrote, "felt a great abhorrence of the mode
by which these unfortunate creatures are torn from their families
and country and have doubted whether any sound policy could
grow out of a system which seemed so vicious in its foundation;
but I am extremely alarmed at . . . the consequences of any innovation upon a long established practice, at a period so full of
dangers as the present." [38]

Wilberforce's noble and unceasing war on the slave trade was
not typical of English ardent Christianity nor yet of the man himself. Outside this subject he was self-righteous, narrow, unimaginative and hardhearted. To forbid trade unions, to prevent rises in

wages, to support the savage Game Laws, to commend brutalities in Cold Bath Prison, to put down freedom of speech, to support governmental spying, and to persecute individuals by means of a "Society for the Suppression of Vice"—these were only some of his enthusiasms, which led to Cobbett's famous farewell on leaving England for America:

"No hangings and rippings up. No Castleses and Olivers. No Cannings, Liverpools, Castlereaghs, Eldons, Ellenboroughs or Sidmouths. No bankers. No squeaking Wynnes. No Wilberforces. Think of *that!* No Wilberforces!"

He, and his most powerful aide, Hannah More, condemned Pitt for fighting an abortive duel with Tierney in May, over a trivial squabble—not so much because it was a wicked and out-of-date habit, but because they fought on a Sunday. His book, *A Practical View of the Prevailing Religious System of Professed Christians in the Higher and Middle Classes in this Country contrasted with Real Christianity,* had been published the previous year and despite its title was having an increasing influence, as was all evangelical and nonconformist writing.[39] The Dissenters had once been a great source of enlightenment—Paine, Richard Price, Priestley, and Gilbert Wakefield were all dissenters of one type or another —but now discontent with the established church, whether as lazy or as Erastian, had been diverted into ways less useful to the world. Justice would indeed be done, the rich and tyrannous would be punished, and the poor and virtuous be rewarded—but in the next world. Then (in the words of a popular pamphlet published this year in Norwich) "the high and the low, the oppressor and the oppressed, shall be reduced to one perfect level. The pampered tyrant, and his indigent vassal; the wealthy peer and the neglected pauper, shall receive an equitable and impartial sentence." [40] The anger and hatred of the dispossessed and oppressed were not transmuted into Christian loving-kindness by the evangelicals; they were merely given a new object. Here is a sadistic hymn that Isaac Watts, using what the eighteenth century believed to be sapphics, wrote in *The Day of Judgment*:

> Hark the shrill outcries of the guilty wretches!
> Lively bright horror and amazing anguish
> Stare through their eyelids, while the living worm lies
>   Gnawing within them.

> Thoughts like old vultures prey upon their heart strings,
> And the smart twinges, when the eye beholds the
> Lofty Judge frowning, and a flood of vengeance,
>   Rolling before him.
> Hopeless immortals! how they scream and shiver
> While devils push them to the pit wide yawning,
> Hideous and gloomy, to receive them headlong
>   Down to the centre.[41]

Like other frustrated emotions this hatred could come near to madness; the examples of Moravian and Methodist hymns and exhortations given in, say, E. P. Thompson's *The Making of the English Working Class*,[42] sometimes need a Freud or Krafft-Ebing to interpret them. Hysteria was recurrent in Methodism; Wesley in his *Journal* records that at Bristol "a vehement noise shot like lightning through the whole congregation. . . . The terror and confusion was inexpressible. . . . The people rushed upon each other with the utmost violence, the benches were broken in pieces, and nine-tenths of the congregation appeared to be struck with the same panic."

Into such ways were channeled some of the energies and enthusiasm of the people who had once eagerly read Paine's *The Rights of Man*. Men who were convinced of the certainty of heavenly justice and of the overwhelming need of securing paradise for themselves had no interest in politics. If they hesitated, the Methodists in particular, both the Wesleys and their two most powerful successors, dreadful reverends called Jabez Bunting and Edmund Grindrod, peremptorily and specifically forbade any association with radical views and persons except to denounce and report them.[43] Another reason for the decline was the passion of patriotism which swept Britain this year; yet another was the internal history of the French Revolution. Who could feel about the Directory what he had felt about the National Assembly of 1789? Fox had said of the French Revolution, "How much is it, by far, the greatest and the best thing that has ever happened in the history of the world"; he had not unsaid this, but it was unlikely that he would have repeated it now, at least in the same words. A further reason was the strengthening of the laws preventing the publication of anything that could be considered seditious. This had followed from humiliating failures of the authorities in 1794 to secure convictions of members of the London Corresponding Society and others who had defended French principles. Acquittals had been won by the eloquence of Thomas Erskine, the steadfastness of the defendants, and the devotion of the London juries to what they called "British Liberty"—their opponents called it "the London disease." To prevent this happening again, acts had been passed making speaking or writing as much treason as overt acts, making inciting hatred of the government a "high misdemeanour," and requiring licenses for all public meetings, political lectures or reading rooms; this year Pitt, who was wise in advance of his time in the mechanics of repression, had an act passed requiring the registration of the names and addresses of the printers, publishers and proprietors of all newspapers, together with specimen copies. It was to be used next year with great effect; even now it was unwise if not impossible to speak or write the truth on any subject likely to offend the rulers.[44] William Blake wrote on the title page of a book by a bishop:

"To defend the Bible in this year 1798 would cost a man his life.

"But to him who sees this mortal pilgrimage in the light I see it, Duty to his country is the first consideration and safety the last."

And then he added:

"I have been commanded from Hell not to print this, as it is what our Enemies wish.

"The Beast and the Whore rule without control."

Hell, in Blake's language, was the giver of good advice; the Beast was the state, and the Whore was the church.

Others followed the advice from Hell, and were silent; but two hundred thousand copies of Paine's *The Rights of Man* had already been sold, and their contents were not forgotten; they were rather stored for the future. Meanwhile, the once-powerful London Corresponding Society was nearly in dissolution; other societies had mostly vanished. There were indeed in some sort of existence societies calling themselves the United Scotsmen and the United Englishmen (or sometimes United Britons) by whom the authorities professed to be greatly alarmed.[45] They caught Arthur O'Connor, the United Irishman, John Binns and two others called Allen and Leary at Margate in February, on their way to present an address "from the Secret Committee of England to the Executive Directory of France" (it was all wind). In April they arrested the remaining leaders of the London Corresponding Society at a general meeting, and secured papers which later convinced the Commons' committee that "it appeared that about forty divisions of United Englishmen had been formed in London" and "many similar" in the provinces. This was almost surely fantasy, or wishful thinking by the secretary; he signed his letters "Health and Fraternity," and was making great efforts to whip up enthusiasm.[46] Francis Place, a man who should have known if anyone did, put the effective membership as about a dozen.[47]

But here too aristocracy retained its privileges. The government, individually and as a whole, could be denounced in public, the behavior of the rich abused, the structure of society condemned and its overturn demanded, if the speaker was of the right descent, wealth or standing. Sir Francis Burdett, M.P., attacked the King's "highly objectionable speech" with material supplied by Thomas Holcroft, one of the defendants of 1794.[48] The Duke of Bedford moved for the dismissal of the government; Sheridan poured acid contempt upon the use of the committee's flimsy revelations to secure the suspension of habeas corpus.[49] Fox (who once had said, "I pay no regard whatever to the voice of the people") gave the health of "The People" at a great meeting instead of "the king." Pitt indeed spent some time working out a tortuous way of sending him to the Tower, but it would not do; all that could be done was to strike his name off the list of privy councillors on May 9; six days later he was blandly chairing the assembly which formed the Chertsey Volunteers.[50] The Duke of Norfolk, at Fox's original meeting, used words which it was surprising any government would permit in wartime:

"Not twenty years ago the illustrious George Washington had not more than two thousand men to rally round him. America is now free. This day full two thousand men are assembled in this place. I leave you to make the application." [51]

The suppression of free speech and free publication was in any case limited by the limited strength of the government. A network of spies was not yet woven; the magistrates had not yet become what they were in the days of Ludd and of Peterloo, nor had the yeomanry. Five years before, in 1793, the London Corresponding Society had compared the situation of Englishmen with that of Frenchmen before the revolution: "Our persons were protected by the laws, while their lives were at the mercy of every titled individual. We were MEN while they were SLAVES." [52] This brief phrase was still in part true, in England and Wales at least, less so in Scotland. All men were supposed to be equal before the law; if the rich were sometimes improperly favored by the courts, the scandal was less than it once had been. There was freedom from arbitrary arrest. There was no absolute ruler—a rare boon, at this period of history (or indeed at any period). There was religious freedom, though not equality—that is to say, there was liberty of conscience, but if your conscience led you outside the Church of England, you lost certain privileges. There had been, until very recently, large liberty of speech and writing, and the curtailment of it was believed to be temporary. All classes had a voice in Parliament, and tyranny could be checked by riot and tumult, for there was no effective police and the use that could be made of the soldiers was limited—so much so that thirty years earlier Benjamin Franklin, a most shrewd American observer, decided that if Wilkes had had a good character and George III a bad, the King would have been turned off the throne. Finally, everyone had the right to trade, to travel and to sell his labor wherever he chose. There were few other countries where these things were true. The Englishman had only to look around Europe to count his blessings, let alone Asia or Africa.

Where the new machines had not destroyed the old methods— still a large area—the plain workingman could even be obstreperous. The *Gentleman's Magazine* printed in June a furious letter from one of its gentlemanly readers, whose contractor could not get carpenters. He blamed the public houses, those "houses of call" from which arose the modern trade unions. The men, he said, "triumph in impudent refusal—saying 'Tis *our* time now'— 'We will come when we like'—'We are not *broke* yet.' " There ought, he considered, to be "a word in season to those publicans." [53] Apprentices also could be uncontrollable; they were indeed notorious and riotous nuisances.[54] The existence of a Londoner, and to a less extent of a citizen of a provincial town, was kept lively by an astonishing number of clubs, meeting usually at taverns and coffeehouses. There were punch clubs where members got drunk; there were lottery clubs to buy state lottery tickets; there were trade clubs; there were cock-and-hen clubs for young men and tarts; there were musical clubs and mutual-assistance clubs; there were chair clubs for singing vulgar songs; and, perhaps most interesting of all, "cutter clubs." "It is customary," wrote a Bow Street officer, "for many apprentices to raise enough money to buy a cutter; with this cutter they go up the river to Richmond or Kew . . . those who cannot buy a boat, they go to Godfrey's and hire. Forty or 50 of these boats go up of a Sunday." [55] Place, from whom much of this information is taken, regrets that nothing could induce the English worker to save when he made good money. All was spent, on ale, on clubs, on women, or on cutters. The artisans and small employers had no resources; good tradesman after good tradesman whom he had known ended as a poverty-stricken wreck.

This universal independence took odd forms. The Clerk to the Bank of England, Mr. Jenkins, died this year. He was an unusual man, eight feet tall, and this peculiarity caused two hundred guineas to be offered for his corpse. The Bank, considering this unseemly, and perhaps fearing body snatching, merely buried him within its grounds; perhaps he is still there. [56] But such almost anarchic permissiveness had necessarily another side. Violence was common; the Londoners' amusements, besides those already mentioned, included stoning to death criminals in the pillory, watching hangings at Tyburn and the whipping of women at Bridewell, and tormenting the lunatics in Bedlam. Life was unsafe for the weak, and even for the merely unwise. John Mellish, for example, the Member for Grimsby, went stag hunting in Windsor Forest in April. The King had not only given permission, but having first ascertained that Mellish "ranked highly in the commercial world" had ordered a deer of "much speed and bottom" to be turned out for his party. As he rode back happily through Hounslow Heath, Mellish was set upon by three ruffians who robbed him and shot him. He was carried mortally wounded into the inn of the Three Magpies, and a surgeon was sent for hastily. When the doctor rode up, the three footpads, who were lying in wait, set on him too and robbed him, though through some scruple they did not shoot him. There is no record of them having been caught and punished, well known though their victim was.[57] They were more fortunate than their colleague Avershaw, who also "worked" Hounslow, was hung in chains on Kennington Common and whose toe and finger bones, as they dropped off, were used by his admirers "as stoppers for their tobacco pipes." [58]

Despite the disorderliness and violence (and few if any countries were much safer) life in British cities was far more civilized than it had been half a century before. About halfway through the century a wide discontent with the filthy, uncomfortable, and insanitary conditions of their towns had seized upon the citizens, and improvement act after improvement act had been demanded of Parliament and forthwith secured. Westminster had its act in 1762, the City of London in 1766, Birmingham and Portsmouth in 1769, Manchester in 1776, Liverpool in 1780—and so on; between 1785 and 1800 no fewer than two hundred and eleven acts were passed and by now the effects had become visible all over the country. London in particular was the admiration of the world, better paved, drained, scavenged and lit than any other capital. "Prodigious . . . twenty two candles in one little shop!" exclaimed a Birmingham visitor.[59] Criticizing the "injudicious" planning of the city, the edition of the Encyclopaedia Britannica completed in 1797 nevertheless said: "The improvements for some years past have however been very great; and the new streets, which are numerous, are in general more spacious and built with greater regularity and elegance. The very elegant and necessary method of paving and enlightening the streets is also felt in the most sensible manner by all ranks and degrees of people. . . . Nothing can appear more brilliant than the lamps, regularly placed on each side at short distances . . . when viewed at a distance, especially where the roads run across; and even the principal streets, such as Pall Mall, New Bond Street, Oxford Street &c. convey an idea of grandeur." [60] Paris (Arthur Young found in 1787) was "vastly inferior . . . streets very narrow and nine-tenths dirty"; as for Madrid even the Royal Palace had no privies at all as late as 1797.[61]

London theaters, though, were not this year in a very good state. Holcroft, whose profession as a playwright and opera writer had not yet suffered unbearably from his political views, wrote in June "our theatres at present are half filled with prostitutes and their paramours; they disturb the rest of the audience. The author, and common sense, are the sport of their caprice and profligacy." But usually the behavior of prostitutes, or at least their principles, he found to be more edifying; two of them in October walking in Newman Street, "praised the goodness of God and, as the weather had been very rainy for some days" prayed that he would "render it fair all the next week so that they might walk the streets in comfort." [62]

Moral lessons and instances of the personal attention of the Almighty abounded for all; perhaps the most dramatic occurred on the stage in Liverpool where "the celebrated comedian, Mr John Palmer," taking the part of The Stranger, delivered the appeal:

> *"O God! God!*
> *There is another, and a better world!"*

and immediately "dropt down dead." [63]

The new practice of sea bathing brought elegance even to seaside villages, and not to Brighton and the south only. In the rough north, William Sutton's "bathing house," which he had built at South Hawes (now Southport) and which had been laughed at as "Duke's Folly," this year became so successful that it stayed open the whole year round.[64]

Sea bathing was but one instance of the enthusiasm for health, and the advance of medicine, of which the British were justly proud. Mr. Thomas Jones this year published the correct method of growing in Britain "true rhubarb" which, "so cultivated as to arrive at 6 or 7 years' growth and properly cured, will possess all the virtues the most sanguine can desire," a belief in which doctors concurred for a hundred years more.[65]

The realization that scurvy could be cured by the juice of lemons, oranges or limes had almost annihilated that once-dreaded disease; when the First Lord of the Admiralty visited Haslar and wished to see a case of scurvy, not one could be found in the hospital.[66]

But it was a victory over an even more dreadful disease for which the year 1798 is remembered. Edward Jenner published a study on smallpox, entitled *An Inquiry into the Causes and Effect of the Variolae Vaccinae.* "*Variolae vaccinae*" means poxes of

the cow, plural, and to Jenner's misfortune his discoveries were
associated with the name of Dr. George Pearson, who became
one of his most ardent propagandists, but disregarded the fact
that Jenner had distinguished two kinds of cowpox, only one of
which could safely be used in what we now call vaccination. He
injected patients indiscriminately, sometimes giving them smallpox rather than curing it, thereby starting a resentment and distrust which is still alive. Jenner's discovery arose from his observ-
ing the truth of a rustic belief in Gloucestershire, where he spent
his youth—that the discharge from certain cases of cowpox, and
what was called "grease" in the heels of a horse, could be a prophy-
lactic against smallpox. After many difficulties he now had made
enough experiments to announce that he had discovered how to
prevent smallpox. He "excited the attention of the medical world
immediately in the most intense degree." [67] It was a discovery,
said *The British Critic,* justly enough, "as singular and extraordinary as any perhaps this wonder-teeming age can boast." The
only criticism that the magazine permitted itself was of the cost of
the book: "utility is sacrificed to splendour. By means of prepos-
terously large margins and loose printing, the number of pages is
doubled," it said, and unnecessary colored engravings made the
price three times what it should be. Dr. Jenner, who did not like
criticism, replied sharply that anyone of intelligence should have
seen that the engravings were essential to an understanding of his
thesis; and the magazine fell silent.[68] Many doctors, as usual, resisted or derided the new discovery; but vaccination was in the
end adopted, first in Britain and then in most of the rest of the
world. Smallpox was either eliminated, or contained. The majority of its victims had been children; the Reverend Thomas Birch
in 1759 had rather callously called it "the poor man's friend who
happens to be burdened with a large family";[69] this was no longer
to be true, but how far Jenner was responsible for the rapid increase in population in the next century has never been decided.
  There were even small signs of progress in the most difficult
area of all medicine, the treatment of the insane. The King's madness in 1788 had made it impossible for the clergy and doctors to
continue to regard insanity as a sign of wickedness. Till then
"mental and moral defect" had been synonymous;[70] but nobody

dared accuse George III. Lunatics had been flogged, purged, and cauterized; they had been chained, half-starved, and left in their own filth; they had been caged and exhibited. The King could not be treated so; perhaps other lunatics should not. Two institutions, St. Luke's Hospital in London and the Manchester Lunatic Hospital, had begun the serious study of mental disorder, and abandoned all force beyond what was absolutely necessary to restrain the violent.[71] This year an institution far in advance of its time, the York Retreat, run by the Quakers, was inspected by a Swiss, Dr. Delarive. "It does not," he recorded with surprise, "give in the least the impression of a prison, but rather that of a great farm in the country; it is surrounded by a walled garden." The patients were treated with inexhaustible kindness and patience; the records which are still extant show "a vivid picture of forbearance." [72] But only thirty, and those all Friends, could be admitted, and it was fifteen years before the Retreat became an example to others. Meanwhile, the old brutalities of Bedlam continued.

Though science was progressing, painting was in a worse way than the drama. Artists of all standing were in greater poverty than they had been for years. But here at least the government felt a duty to help. On the first day of the year, in presenting the "assessed taxes" which preceded his income tax, Pitt found a way to exempt Royal Academicians and their Associates from them. By one of those pleasing devices so common in the civil service, their houses should be classed with lunatic asylums, and so left untaxed. Nevertheless, for the first time in its history the Academy was so pressed for funds (to meet the needs of the R.A.'s who were appealing to it for help) that it had to make a charge—sixpence—for the catalogue of its exhibition.[73] The origin of the distress was simple: because of the war, patrons were no longer buying pictures. Holcroft attended a big auction in June; some of the prices seemed good enough, but in fact the pictures were being bought in by their owner, a dealer called Williamson, notorious as "the worst of that tricking trade." What he wanted was to be able to tell his simpler customers that they fetched such and such a price at auction in 1798.[74]

Otherwise than financially, no art surely could be said to be in a bad way when among its recognized heads were Reynolds,

Romney, Raeburn, Gainsborough, Opie, Stubbs, Rowlandson
and Lawrence. Contemporary verdict on these painters' status,
however, was not the same as ours. The assessments of the 1798
exhibition in the serious London press are unexpected. The
Oracle selected Hoppner as the most successful artist, he having
now definitely outclassed Lawrence. The *St. James Gazette* admitted the apparent triumph of Northcote, but suggested it was
due to a misuse of his position on the Hanging Committee—he
had put all his own pictures in the best places. Opie indeed was a
fine technician, but how could he be forgiven for having painted a
portrait of that disloyal dramatist Thomas Holcroft? The *White-
hall Evening Post* had the perspicacity to single out for vehement
praise "Norham Castle" by the young J. M. W. Turner. But its
commendation was vain; when Turner's name came up in November for election as an A.R.A., the Academy preferred M.
Archer-Shee and the sculptor Charles Rossi.[75] The Academy was
a part of what would now be called "the Establishment"; it was
justifying Blake's comment on Reynolds's *Discourses* to it:

"The Enquiry in England is not whether a Man has Talents &
Genius, But whether he is Passive and Polite & a Virtuous Ass &
obedient to Noblemen's Opinions in Art and Science. If he is; he
is a Good Man. If Not, he must be Starved." [76]

Blake was a genius, or mad, or perhaps both; certainly, he considered himself as under the direction of messengers from
Heaven. He laid down about this time his interpretation or explanation of the condition of English art, philosophy, economics,
and policy, all of which he considered to be intimately interlinked.
What he says is baffling, and yet in a way illuminating:

"I know too well that the great majority of Englishmen are
fond of the indefinite, which they measure by Newton's doctrine
of the fluxions of an atom, a thing which does not exist. These are
politicians, and think that Republican art is inimical to their
atom, for a line or a lineament is not formed by chance. A line is
a line in its minutest subdivision, straight or crooked. It is itself,
not intermeasurable by anything else. Such is *Job*. But since the
French Revolution Englishmen are all intermeasurable by one another: certainly a happy state of agreement, in which I for one do
not agree." [77]

It is easy enough to see what Blake detested in fashionable

painting. There are vapidity, optimism and prettiness er
Reynolds, Raeburn and Romney to suit all Noblemen's Op.
It is not so easy to demonstrate what was wrong in fashionaᵇ
poetry, but there must be few literary histories which do not record the publication this year of *Lyrical Ballads* as a mortal blow
to what is called Augustan poetry. H. W. Garrod, Professor of
Poetry at Oxford, called it "the most important event after Mil-
ton." [78] The book was anonymous, it was small, and the first edition was of five hundred copies only. The authors were two young
men named William Wordsworth and Samuel Taylor Coleridge;
the poems, with the exception of one called "The Rime of the
Ancient Mariner," were short. The preface explained: "the majority of the following poems are to be considered as experiments.
They are written chiefly with a view to ascertain how far the language of conversation in the middle and lower classes of society is
adapted to the purposes of poetic pleasure." [79] These words, written by Wordsworth, were deceitfully modest; the intention was to
put an end to the current style of poetry writing which had declined from Pope's skilled and metallic wit to an automatic stamp-
ing out of rhetorical lines of rigid rhythm, conventionally ornate,
didactic, and with emotion which appeared to be false even when
it was not. It is difficult to select typical examples, because they
are not only unbearably dull to us, but usually also unbearably
long. Here, however, is an indisputable specimen, part of this
year's "Ode for his Majesty's Birth Day," by H. J. Pye, the Poet
Laureate. The "her" in the quotation is, of course, Britain.

> Her laurel'd brow she ne'er will veil,
> Or shun the shock of fight, though numerous hosts assail.
>> Th' electric flame of glory runs
>> Impetuous through her hardy sons.
>> See, rushing from the farm and fold,
>> Her swains in Glory's lists enrolled.
>> Though o'er the nations far and wide
>> Gallia may pour oppression's tide,
>> And, like Rome's tyrant race of yore,
>> O'errun each tributary shore,
> Yet, like the Julian chief, their hosts shall meet
> Untamed resistance here, and foul defeat.

Official poetry is always stilted, even when the emotion it tries
to express is as genuine as patriotism was this year. But there is

ample choice among unofficial poets. Passing reluctantly by Miss
Williams's "Address of the Glacier Goddess to Dr Darwin," in
Volume Two of her *Tour in Switzerland*—

> Stay thy rash steps! my potent hand impels
> The rushing avalanche to gulphs below!
> I can transfix thee, numbed, in icy cells
> Or shroud thee in unfathomed folds of snow!

and even the "Ode to the Spirit of Freshness" (in "the enlarged
edition of Polewhele's *Influence of Local Attachment with respect to Home &c*"), which also appeared this year, choice might
fairly fall on a writer who was no Philistine, Joseph Cottle of
Bristol. He was possibly the most cultured and wide-minded pub-
lisher in the island; he had already advanced Coleridge money for
some poems, and indeed published *Lyrical Ballads* itself, though
he quickly jobbed it off to another bookseller, named Arch.[80] The
subject is the beauties of nature, the emotion again is genuine, the
poem is called "Malvern Hills," and the subsection is entitled
"Musings on arriving at, and quitting, the Summit of the Malvern
Hills early in the morning of Whitmonday."

> Oh what a luxury do they possess
> Who, rising with the morn, taste its first sweets!

he exclaims, and continues:

> Day returns
> And Nature, from a transient rest, assumes
> Her wonted form, and seems to look more pleas'd
> For being seen. 'Tis well to contemplate
> On Providence, whose eye encircles all.
> Parent and guardian of creation round!
> The elephant on thee depends for food,
> And all the intermediate train of shapes
> Down to the mite: and beings, smaller still,
> Possessed of parts peculiar and complete
> To whom the mite appears an elephant!
> All on our common Father call for bread!
> Learn it, astonish'd earth! Shout it, oh Heaven!
> He hears them all!

It is not unfair to compare this with some other musings written
not so far away, a few miles above Tintern Abbey, published in
the new book, and too well known to need quotation at length:

> Once again I see
> These hedgerows, hardly hedgerows, little lines
> Of sportive wood run wild; these pastoral farms
> Green to the very door; and wreaths of smoke
> Sent up, in silence, from among the trees . . .

Coleridge himself later described the conception, birth and intention of the new book.

"During the first year that Mr Wordsworth and I were neighbours, our conversations turned frequently on the two cardinal points of poetry, the power of exciting the sympathy of the reader by a faithful adherence to the truth of nature, and the power of giving the interest of novelty by the modifying colours of the imagination. The sudden charm, with accidents of light and shade, with moon-light or sun-set diffused over a known and a familiar landscape, appeared to represent the practicability of combining both. These are the poetry of nature. The thought suggested itself (to which of us I do not recollect) that a series of poems might be composed of two sorts. In the one, the incidents and agents were to be, in part at least, supernatural; and the excellence aimed at was to consist in the interesting of the affections by the dramatic truth of such emotions as would naturally accompany such situations, supposing them real. . . . For the second class, subjects were to be chosen from ordinary life; the characters and incidents were to be such as will be found in every village and its vicinity, where there is a meditative and feeling mind to seek after them, or to notice them when they present themselves.

"In this idea originated the plan of the 'Lyrical Ballads'; in which it was agreed that my endeavours should be directed to persons and characters supernatural, or at least romantic. . . . Mr Wordsworth, on the other hand, was to propose to himself as his object, to give the charm of novelty to things of every day, and to excite a feeling analogous to the supernatural, by awakening the mind's attention from the lethargy of custom and directing it to the loveliness and wonders of the world before us." [81] The plan of the authors was not perfectly fulfilled; the book is not impeccable. Coleridge's major contribution, "The Ancient Mariner," chief representative of the supernatural, was disfigured by grotesque spellings and archaisms, which were removed in later editions.[82]

Wordsworth's shorter contributions were damaged by his sudden falls into bathos:

> And five times did I say to him:
> "Why, Edward? Tell me why!"

But genius shone through, even where there was moralizing, or propaganda if that word is preferred. The authorship of the various poems was sorted out later; this is one of Wordsworth's:

Old Man Travelling

> The little hedge-row birds
> That peck along the road regard him not.
> He travels on, and in his face, his step,
> His gait, is one expression; every limb,
> His look and bending figure, all bespeak
> A man who does not move with pain, but moves
> With thought — He is insensibly subdued
> To settled quiet: he is one by whom
> All effort seems forgotten, one to whom
> Long patience has such mild composure given,
> That patience now doth seem a thing, of which
> He hath no need. He is by nature led
> To peace so perfect, that the young behold
> With envy, what the old man hardly feels.
> — I asked him whither he was bound, and what
> The object of his journey; he replied
> "Sir! I am going many miles to take
> A last leave of my son, a mariner
> Who from a sea-fight has been brought to Falmouth
> And there is dying in an hospital."

Both men were still republican in sentiment, though the enthusiasm of their pantisocratic days had subsided, and their faith in France had disappeared. They were visited in Somerset this year by an acute observer from Shropshire who admired them as much for their personal character as for their poetry—William Hazlitt. Wordsworth came up to his expectations: "there was a severe worn pressure of thought about his temples, a fire in his eye (as if he saw something in objects more than the outward appearance)" —but Coleridge made a much deeper and more complex impression upon him.[83] He had risen before dawn one day in January to hear Coleridge preach at a Unitarian chapel ten miles from his father's home; the walk was "cold, raw and comfortless," he records. "When I got there, the organ was playing the Hundredth Psalm, and when it was done, Mr Coleridge rose and gave out his text: 'And he went up into the mountain to pray, *himself, alone.*' As he gave out this text, his voice 'rose like a stream of rich distilled perfume' and when he came to the last two words, which he pronounced loud, deep and distinct, it seemed to me, who was then young, as if the sounds had echoed from the bottom of the human heart." Coleridge's sermon was a dramatic plea for pacifism; the young Hazlitt "returned home well satisfied; the sun that was still labouring pale and wan through the sky, obscured by thick mists, seemed an emblem of the *good cause.*" He was overwhelmed when Coleridge came soon after to dinner at his father's house, and spoke very animatedly. He even ventured to offer a remark—that to speak contemptuously of Burke was a sign of a vulgar mind. "This was the first observation I ever made to Coleridge and he said it was a very just and striking one. I remember the leg of Welsh mutton and the turnips on the table that day had the finest flavour imaginable." [84]

Later in the year, he walked no fewer than one hundred and sixty miles (from outside Shrewsbury through Worcester, Upton, Tewkesbury, Gloucester, Bristol and Bridgwater to Nether Stowey where Coleridge was staying, near to Wordsworth's house at Alfoxden). The long journey there and back was worth the effort; the stay was almost an ecstasy. His experiences had been, and still were, "in a manner, the cradle of a new existence." Nevertheless, once when out walking with Coleridge, he had noticed something which later on seemed to him to have been a warning of the coming apostasy.

"It was a fine morning and he talked the whole way. The Scholar in Chaucer is described as going *'sounding on his way.'*" So Coleridge went on his. In digressing, in dilating, in passing from subject to subject, he appeared to me to float on air, to slide on ice. . . . I observed that he continually crossed me on the way, by shifting from one side of the footpath to another. This struck me as an odd movement, but I did not at that time connect it with any instability of purpose or involuntary change of principle, as I have done since. He seemed unable to keep on in a straight line." [85]

3

THE GREAT ANTAGONISTS:

FRANCE

Epochs often have a product, a
fashion, an art or a style associated with them; the French Directory has been unusually unlucky in this way. There are Regency
wallpapers, Restoration comedies, Empire draperies and Jaco-
bean furniture, but there are only Directoire knickers. The curious may like to know that these were (or rather, are, for they are
still listed by the more staid London stores[1]) women's close-
fitting drawers, not pantalettes but ending above the knee, and not
wide like bloomers.[2] It is grotesquely unfair that it should be
these that preserved the Directory's name, but it is explicable.
History records changes, and the most obvious change in France
was a resurgence of frivolity, a general relaxation, and even a
looseness of morals and habits. Republican principles certainly
still ruled, but the puritanism of Robespierre's day—financially,

sexually and sartorially—had been jettisoned. The outside world was indeed actively interested in the politics of the republic, the conflicts between Jacobins, moderates, and royalists, but it was fascinated, as it would not have been earlier, by the gaiety, the morals, and the fashions of Paris. There was, unfortunately for us, no exact equivalent in 1798 to the fashion writers of modern magazines, but there was at least one writer whose reports have survived and served a similar purpose. She would be classified today as a "sob sister" as well as a fashion expert. Her name was Helen Maria Williams, she had traveled widely, knew France well, and unlike her successors was also a poet of "great sensibility"—in fact, her most successful poem was entitled "To Sensibility" and inspired a schoolboy who had not met her, named William Wordsworth, to send to a magazine a poem entitled "On Seeing Miss Helen Maria Williams Weep at a Tale of Distress," which he afterward suppressed. *The Lady's Magazine* this year printed accounts from her which gave its readers what they most wished to read.[3] Here is her description of the costumes at a typical private ball, given by a wealthy Parisian contractor:

"The loose light drapery, the naked arms, the sandaled feet, the circling zone, the golden chains, the twisting tresses, all display the most inflexible conformity to the laws of republican costume. The fair Grecians being determined not to injure the *contour* of fine forms by any superfluous incumbrances, no fashionable lady at Paris wears any pockets; and the inconvenience of being without is obviated by sticking her fan in her belt, sliding in a flat purse of Morocco leather, only large enough to contain a few *louis,* at the side of her neck, and giving her snuffbox and her pocket handkerchief to the care of the gentleman who attends her."

Her readers were probably shocked even if agreeably so (the *Times* had recently declared that for women to wear drawers at all was indecent),[4] and she herself obviously was scandalized by certain extravagances:

"To be dressed *à la sauvage* was to have all that part of the frame which was not left uncovered clad in a light drapery of flesh colour. The bodice under which no linen was worn (shifts being an article of dress long since rejected at Paris) was made of

knitted silk, clinging exactly to the shape, which it perfectly displayed; the petticoat was on one side twisted up by a light festoon.
The feet were either bare or covered with flesh coloured silk
stockings with toes like gloves."

The total weight of a fashionable woman's clothes could be no
more than two pounds, much of it diaphanous, and the need for
Directoire knickers was obvious.

The first view of a traveler entering Paris would confirm the
impression of irresponsible and universal gaiety. "A stranger,"
wrote the same Miss Williams, "entering the city at night by the
bridge of Neuilly would on his right discern the lights of Bagatelle
beaming through the Bois de Boulogne and would pass close to
the brilliant entrance of Idalia. On his left he would be dazzled by
the illuminations of the Elysium, while as he advanced he would
discern above every quarter of the town the tall sky rockets dart-
ing their vivid flash." [5]

But the glitter of Directorial society was as ephemeral as were
the flares of the rockets; in morning light Paris was a dirty town,
dilapidated and uncomfortable. The great houses of the aristocracy were either taken over as public bureaus, or let out in sections by speculators to what tenants they could find. Landlords of
all grades had been hit by inflation, and buildings were in a general state of decay; latrines were choked up and filth thrown into
the road. Artisans and small shopkeepers blocked up the streets,
and there was no authority to stop them. The passers-by, when
the dances were over, were more likely to be shabby than models
of fashion. Wigs and knee breeches had vanished; clothing was
not indeed classless, but nearer to classlessness than it was to be
for many years to come. One could tell by looking at a man
whether he was in his working clothes or not, and whether he was
prosperous or not, but not whether he was noble, or professional,
or bourgeois, or small employer, or artisan. If he was a common
laborer he could be recognized, it is true, for he would be unlikely
to have any but his working clothes to wear.

What was true of Paris was true to a lesser degree of the provinces. Most of the towns had suffered less and were less dilapidated, but the marks of poverty and recent decay were still obvious. There were few balls and routs given by the newly rich, with

their ladies dressed *à la sauvage;* the nobility and upper clergy
who had once set a standard of elegance were either in flight or
careful not to call attention to themselves. The peasants, coming
into town, were immediately recognizable, but they were not miserable or in rags; they were proprietors now. So far from giving a
picture of feverish extravagance, provincial society would have
impressed a spectator as becoming settled and already a little
drab; nor would he have been greatly misled.

The period of the Directory owes its reputation of being at
once frivolous and dull to a double cause—part historians' prejudices, and part natural human love of drama. The Directory's
task, and the aim in which it partially succeeded, was to consolidate the gains of the revolution, and to prevent either a return of
the monarchy or a revival of the Jacobin terror. This was a tedious task, involving great difficulties, complex shifts, unpleasant-
nesses and meannesses; neither at the time nor later could it rouse
enthusiasm. The Directory was (as the historian Alphonse Aulard
summarized it) conservative on property, liberal in defending liberty and the revolution, antiroyalist, anticlerical, and anti-Terror-
ist; the republic, in short, though faded, was still there. But it was
not what it once had been, when

> not favoured spots alone, but the whole earth
> The beauty wore of promise—that which sets
> The budding rose above the rose full blown.

That the reign of liberty had begun for the world had been and
still was a cry which could rouse enthusiasm; that a sound currency had replaced the *assignat* was not. The Directory has had
the further misfortune of being succeeded by regimes which had
each their own reasons for running it down, and under whom
writers almost unanimously spoke of it with contempt. Bonaparte, most adept in annexing other people's credit, needed to
appear as the longed-for savior who rescued a despairing nation
from a sequence of corrupt incompetents; his supporters and historians followed him, and a great many of the successes of the
Directory are still quite coolly ascribed to his Consulate. After he
had fallen, France was governed by monarchists, to whom any
republic was anathema; the Jacobin leaders were hated as savage

giants, the Directors despised as venal dwarfs. The consensus of complacent condemnation was not broken until 1839 when Étienne Cabet, known as the "Icarian" from the name of his socialist utopia, published his four-volume *Popular History of the French Revolution*. His book was almost an explosion. The revolution was not defended in it; it was diligently praised as the best and noblest event in French history. It was a shining contrast to the bellicose, profiteering and vicious regimes that followed it, and still ruled France. The story he told was almost as simple and almost as distorted as the official one; yet in it the unlucky Directory was cast once more for an ignoble role—that of traitor. It was the Directory, he said, which destroyed the Roman virtues of the French citizens of the great days of 1792, '93 and '94. It corrupted and rotted republican morality by the exaltation of the love of money and self-indulgence. "The Directory established the lottery, the source of immorality and of disasters to the People" merely to get money, and all its foreign adventures, especially in Switzerland, were nothing but robbers' raids.[6] By this pimp's work, it opened the doors for the monster who followed it, Bonaparte. The battle for and against the revolution has raged ever since in the studies of French historians, but it was not until the turn of the century that one of real eminence (again Aulard) made a serious attempt to do justice to a despised interlude.

Neglect was made easier by the personal character of the Directors. There were always five of them, and they usually worked fairly successfully as a committee. Like most good committeemen, they tended to be colorless, "faceless" and industrious; there had been one man of genius among them, Lazare Carnot, the undramatic organizer of the victorious armies of the revolution. But during an attempted royalist coup of 1797 he had despite his past remained neutral; he was, inevitably, dismissed and only his record saved him from deportation. The Directors sitting in 1798 were named Merlin, François, La Révellière-Lépeaux, Reubell, and Barras.[7] Merlin (de Douai) was a hard-working but characterless lawyer, whose specialty was the drafting or correcting of constitutions, in which he had plenty of employment this year; François (de Neufchâteau) was the only Director who showed any interest in encouraging production—he arranged an exposition this year[8]—he was replaced halfway through the year by Treilhard, a quarrelsome lawyer; the three remaining Directors were those who were the real center of the government. Only one of them, Barras, had what now would be called a public face, and it was a disgraceful one. They were all genuine republicans (so far as Barras was genuine in anything). None of the five—except again Barras—was corrupt; the Directory was indeed an unusually honest government and when corruption was discovered (as in the case of Schérer, the War Minister, and his brother) it was dealt with sharply. But no government which had Barras in it and Talleyrand as its Foreign Minister could have a good moral reputation.

La Révellière-Lépeaux was a Girondin whose brother had been guillotined; he was strictly honest, industrious, unimaginative, and a frequent and tedious propagandist. Anti-Jacobin though he was, he was more concerned with the danger of reaction. He thought the church a more immediate threat to the republic than the Bourbons; he warred against it with more vigor than sense; he patronized a religion invented by a bookseller named Chemin and called Theophilanthropy. It was deist, met in churches and in its tenets and its ritual anticipated Auguste Comte's Positivist Church; but it did not long survive Lépeaux's fall from power. Reubell was the strongest and best of the Directors; a firm-willed Alsatian, without charm or eloquence, he had been a Jacobin and sat in both the Constituent Assembly and the Convention. He was profoundly republican, though authoritarian in principles and manner. If one studies (for example) the official papers dealing with the Swiss question, it is difficult not to be struck by his industry, his instant comprehension, his clarity of thought, and the decisiveness of his instructions.[9] It was a serious loss when in 1799 he was replaced by the vain and shifty Abbé Sieyès, who (if any one man did) really opened doors to Bonaparte. Barras was an ex-viscount, a handsome man, a onetime army officer who had made a fortune out of the revolution, but remained inordinately greedy, despite his aristocratic mannerisms. He was courageous, and could act quickly at need; he was unusually intelligent. His taste in women was comprehensive and

deplorable; he alone was responsible for the aura of extravagance
and licentiousness that hung around the Directory. His male
friends had no more morals than his female; but their weaknesses,
or strengths, were financial. He was closely linked to a group
which the Directory could not dispense with, known as the contractors (*fournisseurs*).

For the Directors, conquerors abroad, were in perpetual money
trouble at home. When they first took office the *assignat,* the
paper currency based on the confiscated property of *émigrés* or
the church, was almost worthless. A hundred francs of *assignats*
was worth forty centimes, and not enough money could be printed
daily for each day's needs. After repeated and desperate struggles,
the Directory had returned to a metallic currency; the economy
was healthier as a result, but the government was hideously poor,
and with no possibilities of maneuvering. Its contractors, for the
army or for anything else, supplied the goods in advance; the Directory was always in their debt; they had liens on all sorts of
government property, even on the unsold crown jewels; they and
the bankers had the government financially in their power. Neither the morals nor the habits of the *fournisseurs* were republican.[10] The Treasury was hostile and rigid, even to the extent of
refusing ministers money which the Directors ordered it to pay.
For any enterprise, however important, funds might have to be
scratched up by irregular means. General Bonaparte, for example, after his appointment to command the army to invade Britain, called on Tom Paine, now almost starving in a Paris garret,
for a subscription. He told him that a gold statue ought to be
erected to him, and that he (the General) slept with *The Rights
of Man* underneath his pillow; he collected one hundred livres off
him (little more than a matter of shillings)[11] and left contented.

It was not only in matters of finance that the Directory was
shackled. The Constitution of the Year III, under which it oper-
ated, was carefully drafted to prevent either the restoration of the
monarchy or the terrorization of the assemblies by the clubs of
Paris; in a period of external peace and of political calm it might
quite possibly have worked. There were three bodies that shared
sovereignty. The Executive Directory of five appointed and controlled all ministers, and was the directing executive body, as its

name implied. But it could not dissolve or even address the Councils; it could only send messages. There were two Councils: the Elders (*anciens,* forty years old or more, two hundred and fifty of them), and the Council of Five Hundred (thirty years old or more). The Five Hundred passed resolutions of principle, which the Elders then turned into laws. They also provided a panel of possible directors (ten times the names needed) from which the Elders selected the successful candidates. No common sessions of the sovereign bodies were permissible, nor could the Five Hundred appoint any permanent committees, like the terrible Committee of Public Safety. It could suspend the freedom of the press, indeed, but for one year only, and the Directory could arrest citizens without a warrant, but for twenty-four hours only, and only for conspiracy against the republic. The right to vote was restricted more than in the high days of the revolution, but it was more democratic than almost anywhere else in Europe. Anyone who paid any direct tax was an "active citizen" and had a vote, by which he chose an "elector" who attended cantonal meetings where with his fellow electors he chose the members for the area; an elector had to be a thirty- or forty-franc freeholder or leaseholder. (He would not be likely to be able to go to cantonal meetings otherwise; even as it was, the nuisance of turning up at assemblies that occupied days and wasted time over verifications and points of order made attendance irregular and gave opportunities for minority control.) The commune of Paris, a frightening name since 1794, was divided up, as were other great municipalities; political clubs were not forbidden, but they were not allowed to federate or send in collective petitions. Those provisions would deal with the Jacobins; to deal with the royalists was easier. Those *émigrés* who had returned from exile and had been "provisionally struck off" the register of enemies were barred from office; the priests who continued to fight against the constitutional church could be deported.[12] The Councils had power to frustrate any arbitrariness by the administration—as they did in January of this year when the police seized some cloth intended for members' uniforms as "English imports"; they passed a law ordering the Directory to hand the cloth back, and it did.[13]

But there was not secure peace abroad, only an unstable armistice; there was not political calm at home. There were two active groups, Jacobin and royalist, anxious to overturn the Directory; there was a great lassitude in the population of France which made it unwilling even to vote, let alone take any more troublesome activity. The local authorities kept sliding under the influence of one group or the other, and the Directory was drawn into autocratic actions which strained the constitution and which, it may well be, it regretted and disliked.

Since the days of Cabet it has become customary to describe the rule of the Directory as the rule of the bourgeoisie; this is roughly true, but only if the word bourgeoisie is used in a rather different sense from the present day or even Marx's day. The ruling class was still the Third Estate of 1789; its leaders were "officials, lawyers, professional men, proprietors, financiers and merchants." There were scarcely any industrialists, for the economic effects of the revolution had been to liberate trade, not to increase production, in which England was far ahead of France; and even so the commercial element was relatively weak.[14] Writers, actors, civil servants and even artisans were esteemed and listened to as never before; the peasants indeed took no active part in politics, but the authorities would not offend them, knowing their support was indispensable. There were certainly class divisions still, but the classes were mingled more than they were later; in the tall thin houses of Paris the rich bourgeois occupied the large salons on the first floor, the poor man climbed up to the mansard attics.[15] The only groups which had been excluded from power were a minority of the workers, the mostly unskilled sans-culottes who paid no taxes, and the totality of the nobles and upper clergy.

But these two groups, with their sympathizers, were able to use the weaknesses of the constitution to threaten its destruction. The Directory had just had a near escape from a royalist plot, known from the republican name of the month when it occurred as "Fructidor" (roughly, September 1797). It was a genuine plot, and "English gold" did in fact play a part in it; Pichegru, a successful republican general and president of the Five Hundred was its head; its organizations had names like the Friends of Order, Legitimate Sons, and the Philanthropic Institute. They had infiltrated local authorities and had got near to a majority in the Five Hundred; one Director (Carnot) was neutral and one (Barthélemy) a conspirator. It was defeated partly by the invincible stupidity of the Bourbons; what the monarchists in France wanted was the constitution of 1791 with a constitutional king and no feudal laws, but "Louis XVII," the poor child who might have served, had died and his successor, the Count of Provence, who lived abroad and called himself Louis XVIII, declared in favor of absolutism and the *ancien régime*.[16] Both he and "the emigration" as a whole believed that the monarchy was deeply beloved by the people, who were longing for its return. It was untrue; it never had been true; even at the death of the "Sun King," Louis XIV, the people "laughed and drank and sang; they shouted insults and obscenities after his corpse when they saw it borne along the rue de St. Denis. 'I cannot recall it without horror' wrote the duke de Richelieu. 'The death of the most odious tyrant could not have afforded more pleasure.' " And on the death of his successor, Louis XV, called "the much-loved" (*le bien aimé*), there was "the same laughter and drinking and singing and shouting of insults after the corpse along the rue de St. Denis. *'Va-t-en salir l'histoire!'* shouted from the pavement by some nameless drunken genius was his funeral oration." [17] But the more immediate cause of the royalist defeat was the swift action of the republican three, Reubell, Barras and Lépeaux, in calling in not only the army, but retired officers up and down the country. The French army and navy were unlike any other in the world. They were, or had been, the "nation in arms" as no other force had been since Roman days. The old officer caste had been completely eliminated; between 1792 and 1795, 110 division commanders, 263 generals of brigade, and 138 adjutants general had been dismissed. In 1794 the soldiers had passed the unexampled figure of 850,000 armed young citizens; and though wars and desertion had thinned their numbers, this had had the effect of making them more like a volunteer force,[18] and so more politically conscious. But they were not as yet a nationalist force, nor were they moved by the appeals to *"la France," "la gloire"* and such, which degraded French oratory for a hundred and fifty years to come. They were, or believed they were, the forces of freedom everywhere and for everyone. They campaigned under the famous decree of the Convention in No-

vember 1792, "Wherever French armies shall come, all taxes
tithes and privileges of rank are to be abolished, all existing authorities cancelled and provisional administrations elected by universal suffrage." It was unrepealed for them (though less so for
the Directory, which would have traded some of their conquests
for peace). A curious evidence of the dedication of even the common sailors survives in a perplexed note by one of Nelson's rat-
ings named Nicol. In the American wars, he remembered, French
sailors when made prisoners of war were carefree and even merry,
but in 1798 they were "sullen, and as downcast as if each had lost
a ship of his own." The armed forces felt themselves to be, and
arguably they were, more truly the republic than either the sans-
culottes of the Terror or the "electors" of the Five Hundred.[19] Nor
did they ever fall to the level of a praetorian guard, or a modern
South American or African army. When they intervened, it was
because they were called by the civilian power. Nevertheless, at
Fructidor they came; the deputies pointed out by the Directory
were arrested and the treacherous officials expelled. The republic
was saved; the monarchy lost its chance. The three Directors that
day had made it certain that the French monarchy would not in
the end survive, as later history was to show. But they had also
used military force against an elected assembly.

Momentarily, however, they could feel confident. The populace
was prosperous; this year it had what was its traditional demand,
the "Three Eights"—bread at eight sous a four-pound loaf, meat
at eight sous a pound, wine at eight sous a pint. All foodstuffs
were so plentiful that prices were between twenty-five and thirty-
three per cent lower than in 1790, a famous year of abundance.
There was more wine than even the French could drink. The
countryside was less pleased, probably, especially as tax reforms
were halving the one and a half to two years' delay in payment
under the old regime. But after the years of brigandage, devasta-
tion, civil war, and famine even farmers were unlikely to be seriously discontented at luxuriant crops; certainly few citizens would
look back longingly to the days of the "maximum" and food riots.
However, prosperity, though real, was unstable; there would not
every year be harvests as good as the last three, and the enormous
expense of the victorious armies might not be met forever by the

liberated peoples. If the victors returned home and were not disbanded the already shaky finances of the government would be broken into ruins. The Directory was fully aware of the need to protect French solvency at the expense of neighboring countries, even by methods that were difficult to square with the Convention's resolution. There remains, for example, a letter signed by Carnot, Reubell and Barras to General Moreau, commanding the Army of the Rhine, dated 29th Thermidor, Year IV. It says that because of the competition by the Swiss city of Constance with the silk workers of Lyons he is to send to France all high-quality silk-manufacturing machines, to destroy all the others, to wreck all establishments *soit en maçonnerie, soit hydraulique et en mécanique* which could be used for silk manufacture.[20] Afterward the Directory would consider whether there was adequate reason to compensate the town, by diminishing the contribution that it had to pay for opposing the revolutionary armies.

However uncertain, or immoral, such devices might be, there was for the moment peace and comfort, and the revolution could rest and expand. There was an efflorescence of energy, or a relaxation, or a flowering, or what metaphor you please. There is a picture in the Salpêtrière Hospital which symbolizes the freedoms which the revolution had brought; it is of Citizen Pinel, the republican superintendent at Bicêtre, striking the chains off the lunatics kept there. There was a similar sudden disappearance of the chains on men's minds, and the relative calm of 1798 allowed the scientists, philosophers, historians both to pursue their investigations and to publish the results, free of any fear of the monarchy, the church or the guillotine. Cabanis laid the foundations of medical psychology; Berthollet of modern chemistry; Haüy of crystallography. Lamarck, Cuvier, and Saint-Hilaire were teaching and lecturing at the Museum; other names that the world remembers were Monge, Lagrange and Laplace. One advance which even the most Philistine could not deny was made this year; a congress of scientists in the winter at Paris fixed the length of the meter (which was to be one forty-millionth of the earth's circumference) and on that has been based the whole metric system.[21] What that meant in accuracy and human convenience only those can understand who have had to calculate in arpents, sous and quin-

taux. There was less to record in the arts. Great poetry and prose
is written before or after a revolution, but rarely during its progress; the most popular book under the Directory was a translation
of the poems of Ossian, a Highland epic forged by a Mr. Mac-
pherson some thirty-five years previously. In painting, J. L. David
was "almost an artistic dictator"; he was by no means a bad
painter—indeed, his portraits are magnificent—but what he was
admired for was his vast dramatic scenes in the classic manner,
such as his "Oath of the Tennis Court" which is continually reproduced in illustrated histories.[22] Such imitations of what was
supposed to be the style of the ancient world were an inexorable
fashion; other periods were despised. Leonard Defrance, who selected for the nation the pictures to be brought from Belgium,
ignored all the fifteenth- and sixteenth-century canvases as "the
first stages of the slow and difficult progress of art" and left them
behind to become the pride of the Brussels Museum.[23] The only
name unquestionedly of the first rank is that of P. J. Redouté,
"flower painter to the nation," whose exquisite prints (with those
of his brothers) are an unfailing if limited delight to this day.[24]

The defeat of the royalist plot of Fructidor was followed by a
repression which was savage in its threats and enactments, but
less brutal in fact. Death or deportation was decreed for all
émigrés, even readmitted officially, who did not leave France
within a fortnight, and for all "refractory" priests; Sieyès demanded that all people of noble origin should be expelled from
the republic. Deportation was to French Guiana, so unhealthy
that it was called the "dry guillotine." There were, perhaps, a
couple of hundred executions, and some eleven thousand persons
marked down for deportation. But only twenty-five out of every
thousand were ever actually sent to Guiana, and though the mor-
tality there was high, the majority of the deportees were elderly;
deportation moreover ceased entirely in August. The royalists, in
short, were not annihilated, but cowed and deprived of their leadership; the most serious result was that the police now had, and
used, great powers of inquisition into the lives of citizens. The
number of dismissals of mayors, local councilors and local officials is unknown, but in one disloyal department, Sarthe, three-
quarters were ejected and replaced by government supporters.[25]

The government's struggle was more persistent against the church than the crown; it was probably the period of the Directory which made France a lay state; the papal Catholics learned for the first time in history that they must live with others. Their church was weakening far more than its defenders cared to recognize. The constitutional church (which had defied Rome by supporting the republic) was a great deal stronger than later propaganda suggests. Even though it was no longer government-supported, it had forty-four officiating bishops at the beginning of 1798, and in Sarthe, once a center of the "Chouan" rebellion, there were one hundred and twenty-two constitutionalist priests compared with two hundred Romanists. The papal church was hardly recognizable as the rich and domineering church of 1789. Few recruits came in to replace the old priests; education had been taken out of its hands; unused churches were sold; and, what was highly disquieting to its natural and respectable supporters, its priests were giving the example of law-breaking. If the Directory had had more sense, or if the deeply conscientious La Révellière-Lépeaux had not been allowed to direct its anticlerical policy, it might have secured a more complete victory, that which the French called *la laïcité de l'indifférence;* the church could have crumbled even further in a society which was no longer interested in its dogmas, and disliked its hierarchy. But logic and the decimal system drove him forward; laws were passed and decrees enforced requiring the universal observance of the ten-day week, with the tenth day, *"décadi,"* as the day of rest. The constitutional clergy were required to "sanctify" that day instead of Sunday and celebrate mass then (which many of them refused to do), "civic sports" were organized for it, and a large number of other republican festival days were authorized—altogether too many; the result was merely to destroy the value of holidays like Bastille Day which had till then had a real meaning for many of the people. Religious processions were forbidden, pilgrimages were vetoed, bell-ringing was stopped, and priests were not allowed to wear their vestments in the street. The conflict was on between "Monsieur Dimanche" and "Citoyen Décadi"; a less rigidly principled man than Lépeaux would have realized that Mr. Sunday was bound to win. The French people were not going to work nine days a week. The regulations were simply not obeyed; at the best, the workers and peasants rested on both days. The new calendar was an irritation in the lives of almost every citizen; the silencing of the bells and the stopping of religious processions removed from his life color which he missed; moreover, this was not at all the "freedom of religion" which was guaranteed by the constitution. Anticlericalism seemed to be petty persecution, and an attempt to overwork the honest laborer by a trick; the official agents of the Republic One and Indivisible appeared as pettifogging nuisances.

The Directory was, however, soon occupied with what seemed much more immediately serious. The assemblies had to be renewed one-third at a time, and the purge had caused many additional vacancies; an election had to be held. The repression of the royalists after Fructidor had had a result which anyone but the Directors would have foreseen; it increased the power of the Jacobins—in modern political terms, the Left benefited from the defeat of the Right. The Jacobins of 1798, however, were not the same as the "Mountain" of 1794. Since the fall of Robespierre that year there had been an attempted coup by some of them which alarmed the bourgeoisie of France almost as much as the memory of the Terror and the *démocratie sociale* of the Year II. This was the Babouvist conspiracy of 1796. Babeuf and his followers did not fly the red flag, their projects for the public ownership of industry and agriculture by a "grand national community" never came near to practicability, his writings were no more than an uncanny preview of socialist programs a century or so later,[26] and the whole insurrection was so mismanaged that it was little more than a scuffle outside the soldiers' barracks at Grenelle. But it brought a new particular element of fear and dislike to the minds of the anti-Jacobins, from the highest Director to the lowest peasant; to terrorism and the "agrarian law" they now added "anarchy" as an unforgivable political crime, and by "anarchy" they meant Babouvism. The remaining Jacobins were not Babouvists; they had at the most some nostalgic hankerings for price controls and punishments for hoarding and profiteering. They benefited from the genuine revulsion against the royalist plotters, and the belief that they were more vigorous and more reliable republicans than the Directors. They obeyed the laws carefully; they federated no clubs. They only formed "constitutional circles," to which many of the new local councilors belonged, which concerted means of rooting out unrepublican tendencies in the departments. In Le Mans the circle organized what it called "ambulations"; every *décadi* its members congregated in a nearby town where sympathizers had arranged a *fête* to welcome them, which ended always in the formation of another circle. The Directors quickly became alarmed; Merlin was given the job of organizing the election. He fired the chief of police; he sent out special envoys to local *commissaires;* he arranged for the electoral inspectors to make trouble for the electors traveling to the cantonal meetings; he allotted them secret-service funds and provided a list of right-thinking candidates; he encouraged the *commissaires* to make wholesale arrests on suspicion of citizens who seemed likely to be troublesome. His most successful device was to disrupt the cantonal meetings by organizing minority groups which challenged the credentials of their opponents and at need "elected" a rival list which he could accept. He may quite possibly have thereby in fact secured a majority of yes men. But this was far from certain, and the sitting Council members were more to the left than before Fructidor. In short, the constitution was still too democratic for a firm opinion by the electors to be suppressed; the list of successful names was disagreeable. La Révellière-Lépeaux in particular remembered his brother's death; and he was also told in persuasive detail that the terrorists had arranged to murder him. He was to be killed on his regular morning walk through the Jardin des Plantes to call on a botanist friend named Thoin. When the Councils began according to routine to examine the credentials of the newly elected members, and to throw out, one after another, not Jacobins but Merlin's protégés, swift action had to be taken. The Directory sent a message to the Councils, declaring that there was a double conspiracy, of the "White Cockade" and of the "Red Cap," and both must be outlawed. Its spokesmen in the Five Hundred produced an omnibus list of Jacobin members who ought to be excluded—one hundred and six in all—and demanded that they should be expelled without investigation. There were violent debates; "the guillotine is there," shouted one supporter named Crassous, "are you going to walk to it?" (*"La guillotine est prête; voulez-vous y monter?"*) On the 22nd Floréal (May

11, 1790) the pressure was successful; the Council obeyed. The soldiers had not been called in; but the Executive Directory had enforced its will over the elected assembly on a matter which was, if anything was, essential both to its independence and to the freedom of French citizens.

Protected, as it thought, from enemies on either side, the Directory made serious efforts to free itself finally by getting out of the grasp of the *fournisseurs*. Immediately after Fructidor it announced a consolidation of the national debt, one-third of which was entered on a Great Book and could be used for paying taxes or buying *biens nationaux,* while the other two-thirds were represented by more paper. This was called cynically but adequately the Two-thirds Bankruptcy. It set up a tax office in every department, and began seriously the unending war between the French *contribuable* and the tax inspectors. It compelled the cowed assemblies at last to vote unpopular taxes—on patents, newspapers and advertisements, tobacco, doors and windows, salt, registrations and coach tickets. This was not enough to free the government entirely; it was still grotesquely short of money (the Treasury, for example, blankly refused any money for an invasion of Ireland).

Momentarily, however, the liberated countries shouldered the largest expenditure—that on the armies—and even provided something over. Both sorts of internal enemies had been overcome. All was well. It does not seem to have occurred to the Directors that so far from strengthening their position, their actions had undermined it. Nobody admired the Directory; nobody indeed had enthusiasm for any particular group of politicians; it stayed merely because there seemed to be no alternative. There was, however; it was the army, whose generals one day could be called upon once too often.

The Directory had in 1798 a chance to consolidate the republic, to turn it away from war-making and toward internal peace; it could have altered the course of history. But it failed—not because it was frivolous, corrupt or incompetent, but because its members were overnervous, overconscientious, intolerant, unnaturally unimaginative, and plain stupid.

4

"DIRECTORIZATION": THE FATE

OF THE SMALL REPUBLICS

I T IS not true that all revolutions follow the same pattern. But there are certain limited sequences which do appear to repeat themselves; there are situations which recur and are dealt with similarly. In particular when a revolution exports itself, and smaller countries around it are also revolutionized, there is apt to come a time when the revolutionaries in the minor countries are dispensed with, and replaced by those approved by the originating country. This may be done civilizedly or brutally. After the Russian Revolution had passed out of its genuine revolutionary phase it was done brutally. Kostov in Bulgaria, Rajk in Hungary, Slansky in Czechoslovakia and the rest of them did their task in securing total Communist control in their countries; they and their associates were then judicially murdered by more acceptable servants of Russia who took their place. This

process, from the name of its beneficiary, was called "Staliniza-
tion," but there is no name for somewhat similar events which
took place in the year 1798. Perhaps it may be permissible to call
them Directorization. Because Frenchmen are not Russians and
because the eighteenth century was not the twentieth, the men
who were turned out of power in the minor republics were not
killed—they were often not even imprisoned—and although they
were abused in fairly mechanical rhetoric, their reputations
suffered nothing similar to the servile and savage slander of the
later period. But though their fates were not as dramatic or dreadful as those of Rajk or Kostov, and though their names are even
more forgotten, their tragedy was real. They had helped, as they
believed, to raise their country out of slavery and brought it liberty and equality; they saw it falling instead under the rule of a
foreign power. They may easily have thought that their work, perhaps indeed their lives, had been valueless. The changes in the
government of the Cisalpine, Ligurian, Helvetian and Batavian
republics were not crude captures by a foreign center. The inhabitants were not openly taken over by French commissars; they had
the more difficult task of quickly and correctly adjusting their policies and changing their politicians to fit in with the changing policies and rulers of their French masters.

The first and easiest victim was the Cisalpine Republic, whose
territory was the large area of northern Italy captured from Austria by General Bonaparte. Though the treaty with it declared it to
be free and independent (*"puissance libre et indépendante"*)[1] it
was summarily forced to change its governors as early as February. It found a powerful defender, its creator the onetime Jacobin,
Bonaparte. The arrest of several members of its Council and the
proposal to arrest two of its Directors, Moscati and Paradiso
(whom he had approved himself) shocked him into making a formal protest to the Directory. "I feel it my duty to tell you that
France and liberty have no truer friends than these two Directors," he wrote, and added the penetrating comment that "the
disparagement of the Cisalpine government and the loss of its best
citizens" would be a misfortune for France and a triumph for the
Austrian Emperor and his partisans.[2] It was no good; Moscati
and Paradiso went out, and so did their counterparts in the Ligu-

rian Republic, the name now given to Genoa and its hinterland. What the Directory wanted was control; so far from deferring to popular generals it was sending out commissars to control them as in the great days of 1793, though not with equal success.[3] The commissar sent to the Cisalpine was named Trouvé, and he had in his pocket a constitution which was said to be the personal production of the French Director La Révellière-Lépeaux. Before it could be put into force, by submission to a series of "primary assemblies," it was necessary to make a fresh change in policy and governors. On August 13 Trouvé expelled one hundred and sixty members of the Cisalpine legislative Council, and two more Directors, named Testi and Savoldi, who till then had been considered satisfactory. The Cisalpine army had been engaged in a rather ineffective war against the King of Sardinia, who ruled over Piedmont; it was now called back by the French Directory, which announced that in order to protect the King its own army would occupy Turin, in answer to an appeal from him. This it did, adding another satellite to France, but the Cisalpine politicians were still not at rest. The local general, Brune, intervened and dismissed three of Trouvé's nominees from the Directory, replacing them by three of his own, and recalling a number of the expelled members of the old legislative Council. He did, however, put the Lépeaux constitution to the primary assemblies, which naturally accepted it, and for the moment there seemed to be stability.

There is no evidence that the Cisalpinists in general much resented the continual reshaping of their executive and legislature. They had too recently escaped from the medieval prison house of Austria to criticize their liberators at all sharply. But this was not true of Holland. The French minister there, writing home to the Directory, listed almost naïvely the reasons why the revolution could not command the passionate enthusiasm it found elsewhere: "No nobility to overturn, no rich and powerful clergy, everywhere republican habits, long usage of free speech only momentarily chained by stadtholder tyranny, strong traces of ancient frugality and economy, habituation to public meetings and discussion of public affairs." [4] It would be hard to find a more concise summary of the immediate benefits the French Revolution

brought to its citizens; their absence in Holland left the French
with only two trump cards in their hand, the nuisance of the ancient constitution and the objectionable behavior of the exiled
Stadtholder and King, William V. William, whom few even of
Dutch historians admire, had in 1787 used Prussian troops to
turn his position as stadtholder into that of a nearly absolute
monarch, and European capitals had been filled with highly respected Dutch exiles. When the French armies broke in and
chased him out, he fled to Hampton Court near London, issued
instructions to all the Dutch colonies to surrender themselves to
the British, and published proposals for an English invasion of
Holland and the reduction of France to "its size when ruled by
Henry IV." [5] The exiles returned joyfully, and the French, in those
early days, took great care not to interfere with Dutch customs
and institutions. The new republican regime was mild, there were
few confiscations, and fewer revenges.[6] The provinces retained
great powers. Two Dutchmen, or Batavians as they were now expected to call themselves, came into prominence, Schimmelpenninck and Daendels. They were, and are still, more substantial
figures than Moscati and Paradiso; they also played their cards
better, but the game was essentially the same. Schimmelpenninck
presided over the convention which was called in 1796; Daendels
was the premier general—indeed practically the only one of importance.

The country used to be called the United Provinces and the
chief defects of its constitution, indecision and slowness, were due
to the fact that power lay with the provinces and not the central
government. Groningen, Frisia, Holland, Zeeland, and Overijssel
were perhaps the most stiff-necked and obstructive of the provinces. The convention produced a centralized constitution for a
Batavian Republic, one and indivisible; it submitted it to a refer-
endum; the provinces rejected it by 108,761 votes to 27,955 and
Schimmelpenninck resigned. A National Assembly took the place
of the convention and politics seemed to go on in the old way
throughout most of 1797, when conservative policies were in
favor in France; but after Pichegru's conspiracy had been put
down a little more Jacobinism seemed in order. A new French
Minister and the French General Joubert came in January 1798

to an understanding with a Herr Midderich, "a decided Republican," who defeated Herr Meederwort ("who was a Patriot last year but this year is a Federalist") and in the nights of the 21st and 22nd arrested the Foreign Affairs Committee, twenty-two assemblymen and ten others who would not swear an oath of hatred against "Stadtholderism, Aristocracy, and Federation." [7] The French troops were very correct, staying in their barracks, and the new government's proclamation apologized for "the cruel necessity" of arresting M.P.'s and promised not to hurt them "being fully aware of the fatal effects of a system of Terror." The Assembly under its instruction nevertheless produced a new constitution very like the previously rejected one, with a Directory and two Houses; but this time Midderich saw to it that the Dutch voted in favor of it by 153,913 to 11,597. Yet the unfortunate new Directory had only a few weeks to enjoy its power; by June the French Directory had decided, because of "Floréal," that Dutchmen with any taint of Jacobinism had better go. General Daendels got the message sooner than the French Minister; he declared the Assembly ought to be dissolved, the Minister denounced him to the French Directory as an enemy of the people, he drove to Paris, explained the position, and came back. The Minister was recalled "to his great displeasure"; Joubert and his troops walked peacefully about the streets, not firing a shot; Daendels did not so much drive out as gently push out the Dutch Directory, replacing it on July 31 by five harmless men named Hasselt, Haersolte, Hermerins, Hettema and Hooff. They added the word "anarchy" to the list in the oath of detestation, and decreed that "no power should have the right to interfere with banks in the cities of the Republic." Otherwise, they made little mark in history, but Daendels and Schimmelpenninck, who now became the permanent Dutch envoy in Paris, proved to have great powers of survival. Schimmelpenninck became in due course Grand Pensionary and ruled Holland until Bonaparte wanted its throne for his young brother Louis; Daendels became governor of the Dutch East Indies. Their country had reason to be grateful to them; they protected its citizens skillfully during what might have been a period of great oppression; one of Schimmelpenninck's first acts was to secure the French Directory's assent to a general act of amnesty.[8]

The Dutch were more fortunate than their neighbors to the south, the Belgians, because Belgium (previously the Austrian Netherlands) was not recognized by the Directory as a separate entity at all. Most of the inhabitants spoke French, the country had been incorporated into France and divided into departments, and there seemed no reason to treat it or its inhabitants differently from any other part of France. They ought, indeed, to be rather more enthusiastic and grateful than the average Frenchman; had they not received the benefits of the revolution without having to fight for them? Nor were these benefits imaginary; the old feudal distinctions had been wiped out. "New taxes, graduated on income, made no exemption for the nobility and clergy; civil marriage and divorce by consent were recognized; believers, dissenters and atheists were given equal status, and civil hospitals were established." [9] The church property which had been sequestered was often put to excellent use—Baudeloo Abbey, for example, was made a central library of books and its grounds into a Jardin des Plantes—and a new system of education was set up. There were Écoles Centrales now in all nine departments. True, a triumvirate of French artists, headed by Leonard Defrance, had collected something under three hundred of mostly seventeenth-century paintings and sent them to France; but they had never been public property and their absence was hardly noticed.[10] It was more important that William Jacob Harreyns, an eminent painter and the director of the art school of the École Centrale of the Antwerp area, collected some hundreds of paintings from churches for his students, cleaned them and housed them in a secularized convent. This became the nucleus of the Brussels Museum; art was in fact being brought out of darkness and shown to the people.

The people, or some of it at least, remained oddly ungrateful, and the French or French-appointed officials were greeted unpleasantly often by the surprising cry of "Vive l'empereur!" The emperor who was called for was not even alive; he was Joseph II of Austria, whom they had not much liked when he was. Joseph had been an enlightened despot, an eighteenth-century philosopher-king, who had tried to enforce reforms from above, by edict and without popular support. He abolished serfdom, instituted a regular police, reformed the judicial system, drafted a civil code, issued a decree of religious tolerance, and tried to concentrate most of the power of the old diets in his own hands. He dealt particularly firmly with the Roman Catholic Church; he secularized education, severely cut down the power of the Pope, and closed the so-called "contemplative" monasteries and convents. (There had as a result of the last action been a previous massive release of paintings; Reynolds came over to Brussels and Antwerp in 1785 to buy the pictures of the suppressed houses but found them "the saddest trash ever collected together"; only two Rubens and a Van Dyck were worth picking up.[11]) His reforms met with such determined resistance that after a few years he canceled most of them and died. But in his short reign he had sharply disciplined a clergy that badly needed it, and cut away from the church its most idle, useless and parasitical parts; the unforeseen result was that the still furiously resentful priests were much less unpopular in Belgium than in France. The justice, and the profitability, of the secularization of the remaining ecclesiastical property was far less evident to the citizens. The Directory began this year, 1798, to sell the confiscated estates, *biens nationaux*, and found that they went slowly and at poor prices. They were in large units unattractive to small buyers, much being unprotected forest; there was some disapproval on principle; there was also a wide fear that the Emperor—Joseph's successor, Leopold—might return and take back the church's land and even the ordinary estates.[12] Local authorities had been purged of sympathizers with the priests, and the nine commissars appointed by the Directory to the nine departments are described as being "almost absolute"; they were indeed frequently arbitrary, having to chase two enemies, the "anarchists" (Jacobins, presumed to be followers of the late Babeuf) and the Catholic reactionaries. They, and their staffs, were also ill paid, and are described as "avid and taking bribes." [13] Brigandage was rampant in the country and even spread to the large towns, bridges broke down, roads became impassable —the disorganization was such that, as the commissar of La Lys wrote to Paris when the British made their descent on Bruges, "General Championnet cannot understand why the English did not take Ostend, invade the countryside, and burn Bruges and

Ghent." As the year went on, the Directory entangled itself deeper and deeper in a religious conflict with a good half of the population. The commissars tried to force the observance of the ten-day week—shops were closed on *décadi,* and work forbidden; their orders were obeyed for a month or two and then forgotten. "Reunions" were held in churches on that day; nobody attended, but on what had been Sundays services would be held in them, or privately. If necessary, they would be "blind" (that is, without the presence of the proscribed priest). The priests were ordered to swear an oath of hatred to royalty and anarchy; they threw up their hands and declared that to swear hatred was un-Christian. When they were prosecuted they vanished and held full-scale services in the forests. Government agents were sent out to knock down crosses and holy images in public places; crowds either obstructed them or put the crosses and statues back as soon as they had left.[14] In October the Directory decided to extend conscription (for young men between twenty and twenty-five) to Belgium, and this sort of Belgian Fronde became more serious. For a few weeks there was what is rather grandiloquently called a "Peasants' War"; half-armed crowds attacked the centers of various communes, drove out the authorities, and destroyed all the documents they could. They were known as the Roomsche Katholijke Jonkheed, were mainly Flemish, and were directed by the clergy. They were defeated whenever they met the small detachments of French soldiers sent to deal with them, and by the recapture of the town of Hasselt on November 5 the insurrection was effectively over. But the Directory did not get the soldiers it expected, and had to content itself with seizing the church bells in the defaulting communes and sending them to Le Creusot to be melted down for guns.[15] It then issued orders for the annihilation of the real organizers of the discontent; 7,500 "ferocious druids" (as Wirion, the gendarmery's commander, called the priests) were to be deported to Guiana via the Isle of Ré. But the execution of this outrageous decree proved impossible; the lists were wrongly made up, many had to be deleted, most of the rest escaped. Three months later, out of nine hundred marked down in the department of Sambre et Meuse precisely twenty-four had reached the Isle of Ré. All that the Directory had on the credit side was the formation of one Theophilanthropic congregation; it was in the town of Liége.

Switzerland was a republic and had been so far longer than France, ever since 1291, but it deserved that noble name less than Holland and almost as little as the recently destroyed Republic of Venice; it was a complicated oligarchy. Power rested with the original thirteen cantons which had retained their various constitutions (not all democratic); the others were either "allied" or subject (and in one case, Neuchâtel, a Prussian principality). The center of the Confederation was at Berne, which had the canton, or rather *"pays,"* of Vaud as its subject. The defeat of Austria had removed the Confederation's effective defenses, but its rulers were too complacent to realize this. The Vaudois were already in revolt, under an ineffective general named Weiss; the Bernese oligarchy as a sufficient concession to the new spirit of the age had granted Bernese citizenship to two Vaudois families.[16] Everyone else realized that their rule was doomed, especially as a sixteenth-century treaty gave France the right to assure the freedom of the citizens of Vaud.[17] The only question was what would replace it. There were three French residents in various cantons and one chargé d'affaires in Berne; each drew up his own plans for reform, as did General Brune, who was advancing to the aid of the Vaudois with part of the French Army of Italy. (He had decided to divide the country into three.) They might have saved their ink; the matter had been settled on December 8 of the previous year at a dinner in Reubell's house, between him, Bonaparte and Senator Peter Ochs of Basel. The text for a "one and indivisible" Helvetian Republic was already drafted, and revised by the French Director Merlin.[18] The Bernese oligarchy, still in its comfortable daydream, announced that the Vaud "estates" should be summoned next year for a general reform of the constitution, and called for a *levée en masse*, on the French model, to hold back Brune. Most of the Swiss called up did not arrive; those who did shot their own general, D'Erlach; on March 28, a special French representative proclaimed the new constitution, and the old regime was effectively over. Only the cantons of Schwyz, Uri and Unterwalden put up a serious resistance; the Bernese indeed tried a last and typical device—they bribed Talleyrand, the French Foreign Minister. Talleyrand took the money, of course, but neither could nor would do anything to help them.[19] The real power was in the hands of Rapinat, brother-in-law of Reubell, who corresponded directly with the Directory and whose name to the Swiss soon became the equivalent of rapine. He seized the whole Treasury of the Confederation and extracted a contribution of nearly a million pounds sterling from the thirteen cantons (not for himself, but for France; it was used to finance a new campaign by General Bonaparte). The new Swiss Directory (of five, as usual), the old chargé d'affaires reported, "consisted of those whom I had indirectly designated"; this would not do in view of French policy changes, so Rapinat turned two of them out and replaced them by Ochs and a citizen called Donder. He also arrested a number of eminent Swiss merely on his own authority.[20]

The position of the Swiss was not as humiliating as this recital suggests. Their Legislative Assembly declined to accept Ochs and Donder, and though they eventually agreed to Ochs (as well they might, for he was as good and useful a citizen as Schimmelpenninck was to Holland) Citizen Donder vanished from history. The Swiss Directory made direct and vehement protests to the French Directory against Rapinat, culminating in a requisitory listing ten improper actions,[21] and he was recalled. The treaty of alliance offered by France and accepted in September was by no means harsh; it provided, among other things, for French troops to leave the country in three months, and also secured every Swiss the right to work at any trade that he chose. The Swiss indeed lost the four things which they, or at least their rulers, most treasured: their money, their complacency, their social rigidity, and their perpetual neutrality. But, like other nations, they escaped for the moment from a social prison. The Swiss revolutionary movement was an authentic one; a recent historian lists as evidence the names of three men in Zürich alone who found in it their inspiration—Fuseli the painter; Lavater the theologian and physiognomist, and Pestalozzi the educator.[22]

The least live of the new republics was one of the earliest, the Roman Republic. The reasons for this may be disputed. There was certainly little enough love for the Pope and his government of greedy clerics; at the same time there was little ardent republicanism. The Roman clergy's exemption from taxation, the Pope's extravagant fondness for his nephews, the squalid poverty of the ordinary people—these and like reasons for discontent had been too long with them to exasperate the Romans. Some had indeed attempted a riot in December last, with the only result that the French Ambassador, Bonaparte's elder brother, Joseph, had been driven out and a French general called Duphot killed. The establishment of the Roman Republic was a deliberate act of policy of the French Directory. Three members of it, Lépaux, Barras and Reubell, had sent a reasoned letter to Bonaparte while he was still in command in Italy: "15th Pluviose, Year V. You are too much given to reflection, Citizen General, not to have felt as strongly as we have that the Roman religion will always be the irreconcilable enemy of the Republic," it began. "The Executive Directory therefore invites you to do all that you consider possible (without compromising in any way the safety of your army . . . and without rekindling the torch of fanaticism in Italy instead of extinguishing it) towards destroying papal government." [23]

They suggested that he should either hand Rome over to another power, as he had done with Venice, or (which would be better) install an anticlerical government there whose behavior would force the Pope and the Sacred College to go. The expulsion of Joseph Bonaparte gave the necessary excuse; Bonaparte's successor, Berthier, was instructed to invade the states of the church. He was received without interest or opposition by the populace and entered Rome on February 11. Pius VI expressed his willingness to accept any conditions the French proposed, but this was not what was wanted; the local republicans set up a government and demanded that he should go away. The new constitution (once again drafted and revised by Merlin) abolished the Inquisition and other arbitrary organs of papal government; the government confiscated the estates of the religious orders, began to distribute them, and "dispersed the crowd of monks who had in past years flocked to Rome." It was criticized, however, for not closing "the office dispensing bulls and briefs for benefices." [24]

There were, however, soon more serious reasons for discontent. Berthier was replaced by Masséna, later famous as Prince of Essling and Napoleon's cleverest and least likable marshal. He was also the greediest; his robbery and pillage of the wealth of Rome was so gross that the French army mutinied against him, and forced the Directory to recall him,[25] but not before he and his fellow thieves had half stripped the city.

As for the Pope, he was pushed out of Rome, and went first to Siena in Tuscany and then on to a Carthusian monastery near Florence. The old gentleman seemed to his entourage to be more cheerful in distress there than he had been for some while in the Vatican. Outside, the grand opponents of the French, the British, viewed his fate with a divided mind. He was an enemy of their enemy, but hardly a friend. The *Annual Register*, no longer written by Burke but still marked by his style and thought, could not bring itself to defend the head of the Roman Church, the enemy of all freedom of thought and of all Protestant powers; it described him as "hated during the latter part of his reign by his subjects for multiplied errors of conduct both public and private, despised for his puerile vanity, detested for his protection to his nephews who had become the legalized plunderers of the State, and fatiguing the whole world by the involuntary crime of existing far beyond the longest period allowed to his predecessors." But it considered that he had been submitted to some singularly ingenious humiliations which should have been spared him. "The officer charged to notify him that he should leave Rome was a general of the name of Calvin. Monsieur Reinart, under whose control the Pope submitted to place himself, was a Lutheran divine." [26] It produced no evidence, though, that the selection of these persons was purposeful.

SUMMER AND AUTUMN

II

I

NELSON, BONAPARTE,
AND EGYPT

Toulon, the great French naval base, has changed beyond recognition. The old low buildings and houses facing the sea were destroyed in the Second World War; the rest of the town had long ceased to resemble what it had been. But the shape of the port, and the line of the coast, are the same; it requires only a small effort of the imagination to see the harbor as it was on May 19, 1798. Something slightly under or over two hundred ships of war (the figures are variously stated) were sweeping past in a sort of gigantic review in front of the general in charge of the expedition and the admiral commanding the fleet, Bonaparte and Brueys. By an odd chance an Arab poet, Nikula ibn Yusuf al Turki—Nicholas the Turk—watched and recorded the sight. "When the people of Toulon looked at the horizon they could no longer see water, but only sky and ships;

they were seized with unimaginable terror." [1] Terror was the wrong word; it was Oriental good sense to assume that viewers would naturally think instruments of war horrible; pride and admiration were the more probable emotions of the Toulonnais, and of the sailors too. It is almost impossible for a modern writer to describe or even imagine the physical thrill, almost of ecstasy, of standing on the deck of a ship like Brueys's flagship, *L'Orient*, the largest afloat, at the moment when the wind filled its sails and drove it forward, as it did on this cool but clear morning. Stand today on the deck of a small sailing ship, and you may feel a faint approximation of the same sensation; the air fills the sails and pulls them, the mast transmits the energy, all the timber of the boat answers, the strength pulses through the ship, and through your feet into your whole body. You are part of one concerted leap of energy, and the most modern liner seems in comparison nothing but a metal box with an engine in it. For eighteenth-century sailors this integration (as the modern phrase would be) was a matter of every day; but it may well explain why they loved evil old ships with sour captains, why they manned the shrouds and cheered for the slightest reasons, and why the crew under Collingwood (of all commanders) "danced every moonlit night." [2]

The French sailors, their admiral, and even the general had some reason to dance, if they did. The mere departure of the flotilla was a triumph; they had to leave in May or not at all, for in August the Nile would flood and the conquest of the Egyptian delta, their objective, would be almost impossible.[3] It was by great good luck that they had been able to get away; a detachment of the British navy was on the watch, under its most daring commander, Sir Horatio Nelson. But the accidents of wind and weather had played into their hands; Nelson was starved of frigates, which in the days of sail were the eyes of a fleet; and the rumors carefully put about by the French had persuaded the British that the armament's destiny was most probably Portugal or Ireland.[4]

Their luck held; the other units (nearly all from Bonaparte's old Army of Italy) were picked up safely from their embarkation ports of Genoa, Ajaccio and Civitavecchia, and on June 9 the fleet, now of something like four hundred vessels, appeared in front of its first and easiest objective, the island of Malta.[5] Its masts "looked like a huge forest"; the rulers of the island, the Knights of Malta, made hardly a token resistance. Four days later, in decrees of admirable brevity, General Bonaparte ended the feudal system, made all inhabitants equal, abolished slavery, expelled the Knights, annexed their treasury, sent General Berthier around the prisons freeing all held in them "because of opinions," opened a Central School with instructors in "arithmetic, algebra, geometry, astronomy, mechanics, physics, chemistry, navigation and oriental languages," made the hospital start courses in medicine, anatomy and midwifery, and put the islands under a governing commission of nine, of whom eight were native Maltese, to whom no such thing had happened since Phoenician days.[6] He thus completed the first item of his instructions from the Directory, dated April 12, which he had himself effectively drafted. These (abandoning the plan to invade Britain) told him to seize Malta, conquer Egypt, improve the conditions of the natives, cut a canal at Suez, enter into relations with Tippoo Sahib (the sultan of Mysore in Southern India), and return in about six months' time to take command of the army for the invasion of England, by which date the Irish would have risen in revolt.

The man to whom these instructions were issued was as unlike as well could be to the glorious figure of the Emperor of later writers, or to the villainous figure of his contemporary enemies. He was neither godlike nor the incarnation of evil. His most intelligent enemy, Wellington, later said "Bonaparte's mind was, in all its details, low and ungentlemanlike" and compared him to a particular gangster leader, Jonathan Wild, the eighteenth-century equivalent of Al Capone. "Even in the boldest things he did there was always a mixture of apprehension and meanness. I used to call him Jonathan Wild the Great, and at each new coup he made I used to cry out 'Well done, Jonathan!' " [7] There was some truth in this, for in details if not in general principles, there was an element of gutter cunning in Bonaparte all his life; but it was not the full truth. Indeed, probably the present generation is the first that can easily understand Bonaparte; only those who have lived through the days of a later revolution and for whom Stalin has been a contemporary can quickly comprehend him, as he was in 1798 anyway. He was at a stage of development which is not uncommon among revolutionaries; what he was to become later has no bearing on what he was then; hindsight is the greatest misleader of historians. For at this time, against the belief of many historians, against even his own account of himself, there is no reason to believe that he was not sincere.

The list of the considerable library which he had put on board *L'Orient* for his use survives; it gives a clue to his mind. He had already briefed himself fully on his immediate task by studying Near Eastern conditions while he was in Italy; when the great Milan library was taken to Paris it was found that the books on the Orient were covered with notes in his handwriting. The books aboard were for his reading, and they fell into two sharp divisions —military textbooks or military biographies, and works of republican morality, largely (as was the fashion) based on ancient history. All Plutarch, Tacitus, and Livy were included; the poems of Ossian, Tasso, Ariosto, Homer and Vergil; two large books called *Histoire Philosophique des Indes* and *Les Moeurs des Nations;* and for lighter moments the novels of Voltaire, *"Héloïse, Werther, Marmontel,"* and *"40 romans anglais,"* whatever they can have been.[8] This was the library of a skillful and industrious soldier, determined to rise to the top of his profession, but in political matters a rather simple republican with a liking, which of course might not last, for the vague and grandiose. The liking was genuine; a soldier on campaign does not load himself or his transport with stacks of books which he does not think essential.

He did not merely like republican principles; he knew that it was they which had made his life tolerable and his success possible. When he was still Napoleone Buonaparte and Louis was King of France, he was the sort of young man who even today would be instantly recognized—the one intelligent and industrious member who has to provide for a whole voracious, unviable and desperate Italian family. Charles, his father, had been a charmer, a ne'er-do-well, a lawyer of alleged good family, unsuccessful, volatile, pretentious, and perennially hard up, who died in 1785 leaving his wife unprovided for and having fathered a large and youthful family. His flabbiness was compensated for, indeed overcompensated, by her rigidity; Letitia Bonaparte was a type of matriarch whom some will admire, and some detest; but who is often delineated in magazine articles. She was utterly devoted to the family whom she saved by her unremitting toil; she was rapacious, narrow, harsh (she flogged her family, and birched even Napoleon when he was sixteen), and cynical. She despised the family which in her hawklike way she loved; she was sure they were second-rate and shiftless like their father, and when pressed in later years to recognize Napoleon's fantastic success would only answer in a thick Corsican accent, "Supposing it lasts, that is" (*"pourvou que ça doure"*); when he dared to reproach her for not spending the money he insisted on giving her she replied contemptuously that soon he'd be very glad of her savings.

It never entered his mind, naturally, not to accept the burden of this family, which was both large and inept. His elder brother, Joseph, was a fool; the other brothers were at the best mediocre —the only one who showed something of his intelligence and decisiveness was Lucien, and predictably enough they disliked each other. The girls were pretty, bold, and one anyway was no better than she should be. While his father was still alive, and hopes were still grand, Napoleon had been sent to the tough military school at Brienne to become a French officer. The Minim fathers who ran it were ignoramuses, and the genuinely noble French pupils jeered at his Corsican pretensions, calling him "La-paille-au-nez" (straw-in-nose), mocking both his outlandish name and his rustic behavior; he was tormented until by his almost savage reaction he intimidated them.[9] He had only just been promoted to a richer, more advanced and civilized school in Paris when his father died, and from being hard up he became desperately poor. He had not only to provide for himself, but for his brothers and his family—some of whom, like little Louis, would be physically tagging around with him when he moved from place to place. He joined, as early as he could, the regiment "La Fère" at Valence as an artillery officer, so that he at least came on a payroll. Though he was a French officer, his opinions were those natural to a young Corsican who had read Rousseau and was now studying "Voltaire, the Abbé Raynal, Necker, Adam Smith, Herodotus, Strabo, Diodorus Siculus, Plato, Ossian, Homer and Plutarch."[10]

There was in Corsica a noble sandy-haired Highland figure
who seemed to some people to incarnate all the virtues of classical heroes, the General Paoli whom Boswell so admired that he
brought him, with fair success, more than once to dinner with Dr.
Johnson.[11] It was inevitable that Bonaparte should become his
supporter; for, as he wrote to him when he was just twenty years
old, "I was born when my country was dying. Thirty thousand
Frenchmen, vomited onto our shores, were drowning the throne
of liberty in blood." As often as he could (and military discipline
was slack) he traveled back to Corsica both to help his family
and to work for Corsican freedom. Soon the beginning of the
French Revolution modified his thoughts, as it did those of every
young man. Corsica became freer every day, and Paoli more powerful; but great patriot though he was, he was no more suited to
be a ruler of a state than Garibaldi (whom in many ways he re-
sembled). Bonaparte could see this; moreover, what was happening in France was more profoundly significant than any local
events could be.

The world has become skeptical since then of days of dedication, national vows of resistance, vast and theatrical meetings,
solemn covenants, and such paradings of emotion. But sometimes
these have had the importance that their organizers hoped, though
not usually those most energetically organized and best-recorded.
One such occurred on the 14th of July, 1791. On that day, all the
civil, military and ecclesiastical officials, the mass of the people of
Valence, and delegates from twenty-two associations around
swore before a great altar in the drill ground that they would sus-
tain the constitution, obey the National Assembly, and if need be
die defending French territory against invasion. These words, so
commonplace today, broke up in men's minds a whole system of
society, based on loyalty to the king—in the mind of one of those
who swore, at any rate, for Bonaparte wrote: "Until then, I have
no doubt that if I had been given orders to turn my guns against
the people, habit, prejudice, education and the King's name would
have made me obey. With the taking of the national oath, it became otherwise. My instincts and my duty were now in har-
mony." [12] His ideal society, about this time, has been summarized
as one of "equality of station and purse, purity of life and man-

ners, religion without clericalism, free speech and honourable administration of just laws";[13] after one ineffective attempt to reform Corsica on these lines and turn out Paoli, he brought his family out to France, the only country where his vague Utopia might be founded. There, once war had broken out, he was fulfilled; he became a soldier of the revolution. He soon showed he was one of the best. In 1793 his skill and courage were largely responsible for the recapture of Toulon from the British, and the following winter, under the inspiration of Robespierre's younger brother, Augustin, the representative of the Convention in the south, he was largely responsible for the plans being made for invading northern Italy.

The execution of Robespierre the elder stopped the plans temporarily, and checked Bonaparte's career, also temporarily. However, he served the new "Thermidorians" as zealously as the Jacobins; there was no reason why he should not. Historians see in the fall of Robespierre a turning point; it was not so seen at the time. It was more commonly seen as stabilization of the revolution and the end of the Terror. What Bonaparte had most admired, the military vigor of the revolution, was maintained and even increased by Carnot and his colleagues. Bonaparte had not seen the taking of the Bastille; the day of August 10 provoked in him only a technician's contempt for the cowardice and incompetence of a king who allowed a massacre of disciplined soldiers who, properly led, could have dispersed the crowd. The famous surges of Parisian revolutionaries meant nothing to him, and when in October 1795 the cleverest of the new governors, Barras, called on him to organize the defense of the Convention against an attack by the Paris "sections," he wiped the attackers out by artillery fire. He cannot have known he had thereby put an end to a period of history—the people of Paris would never again control the government and alter the world. Nor in fact was the "mob" that he dispersed the same as the heroes of 1789 and 1792; these rebels were the well-to-do; the elite of the rank-and-file revolutionaries was now in the army.[14] In any case he did not get the credit, or discredit, of the "victory of Vendémiaire"— Barras stole it—but he was back in favor now, though as poverty-stricken as ever.

His passion for the revolution was no doubt cooler than it had been—he now saw it as a war upon ignorance (and genuinely so; nothing flattered him more in 1797 than his election to the Mathematics Section of the "National Institute" which replaced the French Academy). This is a milder if more civilized emotion; but it was complemented by one more violent and equally natural to a young man of twenty-six—love for a woman. These two emotions were still the directing forces in the mind of the general who had just sailed into Malta harbor; his character, as it then was, had been formed, and to all appearances fixed, in the winter of 1795 and the year 1796.

In October 1795 he met and fell in love with a woman six years older than him, Josephine de Beauharnais, a widow whose husband had been executed by the Jacobins, and who herself had been in prison till Robespierre died. There she had made a great friend, Thérèse Cabarrus, afterward the wife of Tallien, an eminent "Thermidorian"; the two young women when released were a pretty and predatory pair. Thérèse was a plump dimply blonde, very much to the taste of the nineties, Josephine a lean brunette with a fine profile, much more to our taste. Both were selfish, impeccably mannered in society, clever in a superficial way, fairly promiscuous, and very good-looking, though past their first bloom. Josephine was, or had been, the mistress of Barras, Bonaparte's patron. She lived in a style above her means, and among the theories by which his family, naturally furious, explained Bonaparte's proposal to marry her was that he needed the money she seemed to have. It was not true; with his experience he could recognize at once a penurious pretense at gentility, and indeed sympathize with it. He told Bertrand many years later, "I found out the truth about her finances before I married her, and in any case marriage with a woman of a grand old French family was an excellent thing for me. I was a Corsican, after all." [15] But this explanation was equally false; it arose from his preoccupation at Saint Helena in proving that nobody had ever fooled him, that he had always been the smarter one. No doubt he was flattered by the condescension of one of the belles of Paris, but snobbery or ambition was not the basis of his courtship; he was foolishly, passionately, helplessly in love, and his letters remain to prove it. He

met her in October; he married her in February; at the end of
March he was in agony because she had called him *vous* and not
tu; on April 21 she was *"ma douce amie"* and he sent her from
Italy "a kiss on your heart, and one a little lower, much lower."
Four days later, fearing she did not love him, it was: "Goodbye,
Josephine. For me you are a monster whom I can never understand. . . . I love you more every day." On May 15: "Make
sure to tell me in your letter that you are certain that I love you
more than it is possible for anyone to imagine. That you know for
sure that every instant of my life is reserved for you. That there
never passes one hour in which I do not think about you. That it
has never come into my head to think about any other woman.
. . . A thousand kisses on your eyes, on your lips, on your
tongue, on your . . ." [16] The editor of the imperial correspondence found the last word "illegible."

Josephine reciprocated none of this; the marriage was for her a
matter of calculation. She did not love him; he was indeed not a
lovable figure either in 1796 or now in 1798. He was skinny,
undersized and gauche. He wore cheap and ill-kept clothes, even
his uniform was ill-fitting, his hair was uncombed and unclean
and hung lankily down to his shoulders. He either stood about in
brooding silence, or talked too long and rhetorically in an ugly
Italian accent. He had a prominent bony nose, a hard mouth,
rather alarming dark-blue eyes, and a yellow face, disfigured intermittently by a minor skin disease described as a "tetter." [17] But
everyone knew he was a rising young general; Creole women age
quickly, and she was passing her prime; there was no future for
her as a temporary amusement of Paris politicians; he had fallen
violently in love with her. She had sense enough to seize her
chance, but not sense enough (though she must have seen how
domineering he was) to give him the loyalty and devotion he assumed she would.

The conquest of northern Italy in 1796 which transformed him
from a rising young general to the most successful soldier of the
republic made some change in his character, but not the radical
transformation that is usually supposed. Historians have regularly
pointed to his famous proclamation to his army before the campaign began as evidence of his moral decay—as, indeed, the sig-

nal for the degeneration of the republic itself. "Soldiers, you are
naked, badly fed. The government owes you much; it can give you
nothing. . . . I will lead you into the most fertile plains in the
world. There you will find honour, glory, riches." But this promise and invitation, if indeed he ever made it,[18] seemed to him
merely realism; his wish (as was Lenin's) was to be a more practical revolutionary than the others. If the republican armies were
not fed, clothed, paid and armed they would be defeated; the Directory was bankrupt and could not provide; why should not the
countries they freed support their liberators and defenders? Did
they not owe them everything? And as for the riches that were
taken—the jewels, the gold, the treasuries, the pictures, the wines,
the statues—whom were they taken from? Not the common
people, who never saw them, but the dukes, the nobles, the kings,
the cardinals, and the priests whose power and wealth it was the
central aim of the revolution to destroy. In applying this easily
defensible principle he made a modification natural enough to a
Corsican adventurer, but disastrous in the end. The military helped
themselves; the riches promised did not by any means go only
into the republican treasury. Bonaparte himself was not corrupt;
indeed, he was austere to the point of ostentation (which was not
very wise for the husband of Josephine) but he made a mistake
many have made, he condoned the rapacity of others and even
encouraged it, thinking it gave him a hold over them. Here was
the Jonathan Wild streak in him; it prevented him understanding
the damage it did to his followers. General Marmont, for example, was sent to seize the tax collector's reserves in Pavia,
which had revolted. "We had at that time *une fleur de delicatesse*
which made this duty painful to me. I was afraid of being suspected of turning it to my own profit. I grumbled but obeyed, and
made sure that the money was checked by all the officers I could
find. Later General Bonaparte reproached me for not keeping it
for myself." [19] Marmont did not long retain his flower of delicacy.

Delicacy had never flowered in Corsica; still, the man who had
said to the new Ligurian Republic "the true conquests, the only
conquests that cost no regrets, are those achieved over ignorance" [20] meant what he said, and he sailed from Malta to Alexandria in the confidence that he was commissioned to extend free-

dom and knowledge to the enslaved East and sustained by the love of a noble and beautiful wife and mother who had faced prison and death for her principles a mere four years ago.

His luck held. Nelson, on the watch, had been too swift; he had worked out that Bonaparte must be heading for Egypt, and sailed straight for Alexandria. But when he got there, there was nothing to be seen; only some lackadaisical Turkish or Arab soldiers and merchants who gaped at him. He decided he must be mistaken, and sailed north again, while the French ships were lumbering slowly along. The two fleets, indeed, apparently passed within hailing distance of each other one night. And as a result Brueys's whole expedition anchored intact in the wide bay of Aboukir near Alexandria on July 1.

The journey had been highly disagreeable. Bonaparte had enjoyed (between bouts of seasickness) ceaseless discussions with the mathematicians, geologists, engineers, artists, chemists, biologists, geographers and historians whom he had coaxed into accompanying him; his enthusiasm for the new scientific age was still virgin and he had even communicated it to relatively elderly scientists like Berthollet and Monge, the introducer of the metric system. But he and they were almost alone in their cheerfulness. The transports were vilely overcrowded; the men were sick ("vomiting blood"); provisions went rotten and water ran out; the sailors and their officers were anxious and apprehensive; the weather was abominable. Even on the day of landing the seas were so heavy that a score of men were drowned. There would indeed have been no landing at all if Bonaparte had not given a direct order to Brueys.

He marched his army immediately upon Alexandria, whose apparently classical sky line was silhouetted against the horizon, and took it with ease, his troops suffering much worse from thirst than from the incompetent opposition of the sparse and surprised defenders. They found the city a curious introduction to the gorgeous East, to which they were bringing civilization and freedom, and from which each was to acquire his own reasonable share of Oriental magnificence. There were, to begin with, only about six thousand people in it. "Of the city of Alexandria," says a contemporary account, "built by the architect Dinochares, containing the

library of Ptolemy, and renowned for industry, commerce and activity nothing was left but ruin, barbarism and poverty; stupid-
looking citizens with long pipes indolently sitting in the public
places, half starved and naked children, and the forms of bare-
footed women in blue serge gowns and black stuff veils flying at
the approach of any Frenchmen." There were indeed relics of the
glorious past, but they were broken up or (if marble) sawn up to
construct the hovels the mongrel population lived in. "Nothing
was entire but a bath of black granite, the Pillar of Pompey and
the obelisk of Cleopatra." [21]

It was a disappointment, but not important; the splendor and
luxury would no doubt be farther inland. Bonaparte and his team
of scientists undismayed began their work of revolution at once.
A proclamation was written and printed, from type they had
brought with them; it was a sign of how backward the country
was that this was the first time anything at all had been printed in
Egypt. Its text showed the thought which its author and his colleagues had given to the conditions of Egypt; indeed, the adaptations they had made to attract the natives went almost too far;
years later Bonaparte described it as "charlatanry, but of the
highest quality." [22]

"I have come to restore to you your rights and to punish the
usurpers. I worship God more than the Mamelukes do, and I respect his prophet Mohammed and his admirable Koran," he
wrote. He had arrived, he continued, as a friend of the Sultan of
Turkey, the overlord of Egypt and its rightful ruler. "The French
have shown at all times that they are the particular friends of His
Majesty the Ottoman Sultan (may God preserve his rule!)." Religion having been bowed to and legality affirmed, next came the
economic appeal. "Is there a beautiful estate? It belongs to the
Mamelukes. Is there a beautiful slave, horse, or house? All this
belongs to the Mamelukes. If Egypt be their farm, then let them
produce the deed by which God gave it to them in fee!"

The reference to the Turkish Sultan may not have been wholly
hypocritical. Bonaparte believed that the Sultan would not mind
the restoration of some at least of his now quite imaginary authority over Egypt, and that Talleyrand was on the way to Constantinople to secure his benevolence. He was wrong in both cases.

Talleyrand was not going to any such dangerous place, and the Sultan officially told his Grand Vizier: "When the unhappy tidings from Egypt came to Our Imperial Ear, a full month after that insufferable event had come to pass, such were Our grief and concern that, We take God to witness, it drew tears from Our Eyes and deprived Us of sleep and rest." [23] He sent the British admiral a present of a diamond plume and a pelisse of sable;[24] two hundred coffeehouses in Constantinople were raided, and many of their customers drowned or strangled for expressing a hope that General Bonaparte would capture the city and "effect a revolution" soon.[25]

The references to the Mamelukes were not hypocritical, and, if any Egyptian had read them, might have been effective. For in the extraordinary society into which the French army had been catapulted the one thing immediately clear was that the Mamelukes held all the wealth and all the power, and the rest of the country was in misery. The population was something under three millions at this time; the Mamelukes numbered something under a hundred thousand. They were completely separate from the rest of the people; they were a military caste who reproduced themselves scarcely at all by marriage and almost wholly by the purchase of suitable Circassian or Georgian children, who were trained as soldiers from their youth. They were probably the best cavalry in the world; they were certainly the most picturesque and luxurious. They were often taller and in general handsomer than their Arab and Levantine subjects; their appearance was gorgeous beyond modern custom. They wore wide red trousers, yellow pointed slippers, leather gloves, a chain-mail coat covered by a robe caught in at the waist by an embroidered cloth, and a green cap swathed round by a yellow turban. They were mounted on the finest Arab horses, and each man carried two pistols, a scimitar, a javelin or mace, and a carbine. Their weapons were studded with jewels or inlaid with gold and silver; they had a habit of carrying quantities of gold coins on their persons. No infantry had stood up to their charge for five centuries; they had broken the horsed and armored crusaders of Saint Louis; now the French had sent some more such they were confident that they could do the same again.[26] Murad Bey, one of their two chief leaders, who could

neither read nor write, decided that the invaders should either be
given a present and sent away, or annihilated. As any Mameluke
could cut off an infantryman's head with one reversed stroke from
his scimitar, this would not be difficult.[27] He led a small number of
Mamelukes—some 4,000 perhaps—with about double the number of half-armed attendants to deal with them. He came up with
the French at a place called Shubra Khit or Shebreissa[28] between
Alexandria and Cairo.

Bonaparte's men had had a poor journey southward. Their
General, as usual, had marched them too fast and too far. They
were miserable in their thick serge uniforms under the Egyptian
July sun; they were overloaded; they were parched because the
wells were either dry or deliberately stopped up; if they straggled
they were cut off by the Bedouins who were continually harassing
them. They would then be stripped of all they possessed, and possibly killed—if not, the women (there were far too many camp
followers and wives) would be beaten casually but thoroughly
and the men sodomized, the Arabs exclaiming over their beautiful
white bodies.[29] They were prepared for none of these things, and
even the generals were openly discontented. The army was almost
awe-struck when it came in sight of the Mameluke camp, with its
white tents with brass globes and half-moons on top, its flamboyant standards, and the vast crescent of multicolored horsemen
moving and surging in front of them. The battle began unpropitiously with a cannonade between the French boats on the Nile
and the Mameluke boats. The guns of the latter were manned by
Greeks, whose aim was excellent; several French ships were
boarded and the crews' heads cut off. As usual, the victors held
the heads up by the hair and dangled them in the sight of the
enemy troops on the banks.

The French army, however, did not run away. It was drawn up
in squares, and whenever the Mamelukes charged them, they were
met with a barrage of grapeshot, cannon balls and small-arms fire.
They were unable to get to grips with the enemy at all; their
horses were shot down or they themselves were; their carbines
were no match for this concentrated fire; and they could slice off
no heads. Murad was perplexed; his men came back discouraged
to their original line, and then, when they were ready for another

great charge, a lucky French shot blew up the Mameluke ammunition ship with an enormous explosion. The Mameluke army
thereupon retired, not in the best of order; the French, in their
own time, resumed their march on Cairo. Their progress was as
hot and thirsty as before, and the Bedouins pestered them as
much.

The Mameluke leaders still had no understanding of what they
had to face, but at least realized they must bring up their full
strength. The forces were divided between the two chief beys.
Murad drew up his on the western bank of the Nile, in front of the
Pyramids, at a village called Embaba; his fellow bey, Ibrahim,
drew his up on the other bank, an arrangement typical of their
amateur strategy. Bonaparte naturally ignored Ibrahim and chose
to attach Murad, rather than cross the Nile. He probably did not
in fact point to the Pyramids and say to his army, "Soldiers, forty
centuries look down upon you," and if he did, they could not have
heard him. But that was what he thought; he was bringing enlightenment and freedom to the cradle of civilization; he and his army
were the successors of the Pharaohs and of Alexander the Great.

The battle was a longer and bloodier version of Shubra Khit.
The Mamelukes charged the French squares with unexampled
courage and dash; they did not break one. The French held their
fire until the last moment, and then swept the cavalry with a hail
of bullets. "The soldiers," wrote Lieutenant Vertray, "fired with
such coolness that not a single cartridge was wasted, waiting until
the very moment when the horsemen would have broken our
square." Before long Murad's Mamelukes were lying dead in
heaps, and the rest of the army was a wreck; some fled with
Murad south into the desert, some tried to escape by swimming
the Nile to the other bank, where Ibrahim's army could do nothing but scream, and cry to Allah. The French soldiers at last got
some of the opulence they had been promised; from the bodies of
the dead they got not only jeweled weapons but gold pieces—
"three, four or five hundred," according to Bonaparte.[30] It did not
matter that they were not eager in pursuit; Ibrahim realized what
had happened, hastily went back to Cairo, collected his harem,
his guards and their women, and the Sultan's representative, and
then fled eastward. The refugees who followed him were raped

and robbed by the impartial Bedouins; the people of Cairo set his palace and Murad's on fire. Seldom had a ruling class been more swiftly destroyed; the battle had lasted little more than a couple of hours.[31] Bonaparte entered Cairo formally on July 24. Ibrahim Bey and what remained of his army were chased right out of Egypt into Syria. Murad continued southward with the wreck of his. To a summons to surrender he answered, with a certain sublimity, by offering once more to give the French a present to go away; but he was too far off and his troops too disorganized for him to be thought a serious threat.

The French Republic was probably at this moment at the height of its power, in Egypt and elsewhere; Bonaparte too was in some ways at an apex. He was ruler of Egypt, a country of fabulous wealth and importance; for his work of liberation and renaissance he had a team of experts such as had never before been assembled.

Though his task might appear easier than his revolutionizing of northern Italy two years earlier (for there were now no Austrian armies threatening him) he already saw certain obstacles. "It would be difficult," he reported to the Directory, "to find a richer land, and a more ignorant, wretched and brutish people." Once the soldiers had collected the gold coins found on the bodies of their dead enemies, and once their officers had billeted themselves in the available beys' palaces, the French were unpleasantly disappointed with the capital of the gorgeous East which they had taken over.

"When you enter Cairo," wrote one of them, Major Detroye,[32] "what do you find? Narrow, unpaved and dirty streets, dark houses that are falling to pieces, public buildings that look like dungeons, shops that look like stables, an atmosphere full of dust and garbage, blind men, half-blind men, bearded men, people in rags, pressed together in the streets or squatting, smoking their pipes like monkeys at the entrance of their caves: a few women of the people—hideous, disgusting, hiding their fleshless faces under stinking rags and showing their pendulous breasts through torn gowns; yellow, skinny children covered with suppurations, devoured by flies; an unbearable stink, due to the dirt in the houses, the dust in the air and the smell of food being fried in bad oil in the unventilated bazaars. When you return to your house, no comfort, not a single convenience. Flies, mosquitoes, a thousand insects, are waiting to take possession of you during the night."

Clearly, the first thing to do with such a city was to give it a municipal government, and this Bonaparte did at once. It was called the "Divan" and had to be made up of sheiks, lawyers and ulemas (scholars—that is to say, Islamic theologians, for in Egypt there was no other learning) because nobody else was available, but a French observer was appointed to make sure that it at least attempted to do its job. After August, this observer was Tallien, the former Director and current husband of Josephine's best friend, Thérèse, who was sent out by the Directory, as some thought, to spy on Bonaparte. Anyway, he did his official work inconspicuously and reasonably well. In September, Bonaparte made a further effort to force freedom upon the Egyptians; he called a "General Divan" for the next month. It was to be the equivalent of the constituent assemblies in the liberated countries of Europe, but already the French had realized that they could not expect the same automatic reaction from the people. Direct elections were impossible. Each province was required to send three lawyer-sheiks, three merchants, and three representatives of the peasants, the mayors and the Bedouins; the French provincial commanders were told to see to it that these delegates were in fact representative.

This General Divan was meant to be, and might conceivably have become, the origin and guardian of freedom, the Egyptian Long Parliament or Estates-General; but almost at once the French saw that this was unlikely. The reaction of the natives to this, as to every reform, was either null or hostile. The members of the General Divan listened impassively to every proposal put to it, objected to or deferred deciding on any changes, and took only one definite action—they prevented the estates of the defeated Mamelukes from being divided among the peasants (the *fellahin*). The landlord system, they insisted, was the only thing that made the collection of taxes possible, and to preserve this they agreed to an estate duty. After a couple of weeks' wasted time, Bonaparte sent the delegates back home. The chance (if there ever had been one) of popular support for the new regime had been destroyed by the single decision they had made.

Egyptian governors, with French assistants, had already been appointed for the provinces, to replace the Mamelukes. The system of tax collection was reformed, and bribery in the courts was put down. Whipping of the accused to secure confessions was forbidden, and even stigmatized as "barbarian." [33] The canals were cleared, the streets were cleaned, sanitary regulations were introduced, water mills and windmills were built, and an even more startling invention, the wheelbarrow, was introduced into building operations; the police were reorganized and open violence in the streets came to an end. Almost every one of these reforms was unpopular. The taxes, as always, were collected by the Copts (the native Christians, and probably the true descendants of the ancient Egyptians) and the Greeks, since they alone could read and do arithmetic. They were already disliked and the effect of the French reforms was to make it more difficult to bribe them; "they behave like high officials," recorded an indignant Moslem, "they send you to prison." [34] The new police were almost as brutal as the old; Barthelmy, the Greek who was appointed as police lieutenant, presented General Dupuy, the military commandant of Cairo, with a sackful of heads of suspected Beduoin robbers just as he was sitting down to dinner. (It spoiled the General's appetite.) To be prevented from throwing rubbish into the street or burying dead relatives in the square and to have the sick almost forcibly attended by infidel doctors instead of being prayed over were insolent interferences.

Propaganda by example met as much resistance as decrees. Standards for bread were enforced and a higher quality was baked for the hospitals; severe penalties were enacted for anyone who supplied this bread "under any pretext whatever to the Commander in chief Bonaparte, or any other officers, including even the Quartermaster General"; the Egyptian staff marveled at this idiocy and stole it on a large scale.[35] Dr. Desgenettes, to show how baseless was the panic which isolated lepers and left them to die in huts or out in the desert, deliberately cut his arm with an infected scalpel; only the soldiers were impressed. Vehement orders to the troops against rape were issued, and enforced when needed; but their effect on Egyptian opinion was slight. Nobody, indeed, would wish to rape the lamentable hags in the streets, and the professional belly dancers needed no raping. In fact, what the invaders were accused of was a fatuous indulgence toward women. The Frenchwomen set an example of female emancipation, going about unveiled, riding horses, moving and talking freely, and arguing openly with men. Soon this example was followed by the detestable Coptic, Jewish and Greek women; eventually the infection even spread to Moslem women. It was unnatural as well as dangerous, in the opinion of the observer quoted before. "The French prided themselves on their slavery to women, and showered them with gifts, so that our women began to enter into relations with them," he recorded. "They disposed of all the wealth in the country and were submissive to the women, even if the women beat them with slippers." If they had slippered the women, and ravished small boys, they would have made a better impression upon the Egyptians.

There can rarely have been so concentrated, so intelligent and so unsuccessful an effort to drag a medieval society out into the modern world. The admirable team of savants which Bonaparte had brought with him worked enthusiastically, incessantly and in complete independence. When Bonaparte tried to intervene in a discussion on chemistry, the head of the Medical Section, the same Dr. Desgenettes, snubbed him openly. (*Bonaparte:* "Chemistry is the kitchen of medicine, and medicine is the science of killing." *Desgenettes:* "Indeed, General? Then what is your definition of the science of generalship?") They were organized into an "Institute of Egypt," the equivalent of the French Academy;[36] they were housed in the palace of Kassim Bey ("at least as luxurious as the Louvre") and provided with laboratories, a museum, an observatory, an aviary, a zoological garden, and a library unique in the East. The list of what they did, what they attempted, and what was printed on the two printing presses (which were themselves perhaps the most fundamental innovation) could not possibly be given here. At random one can cite the topographical survey of the Alexandrian area, the surveying, maintenance and clearing of the canals, the siting and designing of barrages and dams on the Nile, the study and selection of new crops and new methods of agriculture, the identification, description and illustration of the birds and fishes of the Delta region ("I live in the centre of a flaming core of reason," wrote Geoffroy Saint-Hilaire, the author of this monumental work), the preparation of a completely new educational system, the foundation of hospitals, and certain archeological and historical discoveries that need separate description.

The Egyptians listened to them, visited their library, watched their experiments, and even sometimes attended their lectures. They gave the appearance of being impressed, as was only prudent; but in fact were not even interested. Sometimes they let their real feelings be known; when Saint-Hilaire finished reading his paper on the fish of the Delta to the Institute, a sheik in the audience asked permission to speak. It was all wasted labor, he said, for the Prophet had declared that God had created 30,000 species, of which 10,000 inhabited the land and 20,000 the water; there was therefore no more to be said.[37]

Bonaparte to the end of his life could not quite believe in this utter noncomprehension. Even at Saint Helena he still thought the scientists might have been just on the verge of a breakthrough. "They were frequently in contact with working men, to whom they taught some elements of mechanics and chemistry." The Arab laborers had seen the advantages of the wheelbarrow, and some even more complicated devices, which their sheiks had not; would they not soon have seen the advantages of liberty, equality and fraternity? Perhaps they might have; but in fact it was the workingmen who were most openly hostile; it was they who broke out into open insurrection in Cairo on October 21, after the General Divan had dispersed, killed General Dupuy, and held the city for nearly two days. And the operative causes of their revolt seem by all accounts to have been the enforcement of street lighting, the sanitary regulations, the new estate tax, and the way women were being allowed to go about unveiled.

The most permanent, possibility the greatest, certainly in the long run the most sensational achievement of the French Republic in Egypt was one that the natives could hardly have been expected to appreciate. It was some years, in fact, before anyone did. It added a thousand years—much more indeed—to the known history of the world. A modern reader, conscious from his school days of the vast temples and carvings of ancient Egypt, and the imposing procession of dynasties reaching back into the earliest darkness, cannot easily project himself into the year 1798, when pretty well all that men knew about Egypt, south of Cairo at least, was drawn from the Bible, from the stories of Herodotus (whose accuracy was underestimated) and from some descriptions by the Greek geographer Strabo. The discovery was almost accidental; Murad and his Mamelukes were learning in their distress the art of guerrilla warfare, and had become a considerable nuisance, raiding in from the Fayum oasis or elsewhere in the desert, and even threatening a serious attack. Bonaparte sent his ablest general and closest friend, Desaix, up the Nile with some 4,000 men to catch Murad and inflict on him a defeat sufficient to end his power to annoy. As all republican enterprises were also civilizing expeditions, a member of the new Egyptian Institute was sent with it; his name was Vivant Denon; he was a young, nervous and rather dilettante artist and archeologist, handsome, with curly black hair. The campaign itself was neither important nor successful; the French chased Murad hundreds of miles as far south as Assuan, beyond which were nothing but unknown wastes. Only once did they succeed in pinning him down; otherwise the campaign is a confused story of running battles along or near the Nile banks, in which the Mamelukes escape before they can be crushed. Certainly, they were nearly exhausted, but as the months went on the French were in little better condition, in their hot uniforms under the terrifying Egyptian sun. Nobody, however, was more frustrated by this rushing to and fro than Denon. No sooner had he discovered a new marvel and got out his drawing board than the army would have to move again; on occasion he would be almost physically lifted up and taken away for his own safety.[38] Desaix gave him all the help he could, leaving a guard of soldiers sometimes with him as he finished his measurements and drawings, sometimes accompanying him as he explored great passages and underground chambers that no man had seen for a thousand years. There were huge, stiff, menacing statues, great temples silted up with sand—if he had time, and a few helpers, how he could have cleared them!—monuments toppled on their sides, formalized paintings still with their original brilliant colors, and all those unending incomprehensible inscriptions, half pictures, half unknown letters. Even in their untended state, disfigured by filthy Arab huts and village mess, some places were so awe-inspiring that the common soldiers of their own will halted and were silent. Denon hurriedly saw, recorded and described Dendera, Luxor, Karnak, and many other sites; at Philae he was able to spend some time. His drawings and descriptions were beautifully and carefully done; but he was more than a delineator and reporter. He began to understand what he had discovered. The size and majesty of Karnak did not conceal from him the rigidity and inhumanity of Egyptian civilization. "Not a circus, not an arena, not a theatre! Temples, mysteries, initiations, priests, victims!" [39]

But he was not to return to clear out the sand-choked temples, nor were his colleagues to be allowed to interpret the picture-writings. All the projects of the savants were to be canceled, the plans for health, for drainage, for roads and canals were to remain plans, the half-finished buildings were to stay half finished, the conferences, investigations, and learned papers were to cease. In one night the long lifeline on which they all depended was turned into a rope which was pulled; the noose was tightened; strangulation had to follow, and did. Rear Admiral Sir Horatio Nelson's squadron reached the Bay of Aboukir, between Alexandria and one of the mouths of the Nile, late in the afternoon of August 1, 1798.

This landfall marked for the Admiral the end of a period of great frustration and even greater anxiety. Misfortune and disappointment had followed him for weeks; he knew that his task was of almost immeasurable importance to his country. "Before this time tomorrow," he is reported to have said when he saw Brueys's sails in the bay, it would be "a peerage or Westminster Abbey" for him.

The phrase was justified, and not merely an example of his picturesque exaggeration. Nelson and his character have been discussed almost as extensively as Bonaparte; for though he was a simpler man, and probably to most people a more lovable one, he was certainly one less comprehensible or even imaginable in this century. In his lifetime, and for a century and more later, affection and near-adoration were only diminished by what his classic biographer called "displeasure at his flagrant moral aberration" [40]

—that is, his later infatuation for Emma Hamilton—and it is precisely that which the present generation finds it easiest to forgive.
Otherwise, it is as difficult for us to understand him as it is easy to
understand Bonaparte; we have to transport our minds into the
eighteenth century and accept its habits of thought. His unthink-
ing national hatred, for example: "my blood boils at the name of
a Frenchman," he wrote to Prince William, and, instructing a
young midshipman, he said, "You must hate a Frenchman as you
do the devil." Pietism: he had the habit, which the Kaiser was
almost the last to possess, of presuming that God was fighting on
his side. "Almighty God has blessed His Majesty's arms" began
his despatch on this occasion. "Almighty God continued to bless
my endeavours," he wrote to Lord Minto.[41] Still, it was a genuine
conviction, and though it is often unpleasant reading today, it can
have its dignity. It is hard to find from the pen of twentieth-cen-
tury leaders—Hindenburg, Haig or Foch; Eisenhower, MacAr-
thur, Montgomery or Zhukov—anything to compare with Nelson's last entry in his diary before Trafalgar. "May the Great God
whom I worship grant to my country and for the benefit of Europe in general a great and glorious victory, and may no miscon-
duct in anyone tarnish it, and may humanity after victory be the
predominant feature in the British fleet. For myself individually, I
commit my life to Him who made me, and may his blessing light
upon my endeavours for serving my country faithfully. To Him I
resign myself and the just cause which is entrusted to me to defend. Amen. Amen. Amen."

Politically, he was not so much reactionary as null, void of all
ideas beyond the words God, king and country. None of the ideals
which moved the French revolutionaries had any meaning for
him; he can scarcely have understood, if he ever read, any of
Bonaparte's proclamations. "Equality" in particular as a principle
seemed to him merely senseless and meaningless. This blindness,
added to his devotion to Emma and Emma's royal friends, was to
be responsible for his part in the cruel slaughter at the fall of the
Neapolitan Republic next year.

Vain he was also, to the point of ridicule. "The foolish little
fellow has sat to every artist in London," wrote his grim superior,
Lord St. Vincent. He was impatient for honors and decorations,

even indicating sometimes what he considered he deserved. And yet, with all this, he was universally loved and admired. One reason for this was given by the Duke of Wellington in conversation many years later with J. W. Croker: "Lord Nelson was, in different circumstances, two quite different men. I only saw him once in my life and for, perhaps, an hour. It was soon after I returned from India. I went to the Colonial Office in Downing Street, and there I was shown into the little waiting room on the right hand, where I found, also waiting to see the Secretary of State, a gentleman whom from his likeness to his pictures and the loss of an arm I immediately recognized as Lord Nelson. He could not know who I was, but he entered at once into conversation with me, if I can call it conversation, for it was almost all on his side, and in, really, a style so vain and so silly as to surprise and almost disgust me.

"I suppose that something I happened to say may have made him guess that I was *somebody,* and he went out of the room for a moment, I have no doubt to ask the office-keeper who I was; for when he came back he was altogether a different man, both in manner and in matter. All that I have thought a charlatan style had vanished, and he talked of the state of the country and of the aspect and probabilities of affairs on the Continent with a good sense, and a knowledge of subjects both at home and abroad that surprised me equally, and more agreeably, than the first part of our interview had done. In fact he talked like an officer and a gentleman.

"The Secretary of State kept us long waiting, and certainly for the last half or three quarters of an hour I don't know that I ever had a conversation that interested me more. Now, if the Secretary of State had been punctual, and admitted Lord Nelson in the first quarter of an hour, I should have had the same impression of a light and trivial character that other people have had. But luckily I saw enough to be satisfied that he was really a very superior man. Certainly, a more sudden and complete a metamorphosis I never saw."

A further reason for our indulgence is that Nelson's faults are so forgivable—they are those that we forgive in ourselves and they are accompanied by a courage, kindness and brilliance that we wish we had. The charm of the man still shines through after more than a century and a half; it is almost impossible not to like him after reading his own letters and what others wrote about him. Many people regretted many things about him; most excused them; King George III seems to have been almost the only man who really disliked him. He was the darling of the fleet—not of the officers only, but of all ranks; the letter of a sailor after Trafalgar is well known. "I never set eyes on him, for which I am both sorry and glad, for to be sure I should have liked to have seen him; but then, all the men in our ship who have seen him are such soft toads, they have done nothing but Blast their Eyes, and cry ever since he was killed. God bless you! chaps that fought like the Devil sit down and cry like a wench."

There were three ways in which Nelson was like his opponent. Both were small men—Nelson was scarcely five foot six—and both had married widows older than themselves, and to their disappointment had had no children. Both were the sons of professional men with limited resources, Bonaparte of a lawyer and Nelson of a country clergyman. But there the resemblance ceased. The placid and self-confident Reverend Edmund Nelson was as unlike as well could be to the volatile Carlo Buonaparte; Nelson's relations with his wife, Fanny, were wholly different from Napoleon's with Josephine. His was a reasonably successful, humdrum marriage, based on affection, not passion; so it had been from the beginning. While they were still engaged, Nelson wrote to her that "His Royal Highness" (the Prince who was afterward William IV) "is sure I 'must have a great esteem for you and that is not what is vulgarly called love'; he is right, my love is founded on esteem, the only foundation that can make the passion last." [42] Fanny, Lady Nelson, was not very intelligent [43] and may by now have been losing her good looks; she did not, after ten years, give her husband all the praise and admiration that he called for so abundantly, but she was a devoted and completely loyal wife. She was however a complaining woman and had the exasperating habit of announcing she was ill and going to bed when anything went wrong or vexed her. Her poor health was not imaginary; still, she outlived her son (Joseph, an oaf who became a burden to his stepfather) and many of her grandchildren, spending a large part of her life on a sofa. But as yet neither of them was discontented or disappointed with their married life; Nelson wrote to her vividly and at length. Lady Hamilton at this date meant nothing to him, though it is true he had not been strictly chaste; on one of his long voyages he had taken up with a loose woman in Leghorn and "Nelson and his dolly" for a little while caused surprise and amusement. But this escapade, and a sailorly habit of swearing, were "the only dark specks discoverable in the bright blaze of his moral character." [44]

Physically, he had none of the toughness and relentless energy of his enemy. He was ten years older, thirty-nine, and had always been the runt in his family; his uncle, Captain Suckling, asked to find him his first job, wrote, "What has poor Horatio done, who is so weak, that he above all the rest should be sent to rough it out at sea? . . . But let him come, and the first time we go into action a cannon ball may knock off his head and provide for him at once." He was seasick, he was more than once wretchedly ill with fever, and he had lost the sight of his right eye in 1794. His face was deceptively weak and feminine-looking, with high and strongly marked eyebrows; he was shockheaded, with sandy hair which turned white after his loss of his right arm the year before this, 1797. He was still laboriously learning to write with his left hand, and accustoming himself to having his food cut up for him like a child. His arm had been clumsily cut off and pain was recurrent; in moments of anxiety or wrath he agitated the stump. "The admiral is working his fin again," his crew used as a storm warning. His moments of exhilaration in action and success were balanced by periods of equally extreme distress and despair; he was only just emerging from one of these. "A left-handed Admiral will never again be considered as useful," he had written the previous August to his superior, Lord St. Vincent; with unusual perceptiveness the thickset old man answered, "I will come and bow to your stump tomorrow morning, if you will give me leave"; and sent him back home to rest.

It was at the end of a similar bout of melancholy, he used to tell his juniors, that he had found his vocation. In 1776 he was sailing back from Bombay, more dead than alive with fever, a midshipman with no success behind him and no prospects for the future. The captain was kind, the voyage took six months, and he had time for reflection. Midway, "a sudden glow" was kindled in him; and his mind "exulted" in the idea of king and country. There was "nothing else for it," he felt, and exclaimed: "Well, then, I will be a hero." He added that, confiding in Providence, he decided he would brave every danger; his sincerity was so obvious that despite its naïveté no young officer is ever recorded as having smiled at his avowal.[45]

It was not only for his unwavering bravery in his weak body that his sailors loved him. The humanity that made him sick when he was taken to a bullfight also made him watch like a father over the health of his seamen. It was, of course, not he but Professor Lind of Edinburgh who discovered limes and the other remedies for scurvy, rickets and similar plagues of naval life; but it was he who enforced them and "no officer could hope for his approval who did not follow him in the letter, if not in the spirit." After a ten weeks' chase to the West Indies, he wrote with glee "we have lost neither officer nor man by sickness since we left the Mediterranean; the French and Spanish landed a thousand sick at Martinique and buried full that number." [46] He was, like all eighteenth-century commanders, a disciplinarian, but a mild one, and he saw that the discontents of the seamen were at least in part due to the "infernal plan" by which men were moved from ship to ship "so that Men cannot be attached to their Officers, nor the Officers care two pence about them."

He trained his subordinates, especially the midshipmen, whom he called his children, in the gentlest manner, never asking them to do anything he did not show he would do himself. If he saw one timid "I have known him say" (wrote the wife of an admiral under whom he served) " 'Well, Sir, I am going to race to the masthead, and beg I may meet you there.' No denial could be given to such a wish and the poor fellow instantly began his march. His lordship never took the least notice with what alacrity it was done, but when he met at the top began instantly speaking in the most cheerful manner, saying how much a person was to be pitied who could fancy there was any danger or even anything disagreeable in the attempt. After this example I have seen the timid youth lead another, and reproduce his Captain's words." [47]

Perhaps most important, in this year, were Nelson's relations with his captains. Their average age, in this fleet, was under forty; they all knew each other and knew him; they were, in the phrase he liked to quote, "A band of brothers." He referred to them as "my friends" even in his reports to the Admiralty;[48] during the fleet's long search for Bonaparte's convoy their unity had become closer than ever; they worked now with the highly trained precision of a professional team. A sailing fleet had innumerable disadvantages compared with a modern one—it was slow and could not even move without a wind, for example—but one advantage accompanied these, ease of consultation. Whenever the fleet was slow or becalmed, Nelson called his captains into conference and they rowed over, thereby "becoming acquainted with the masterly ideas of their admiral" and gaining a knowledge of what to do in all probable situations, so that "when surveying the situation of the enemy, they could ascertain with precision what were the ideas and intentions of their Commander, without the aid of any further instructions, by which means signals became almost unnecessary." These are the words of one of them, preserved in manuscript in an odd but not unsuitable place, framed page by page on the walls of a London public house.[49]

The decision to send a powerful fleet into the Mediterranean, taken at the beginning of the year when the French invasion of England was in actual preparation, was an act of hardihood comparable to the sending of tanks to Libya by the Churchill government in the autumn of 1940. It was taken against the best naval opinion;[50] St. Vincent, the Admiral in supreme command, wrote to Nelson in January, "I am much at a loss to reconcile the plans to augment this fleet and extend its operations" (to the Mediterranean) "with the peace which Portugal seems determined to make with France." Gibraltar, he added, was "an unsafe depot," and if Tuscany or Naples gave the smallest assistance to the British fleet the French would destroy them at once. A Mediterranean fleet would have no base. But the Admiralty overruled him. "The circumstances oblige us to take a measure of more decided and hazardous complexion than we should otherwise," the First Lord, Lord Spencer, wrote to St. Vincent at the end of April. "The appearance of a British squadron in the Mediterranean is a condition on which the fate of Europe may at this moment be stated to depend." If St. Vincent did not go himself, he added even more peremptorily, it was "almost unnecessary" to say that Nelson should be sent.

With such a weight of responsibility, Nelson had till now met nothing but calamity. To begin with he had dismasted and almost wrecked his own ship in a storm. "I ought not to call what has happened to the *Vanguard* by the cold name of accident; I believe firmly it was the Almighty's goodness, to check my consummate vanity," he wrote to his wife. "Figure to yourself a vain man, on Sunday evening at sunset, walking in his cabin with a squadron around him, who looked up to their Chief to lead them to glory. Figure to yourself this proud, conceited man when the sun rose on Monday morning—his ship dismasted, his fleet dispersed, and himself in such distress that the meanest frigate out of France would have been a very unwelcome guest." Next, his frigates, thinking he would return to Gibraltar for repairs, had left him, thereby depriving him of his power of reconnoitering. Finally, he had made the grotesque mistake of arriving at Alexandria too soon, and leaving with equal impatience. By now he could scarcely sleep, and had made the lives of his officers of the watch unbearable. The sight of Brueys's ships spread out along the wide half-circle of Aboukir Bay was an unspeakable relief to everyone else as well as to him; with his usual common sense the first thing he did was to order dinner to be served. (It was probably a good dinner, too; unlike Bonaparte, who wolfed his food and drink, Nelson had a palate and one ate and drank well under his command.)[51]

The prospect would not have been wholly pleasant to a conventional commander. It would be late afternoon, or evening, before the fleet could engage the enemy, and the French fleet was not only distinctly superior in numbers and heavily so in gun power, but anchored in what at first sight appeared to be a very strong position. It was spread out in a half-moon, with the most powerful ships, including the huge flagship, *L'Orient,* in the center. There was but a relatively small space, enough for the ships to swing at anchor, between the fleet and the long slow curve of the beach behind. Darkness would soon come down, and defeat any tricky maneuvers Nelson might have in mind. Brueys was sure there would be no fighting that evening, and did not even call in effectively all of the parties of seamen who were ashore foraging for supplies.

Yet his position was not as secure as he thought, and he should not have been there at all. Bonaparte, though he was no sailor, had told him to quit those exposed roads and either take the fleet into the old port of Alexandria through its narrow neck or, if this was technically too difficult, sail off in the direction of Corfu. It is untrue, as some historians have said, that Bonaparte invented these instructions later, so as to shift the blame for the disaster onto Brueys, who was dead, and could not answer; the documents are there. July 3: "The Commander-in-chief wishes the squadron to enter the Port, and he thinks meanwhile you should set sail and approach it." July 30: "I hope that by now you have entered the Port"—adding that if he could not do so "at once" Brueys was to proceed quickly to Corfu. Brueys had done neither.

The wind was north-northwest, blowing directly along the line of the enemy's fleet; Nelson instantly appreciated the importance of this. He would not oblige Admiral Brueys by a frontal attack on his crescent of ships; he would attack the western wing, the van, and proceed to the center, destroying as he went; the French ships at the eastern end would watch helplessly, or if they were alert enough and able enough to lift anchor and somehow tack around, they would be too late. And if the sea between the French ships and the beach was wide and deep enough for them to swing at anchor, then there must be room enough for British ships to slip in and attack them; the French ships could find themselves cannonaded from both sides at once. "By attacking the enemy's van and centre, the wind blowing directly along their line, I was enabled to throw what force I pleased on a few ships. This plan my friends readily conceived," Nelson wrote later to Lord Howe. And as for the coming darkness: "I had the happiness to command a Band of Brothers; therefore, night was to my advantage."

The attack commenced unpropitiously. Troubridge, always Nelson's unluckiest captain, ran his ship, the *Culloden,* onto a shoal, while leading the attempt to get around behind the French; he remained stuck on it throughout the battle, furiously and desperately trying to get off. But his lights at least acted as warnings to the following ships, which were able to take their places without accident. Nelson in the *Vanguard* fell back to sixth in line, to watch how his first five placed themselves and to signal to the remaining ships at need.[52] There was no need. The first two French ships, *Guerrier* and *Conquérant,* were almost at once overwhelmed—within ten minutes, according to Mahan. Nelson put himself up against the third, *Spartiate,* which was already being attacked from the land side by the *Theseus.* The sun was now setting, and some of the other British ships taking their places farther along the French line were less fortunate, in particular the small *Bellerophon,* which found itself up against the overpowering force of *L'Orient,* lost nearly half its crew, and was before long forced to cut its cable and float out of range. But this was no matter; nor was another event which in any other fleet might have been disastrous. A fragment of shell struck Nelson on the forehead, cutting a flap of skin which fell down over his one good eye. Blood poured out; blinded and in acute pain, he thought he was mortally wounded and was carried below. The surgeon ran to attend him; he forbade it and insisted on taking his turn among the injured. The fleet was thus for the moment without a commander. But the captains knew exactly what to do; the *Alexander* and the *Swiftsure,* from the second half of the fleet, came up against *L'Orient* and its neighbor the *Franklin,* and when *Le Peuple Souverain,* another big French ship next to the *Franklin,* had her cable cut by a shot and drifted out of line "the *Leander* glided into the gap, fixing herself with great skill to rake at once the *Franklin* and *L'Orient.*" [53]

Darkness was now complete, illuminated only by the incessant flashes of the guns, but obscured again by rolling billows of smoke. Soon there was a more sinister light perceived; Nelson, whose wound had been bound up but who was in fact unfit to move from bed, was informed of it. "At 10 minutes after nine," writes the observer already quoted,[54] "a fire was observed on board the *Orient,* the French Admiral's ship, which seemed to proceed from the after part of the cabin, and which increased with great rapidity, presently involving the whole of the after part of the ship in flames. This circumstance Captain Berry immediately communicated to the Admiral, who, though suffering severely from his wound, came upon deck, where the first consideration that struck his mind was concern for the danger of so many lives, to save as many as possible of whom he ordered Captain Berry to made every practical exertion. A boat, the only one that could swim, was immediately despatched from the *Vanguard;* and other ships which were in a condition to do so, followed this example, by which means, from the best possible information, the lives of about seventy Frenchmen were saved. The light from the fire of *L'Orient,* falling on the surrounding objects, enabled us to see more easily the situation of the two fleets, the colours of which were clearly distinguishable. The cannonading was still partially kept up to leeward of the centre till about 10 o'clock when *L'Orient* blew up with the most tremendous explosion. An awful pause, a deathlike silence, for a good three minutes ensued, when the wreck of the masts, yards, etc, etc, which had been carried to a vast height fell down into the water and on board the surrounding ships."

The moon had just risen in the clear Egyptian sky, and the sight is said to have been, as we may well believe, awful beyond imagination.

After the sudden silence, which some remembered as lasting as long as ten minutes, the cannonading was resumed; but the result of the battle was no longer in doubt. When dawn came, Villeneuve, commanding the far end of the French fleet (which had not been in action), saw an appalling scene. His two ships and two frigates were all that remained of the fleet; six of the French ships of the line had surrendered, the others were all either destroyed or driven ashore and wrecked. He did the most sensible thing he could; he spread his sails and fled. That even this remnant escaped was a vexation to Nelson; distracted and dizzy he had been sending messages in the small hours of the morning to his ships (for which he has been criticized[55] by those who think he should have appointed a deputy) and believed if they had been obeyed no ship at all would have slipped away. It is unlikely; the sailors were too exhausted for further efforts. "My people," said the captain of the *Theseus,* "were so extremely jaded that as soon as they have hove our sheet anchor up they dropped under the capstan bars, and were asleep in a moment in every sort of posture, having been then working at their fullest exertion, or fighting, for near twelve hours."

It was the most complete victory, perhaps, in British naval history; it was celebrated immediately. On the day after the battle the schoolmaster on the *Vanguard* (there was such a person) wrote a poem which began:

> The foe was ranged in dread array.
> "Conquest or sleep!" the Atheists cry.

And continued:

> "God save the King!" and "Hearts of Oak!"
> We cheared as down the Bay we ran;
> But soon involved in fire and smoke
> Our foe's decided fate began.[56]

Its importance was incontestable; if an analogy is to be sought, it was as if the R.A.F. in 1940, in the Battle of Britain, had not only beaten off the Luftwaffe but destroyed a good half of it. The shadow had moved away from Britain; the dark threat had been destroyed; anxiety was at an end for some long time at least. Its significance was realized in London as soon as the news arrived. Lord Spencer, the First Lord of the Admiralty, fell flat on his face outside his office door; more remarkable still, George III was completely silent for several minutes. The enthusiasm of the common people was wild; there were vast public rejoicings and illuminations—though, as always, there was a section for whom all this meant nothing. Holcroft's diary entry for October 3 reads: "Second illumination night for Nelson's victory. Passed through the mean streets leading to the Seven Dials. The poor did not illuminate."

There was one other man, at least, who understood the gravity of what had happened. It cannot have taken Bonaparte long to realize that he and his army were now cut off from France; he did not need the formal message the Directory sent him in due course[57] saying that it could send him no further help. From conquerors of an empire he and his army had become prisoners isolated helplessly in a useless corner of the world. His mind was still bemused with the campaigns of Alexander, and he may possibly have had momentary dreams of bursting out through Syria and conquering Turkey and Persia—his actions next year could be interpreted so—but so practical a man could never long or seriously have cherished such fantasies. It was, anyway, not many weeks before he realized that soon he would have only two choices. One would be to stay with his army, slowly withering to an ultimate defeat, or to a just conceivable rescue by a victorious Directory from Europe. The other would be to find some excuse to abandon his army and return to France. Defeat or desertion, or both: to that had come the glory for which he had fought so hard in Italy, and which he valued above everything else.

But this prospect of humiliation and failure was not the sole or probably even the main reason for the change in Bonaparte's character that seems to have come in this year. The heart of any man is inscrutable in the last analysis, Bonaparte's perhaps even more than most; but we have his own incautious word for it that such a change did happen. A Victorian writer would have summarized it bluntly. He would have called it a moral breakdown because of a loss of faith; for lack of a more fashionable phrase let the words stand. The foundations of his beliefs broke down; his character changed with them. He learned cruelty from his surroundings and the habits of his Oriental enemies and subjects; a horrible and deliberate massacre of prisoners in Jaffa next year was to show it. He accepted at last that his republican theories had not worked. A whole population had proved totally unresponsive to freedom, reason, equality, humanity and knowledge. All that men could do had been done. The works of Voltaire, Paine, Plutarch, Volney, Livy, the Abbé Raynal and all which he was carrying around with him, were so much lumber; they were guns which did not fire; they should be jettisoned. To this disillusionment was added a more sudden one, very violent and hard to bear by a vehement young man. He found that his remaining inspiration, his adored and noble wife, was no better than a whore. (She was at the moment sleeping with a young man called Hippolyte Charles.) What exactly was the evidence which convinced him is not known; but that he was so convinced is known, and even the approximate date—it was about the end of July. His reaction was predictable and forgivable; at a dinner soon after he picked up a plump, blonde woman, on whom he already had his eye, Pauline Fourès, and took her suddenly upstairs. He swived her there until long after the guests had shrugged and gone home, working off with her both his shock and his months of unnatural chastity. He sent her husband on a mission to Paris, and kept her by him as an almost official concubine. Ever afterward he treated women with casualness. His letters to Josephine changed abruptly in tone; there was no more devotion or love-making; they were "short, polite, sometimes bantering." [58]

It may have been his aide-de-camp, Junot, or even his brother Joseph who sent him the evidence; it was anyway Joseph whom he told that, at the age of twenty-nine, he had exhausted everything. Glory he was tired of. There was "nothing else for it; well, then," he declared, in an unconscious parody, "I shall be a complete and thorough egoist." [59]

So it was; like Nelson he became what he said he would. The man who had left Toulon harbor had been a revolutionary soldier; the man who returned next year was perhaps, as Wellington said, a Jonathan Wild, or maybe rather a Stalin.

2

IRELAND:

"WHO FEARS TO SPEAK OF '98?"

W<small>ELL</small> before this, the event which had been prophesied for Bonaparte's victorious return was past and over. To him, as to most observers, it probably seemed no more than an incident in the struggle between Britain and France. But it was more; it was the Irish revolt of 1798, and the hatreds rising from it poisoned, and still poison, a large part of the Western world.

To explain this a historian is forced, as so often with Ireland, to go back to past history, in this case for at least some thirty or forty years. The story of Ireland during those years was something like a drama played on the two floors of a house. The upper floor was occupied by a civilized, leisured, Protestant class. In Dublin, Cork and Belfast (the last being then the "Athens of Ireland, the focus of liberality") there was a society which was cultured and free-spoken. A member of it could go about repeating almost open sedition; no one would interfere with him. If a viceroy had had the whim of attempting to muzzle him, only the most servile Protestants would have approved. Throughout the century and even during the rebellion of this summer this class kept many traces of its original civility and restraint in dealing with its own members, and there are instances of the oddest and most unexpected chivalry and courtesy. But while this moderated conflict was waged in one class, below it went on a warfare which knew no rules. Judicial assassinations by the use of professional witnesses, and break-of-day visitations of poorhouses and the throwing out of their inhabitants into the fields, were answered by pitchfork murders and ambushes on dark nights. The same men who would let a noted rebel escape through delicacy about entering a lady's boudoir would countenance and even encourage sickening violence among or against "the lower orders," and would ride into a Leinster town with the finger of a murdered Catholic peasant brandished on the tip of their leader's saber.[1]

Such class division was not, of course, peculiar to Ireland. In England, also, there was a sharp division between the gentlefolk and the common people. What was peculiar to Ireland was the further complication of religion. Into the class of the oppressed was thrown a vast body of the population—three millions at least, by the general calculation—by the mere fact that they were Roman Catholics. Their ablest defender, Wolfe Tone, said that the great majority of them were, in mind and habits, reduced "lower than the beasts of the field." [2] The spirit of their remaining gentry was broken, and there was an alert servility, even in ancient families with authentic titles of nobility. The Catholic peasants were frequently the tenants of Protestant landlords, who had already begun to depute their responsibilities to bailiffs; they were powerless to make any resistance beyond sporadic rioting and occasional assassination. Some trade and some manufacture had of necessity fallen into the hands of Catholics, and the relatively well-to-do Catholic merchants lived an easy but cautious life. There were also several Catholic doctors who in the general inertia wielded a disproportionate influence. But they all considered that the central government was their only protector against the rapacity of their fellow Irishmen, and while they believed this, the administrators of Dublin Castle, in the words of Tone, walked, as it were, on a carpet.[3]

They had reason for their belief. The penal laws, which the English viceroys sometimes conveniently forgot but to which any bigot might theoretically at any time appeal, contained almost incredible provisions. No Catholic could be a member of Parliament, a magistrate, a solicitor, a lawyer, a soldier, a sailor, a juryman, a voter, a sheriff, a constable, a schoolmaster, or even a private tutor. No Catholic education was permitted; no Catholic child could be sent abroad to receive the education refused him at home. No Catholic could buy land, inherit it, or receive it as a gift, from a Protestant. Except in the linen trade, no Catholic manufacturer might employ more than two apprentices. No Catholic might marry a Protestant. Death was the penalty for converting a Protestant to Catholicism. No Catholic might own a horse of greater value than five pounds; should a Protestant see a valuable horse belonging to a Catholic, he could give him a five-pound note, and forthwith the horse was his. Elaborate enactments endeavored to break up the solidarity of Catholic families. If the eldest son became a Protestant, the property at once passed to him and his father became merely a tenant. If the wife became a Protestant, she was thereby freed of her husband's control, and the chancellor could assign to her a portion of his property. If any child, however young, professed Protestantism, he was taken away from his father's control and a portion of the property seized for his benefit.

In face of such statutes, the Catholics may well have been glad that their Protestant oppressors were divided. The most privileged of these were the members of the Church of Ireland, called sometimes just "Protestants," sometimes "Lutherans," who in modern England would correspond to Anglicans, in the United States to Protestant Episcopalians. They were more powerful in the south, and there, scattered among a great Catholic population, they were directly dependent upon Dublin Castle. Their views reflected immediately the policies of the English government, and independence could not be expected of them. They included the majority of the officials and of the nobility, a number of landed gentlemen, some traders, and a regiment of beneficed clergy, with churches and tithes all over Ireland, but with scanty congregations. More numerous and less tractable were the Dissenters or Presbyterians, whose center was Belfast. Cromwell, when he planted Northern Ireland and drove the natives to "hell or Connaught," used troops of marked republican sentiments. Their tradition was still strong among the Ulster Presbyterians. They kept down the Catholics, casually and as a matter or duty, because they saw in them not only heretics but the instinctive supports of despotism.[4] But they also greatly resented both the Anglican domination, and the corrupt condition of politics. The Irish Parliament was in any case subject to the British Parliament, but it was, in addition, a purchased preserve of the Episcopalian landlords. "The state of representation is as follows," said an address in 1792. "Seventeen boroughs have no resident electors; sixteen have but one; ninety-eight have thirteen electors each; ninety persons return for 106 rural boroughs—that is, 212 members out of 300—the whole number; fifty-four members are returned by five noblemen and four bishops; and borough influence has given landlords such power in the counties as to make them boroughs also."

Indignation filled many Presbyterian minds at such sharp practice, and warm appreciation awaited any prominent man, whether Dissenter or Episcopalian, who affronted Dublin Castle. No man, probably, received more of this applause than the famous lawyer John Philpot Curran. Many stories of his wit and defiance were circulated. Once when the presiding judge attempted to coerce him by instructing the sheriff to be ready to take into custody "anyone who should disturb the decorum of the court," Curran answered in a sentence which thrilled the listeners. "Do so, Mr. Sheriff," he thundered, turning his back on the judge and staring at the unhappy official, "go and get ready my dungeon; prepare a bed of straw for me; and upon that bed I shall to-night repose with more tranquillity than I should enjoy were I sitting upon the bench with a consciousness that I had disgraced it." [5]

In the south, apart from two or three big towns, there were but three classes—the landlords or the "church lords," who were mostly Protestant, their tenants, and the laborers, who were prac-

tically all Catholics. But in Ulster there were in the towns the
ramifications of several industries, of which the most widespread
was the linen trade, and in the country big landlords, tenants,
small holders, laborers, and all sorts of gradations and subclasses
which shaded one into the other. Most of the inhabitants were
Dissenters, but there were plenty of Episcopalians and a number
of Catholics. It was in this complex society that an unimportant
nobleman took the first step which led in the end to the insurrection of 1798. Lord Downshire, the biggest landowner of County
Down, was a rather stupid peer, leading a wasteful life in London,
never seeing his estates, but calling on them incessantly for fresh
drafts of money. Early in the sixties, being pressed by his credi-
tors, he applied a new system of renting, which became known as
"rack-renting." As each lease fell in, he reduced the rent, but required at the same time the payment of a large "fine," equivalent
to many years' purchase of the reduction. Thus he had his money
in hand, but the farmers were in sudden distress. Scarcely one possessed ready money enough, and the majority of them appealed to
city speculators, who paid Lord Downshire his fine, took the
farms and relet them to the farmers on short leases. The rents
they pushed up from year to year to the highest possible point.
Landlord after landlord followed Downshire's example to get
ready money, and the Belfast merchants raced each other to secure such profitable investments. Though they were of the same
religion as the farmers whom they bled, no scruples held them
back. They held morning and evening prayers in their families,
with their servants in compulsory attendance, where "they read
the very texts condemning the acts that they would do as soon as
they rose from their knees." [6]

The harried farmers belonged to a section of society which was
not used to submission. They retaliated on their oppressors,
elders of the Chapel though they might be, and organized a body
called the Hearts of Steel, which dealt sharply with the tenants
whom the speculators put in to take the place of farmers that their
rapacity had driven out. The Hearts of Steel soon had bands in
most places where rack-renting had begun, and the names of their
captains varied as the object of their journeys changed. Captain
Pitchfork led them to toss out hay to the rain, Captain Long-

scythe to cut the corn before it ripened, Captain Firebrand to burn down barns and houses. Sometimes a bullet whistling past the ear of a rack renter warned him of what would come if the farmers were driven to despair; but as yet murder was rare.

From the country distress was spread to the Ulster towns by the American war. The Ulster Protestant had watched with satisfaction the rebellious spirit of New England. The majority of Americans shared his beliefs in religion, and he was well pleased to share theirs in politics. "No taxation without representation" and contempt for bishops and lords were principles easily popularized in Ulster. Sympathy was reinforced by anger at the results of the government's war. The linen trade, main source of Ulster prosperity, was half ruined by the disappearance of the American market. The collapse of the linen trade spread disaster all over the province. Wool, cattle and land fell sharply in value, and in 1775 "the public credit was almost extinct." At the same time the linen trade's prospects of recovery were damaged by the introduction of cotton spinning. The early factories were small and inefficient, but they were enough to undercut the linen industry. The earnings of a linen weaver fell to as low as five shillings a week. The conditions in the new factories, where child labor was extensively employed, were atrocious; foul fumes, cotton dust, beating by managers, and fantastically long hours were common, while the fathers of the children who were suffering from these conditions were helplessly walking the street. Numbers of them sailed across the sea, with the avowed intention of joining the army of Colonel Washington.[7]

Within three years the government which had ruined them appeared to be helpless. So far from conquering the Americans, its armies were entrapped in the forests and wasted away. It seemed unable even to protect Irish shores. The American John Paul Jones, in the privateer, *Ranger,* actually sailed around the sloop of war *Drake* in Belfast Harbor and carried her off in April 1778. In August of the same year the "Sovereign," that is, the Mayor, of Belfast, receiving rumors of another descent, anxiously asked Sir Robert Heron, Secretary of State, for military protection. The answer was ungrammatical and alarming: "His Excellency cannot at present send no further military force to Belfast than a troop or

two of horse, or part of a company of invalids." There had been
some drilling and arming already; on the publication of this letter
it multiplied wildly, and the Irish Volunteers were born. Since
Belfast, Cork and Dublin were at any moment liable to be rav-
aged by French pirates, merchants, gentlemen, and even workingmen hastily put on scarlet uniforms with black facings, learned
sword play, horse riding and drill, and in some cases purchased
cannon and were instructed in gunnery. Within a year they numbered 42,000 and a year later were believed to be as many as
80,000. Since all classes were affected, it seemed to some of the
Volunteers unreasonable to exclude Catholics, especially since a
decent Papist, when one met him, seemed, after all, not unlike a
Protestant gentleman, and as willing as oneself to drink the King's
health and damnation to the French. Before long the Volunteers,
in Leinster and Munster especially, contained a sprinkling of
Catholics, though to the very end they were chiefly a Protestant
force.[8]

All their emblems, all their resolutions and all their meetings
were on the surface ardently loyal. But they were before long
aware that they were the only armed force in the country, and
that the government, if they chose, was at their mercy. Their
power was most dramatically shown to them and to the world by
James Napper Tandy, commanding the Dublin Volunteer Artillery Company. No object was dearer to the heart of the average
Volunteer than the abolition of the embargoes and restraints by
which England hampered the trade of Ireland. Tandy paraded the
Volunteer Artillery in Dublin in silence and without speeches or
proclamations. But from the round, black mouth of each cannon
hung a notice, "FREE TRADE OR ———." Tandy's fantastic face, with
a straight, overhanging nose far too big for his other features, a
long jowl and big mouth twisted beneath this monstrous nose into
a permanent sneer, and a receding forehead, gave him a crowlike
and sinister appearance that impressed itself on every observer as
he stalked a whole afternoon silently up and down before the mute
threat of his guns. Free trade was granted, and the Volunteers
realized that nothing could be refused them. Their conventions
became filled with a racket of audacious proposals. The first and
greatest was no less than to secure Irish independence. The sub-

The Adelphi Terrace, London
From T. Malton, *A Picturesque Tour through London and Westminster,* in the British Museum

"A Sailor's Prayer before Battle," satirical cartoon showing the favored position of officers. Victory Museum, H. M. Dockyard, Portsmouth, England

EQUITY OR A Sailors PRAYER before Battle. *Anecdote of the Battle of* TRAFALGAR

Napoleon Bonaparte accepting the surrender of Malta
Musée Carnavalet, Paris

View of Rosetta with French soldiers
From *Egypt Delineated*, 1826, London Zoological Society Library

Interior of the Temple of Apollinopolis at Edfou
From *Egypt Delineated*, 1826, London Zoological Society Library

The British and French fleets at the beginning of the Battle of Aboukir. National Maritime Museum

Wolfe Tone
Ulster Museum

Napper Tandy
Mansell Collection

The United Irish Patriots. Left to right: *Samuel Neilson, Michael Dwyer,*
John Sheares, William Corbett, Arthur O'Connor, A. H. Rowan,
William Jackson, W. J. MacNevin, Matthew Teeling, Robert Emmet,
Henry Sheares, T. Wolfe Tone, J. Napper Tandy, T. A. Emmet,
James Hope, Thos. Russell, H. J. MacCracken, Lord Edward Fitzgerald
Mansell Collection

Lord Edward Fitzgerald
Ulster Museum

The last full parade of the Irish Volunteers, Belfast High Street, 1792
Ulster Museum

*Roger Griswold
and Matthew Lyon
dueling in Congress
at the time
of the XYZ affair*
Culver Pictures

King Ferdinand, Sir William Hamilton, and Lady Hamilton watching a floating rebel corpse in Naples Harbor. Museum of San Martino, Naples; Mansell Collection

Ferdinand, King of Naples
Victory Museum, H. M. Dockyard,
Portsmouth, England

Touissant L'Overture
Radio Times Hulton
Picture Library

An assignat

République Française.

Assignat de cinquante LIVRES.

De la Création du 14. Déc.bre 1792.
Hypothéqué sur les

l'An premier de la République.
Domaines Nationaux.

série 2484

n.º 10

50

50

50

50

n.º 10 LIBERTÉ ÉGALITÉ série 2484

LA LOI PUNIT DE MORT
LE CONTREFACTEUR.

LA NATION RÉCOMPENSE
LE DÉNONCIATEUR

jection of the Irish Parliament to the British was affirmed by a
relatively recent act, the sixth of George I. This, on the instigation
of the already famous Parliamentarian Henry Grattan, the Volunteers demanded should be annulled, and in 1782, a little to their
surprise, their request was meekly obeyed.[9]

The newly freed Parliament seemed subservient, for the moment, to their wishes. Grattan had urged them to promote "an
affectionate coalition of the inhabitants of Ireland." Their own
troubles had led them to regard with a more sympathetic eye the
sufferings of their Catholic countrymen. Already, under their
pressure, an act had been passed in 1778 making it legal for
Catholics not, indeed, to own land, but to lease it for nine hundred and ninety-nine years. Now in a bunch bills were passed
repealing the acts which prohibited celebrating or hearing mass,
subjected priests to the necessity of registration, made it penal for
Catholic bishops or regular clergy to live in the country, levied
from Catholics the damages caused by any enemy privateers, and
enabled Protestants to take a Catholic's horse on payment of five
pounds.

After this the Volunteers went daringly on to consider the reform of the Irish Parliament. At the once-famous Dungannon
Convention, the same which by its resolution of February 15,
1782 forced the concession of Irish independence, it was decided to require "a more equal representation of the people," and
though further action was adjourned till the next year few Volunteers doubted that reform was as good as won. These two years,
1782 and 1783, were years in which the scarlet-and-black uniform was the pride of every town. Its wearers carried themselves
with conscious dignity in the streets. They had shown themselves
generous to their oppressed Catholic fellow citizens, loyal to their
King and country, and firm in securing liberty. No bloodshed had
marked their victory, and no weakness or selfishness had been
shown in their demands. Their astuteness had been as remarkable
as their courage, and wherever they showed themselves they were
greeted by the admiration of the people. Years afterward old
members of the Volunteers remembered the time as one in which
righteousness and toleration had walked the street in arms, and
wickedness and corruption had fled before them. They would take

from the closet the old and faded uniform and handle it with an affection shared by every spectator. Yet, though no shot was fired, the underlying threat of force was hidden from nobody. Napper Tandy's cannon carried a message that for a hundred and fifty years was listened to by every Irish rebel and put into a verse which later was in everyone's mouth:

> Remember still, through good and ill,
> How vain were sighs and tears
> How vain were words, till flashed the swords
> Of the Irish Volunteers.

The national convention of 1783, which was to complete and crown the victory, met in Dublin in November. The program of reform was clear, and the arrangements were in the hands of a subchairman, Colonel Robert Stewart, whose hatred of corruption and rotten boroughs, and deep liberality of sentiment no man could doubt. (His name was afterward Londonderry, and his son's was Castlereagh.) On November 21 he produced, after deliberation with a committee, an extensive and drastic plan for parliamentary reform, which anticipated and in many ways improved the famous English bill of 1832. Yet, as it was read over, certain listeners were arrested by a recurrent phrase—"every *Protestant* possessed of a freehold," "every *Protestant* possessed of a leasehold of the yearly value of £40," "every *Protestant* in any decayed borough." There were now 150,000 Volunteers, and among their number (though not among the delegates) was a fair leavening of men who were not Protestants. Reflecting on this fact, certain delegates proposed to extend the franchise to the Catholics. The audacity of this proposal at once caused the assembly to pause. Every Volunteer, by now, rejoiced in the thought of toleration, repudiated sectarian bigotry, and had promised his devotion to a fraternal affection for Irishmen of all religions. But the drastic character of this amendment, which would hand over power to a sect whose members had only recently, and in relatively small numbers, shown a devotion to constitutional liberty, caused even the resolute Colonel Stewart to hesitate, and the debate was prolonged.[10]

Now there was in Dublin a half-dead organization called the

General Committee of Catholics. It had been brought into existence soon after 1750, and was chiefly composed of noblemen and the higher clergy, with a few merchants. It had confined itself, up till now, to presenting adulatory addresses (sometimes unanswered) to viceroys, and occasionally petitioning, in humble tones, for the alleviation of some of the more oppressive burdens. Its present leader was Lord Kenmare, and through him the Committee now issued a statement. The Catholics were, he announced, "so grateful for the great concessions already made" to them that they "could not think of asking for the elective franchise." This declaration paralyzed the most ardent Volunteer advocates of the Catholic case. "They are like the Cappadocians, who prayed for slavery," exclaimed one. It was forthwith agreed that servility was too deeply ingrained among Catholics for it to be safe to enfranchise them. The anger of the Bishop of Derry, the indignation of untitled Catholics at Lord Kenmare, the protests of his lordship himself (which may well have been truthful) that the announcement was unauthorized were all ignored; and the amendment was rejected.[11]

But if that was laid aside, nevertheless there was the general plan of reform to be considered. The Volunteers, whose present chairman was the timid and exquisitely courteous Lord Charlemont, were surprised to find themselves the sudden victims of a torrent of abuse. The place holders and pensioners who fed like liver flukes on the corruption of public administration had been indifferent spectators of the grant of Irish independence. Some may even have rejoiced at the thought that they had no master now but themselves to regard. But at the proposal for a reform which would at one frightful slash cut away all their offices, they turned on the Volunteers with a specially vicious fury. The House of Commons refused Harry Flood leave even to bring in a bill for reform on the ground that the Convention was an illegal body. John Fitzgibbon, a lawyer member of the ascendancy group, abused the astonished Volunteers in such terms that Curran called him to his face a raving maniac and an incendiary. Even Grattan declined to go further with the Volunteers. He did not like to see a House of Commons coerced by an armed body, he was wholly convinced of the sincerity of Dublin Castle's reformation,

and he had his own place bill by which he hoped, as Burke did in
England, to end corruption without constitutional reform. There
were several Volunteers in high places who were equally distressed, and they sought some way to settle their now divided
allegiance. The House's refusal to Harry Flood meant that the
Volunteer Convention must forthwith either dissolve or take some
action—however gentle in appearance or symbolic in character—
that would remind the House where the armed force of Ireland
was. Lord Charlemont could not contemplate this without
horror. It was represented to him that two dangerous agitators,
Flood and the nonresident Bishop of Derry, were hurrying the
Volunteers into ill-considered actions which would turn out, in
fact, to be rebellion. When on the last day of November, a Satur-
day, he declared the Volunteer Convention adjourned till the
Monday, he had already made a momentous decision. On Monday, December 2, 1783, he, together with a few of his personal
partisans, came down to the Rotondo, the meeting place, well
before the usual time of meeting. They passed a few innocuous
resolutions and then declared the Convention dissolved. They left
the building, bolting the doors behind them. Gradually the other
Volunteer delegates appeared, later than usual, perhaps, from
their weekend amusements. They found the hall empty and with
closed doors. The news was passed from mouth to mouth, groups
formed for some little while, but soon, in relief, perplexity or an-
noyance, they dispersed.

From that morning the power of the Irish Volunteers was over.
After they had scattered to their various homes, they paraded
more and more infrequently, they fidgeted about with the design
of the uniform, they stored their cannon and forgot their artillery
drill. The nuisance of continual military activities was a great
consideration to merchants and lawyers; moreover, they had for
some time good reasons for arguing that their influence was no
longer needed. It was two years before Grattan, in a pathetic
speech in the independent House, confessed that he had been deceived. The Devil had been very sick, and for a long while he
remembered to say his prayers. Dublin Castle was on its best behavior, and the opening years of the independent Parliament
showed an unexpected level of decency and attention to business.

Even if the Castle had been less discreet, the essential strength of the Volunteers had been ruined when dissensions entered their ranks. The Bishop of Derry's proposals on behalf of the Catholics and Harry Flood's motion for parliamentary reform (introduced as a bill in 1784 and again rejected) raised questions which could not be avoided, and on which the average Protestant Volunteer could not make up his mind. It was only gradually that the power of the Volunteers faded away, but by, say, seven years after the Dublin Convention, it was clear to everybody that the old regime was in the saddle again. Power now lay more in Dublin than in London, but it was no easier to attack. Viceroys came and went, but always the same clique, "the Beresford faction," was in control. Its chief, John Claudius Beresford, was not a man who concerned himself greatly with political ideas. All he cared for was appointments and perquisites; political memoirs give us a fleeting picture of a heavy man, greed and anger the chief expressions of his overfed, hanging, red face, driving about Dublin or London in an open carriage. When some grave disturbance, as in 1798, forced him into political action, he showed a butcher-like methodical brutality.

Another of the faction was Fitzgibbon, whom Curran had so bitterly attacked. He became Lord Clare, and in 1789 lord chancellor, when he showed his spite by openly driving Curran from his court. He let it be seen that no client who employed Curran had the least chance of a fair hearing, behavior which was said to have cost Curran £30,000 a year. Once an independence man, he grew slowly possessed of a restless parvenu hatred of the Irish people. He boasted that he would make them "as tame as cats"; the boast was repeated, and when he died in 1802, the people broke through the funeral cortege and threw dead cats onto the coffin as it was lowered into the grave.[12]

No two characters in the Beresford faction could be more contrasted than Arthur Wolfe and John Toler, who became attorney-general and solicitor-general respectively. Arthur Wolfe, later Lord Kilwarden, was as respected for his legal talents as he was loved for his sweetness of nature. He owed his promotion to the need that the faction felt for some men of integrity to protect it, not to his own pliability. His behavior in court on the occasion of

the trial of a number of young men for treason had endeared him
to the common people of Dublin. He had examined his papers
and seen nothing unusual in them. He was about to open his case
when the Chief Justice of the King's Bench, the usual hanging
judge, said to him, with an attempt at joviality, "Well, Mr. Attorney, I suppose you're ready to go on with the trial of these tuckered traitors." The odd phrase caught Wolfe's ear, he examined
the row of prisoners more closely, and saw that they were all
under twenty years of age, and that some were mere boys who
were actually wearing a rustic bib and tucker. "No, my lord, I am
not ready," he answered, with an unexpected sharpness, and
walked across the court to the defending counsel, with whom he
held a short talk. "That man," he said, indicating the judge, "shall
never have the gratification of passing sentence of death upon a
single one of these *tuckered traitors.*" He resumed his place and
proceeded with the case, pressing it as gently as possible, and at
night going to Dublin Castle with an urgent demand for pardons.
Within a few days he had pardons for all the prisoners, on condition of their leaving Ireland. There was one boy who would not
accept the condition. It is too long ago now, and the record is too
confused, for us to find out why. Perhaps he was a slow-witted
farmer's boy who could not understand that here was his only
chance: perhaps he was an ardent rebel whose patriotism refused
any compromise. For these or some other reasons he declined to
promise to emigrate. Wolfe could not save him and he was
hanged. His name is said to have been Shannon; years later, this
accident was the strange cause of Wolfe's death.[13]

   If the Solicitor-General, John Toler, had been in charge of the
case, every boy would have hanged. To strain the law, to ruin
defendants by the piling up of legal expenses, and even to cover
and facilitate the packing of juries were the necessary and easy
tasks of Toler, who seems in addition to have been naturally
cruel. "Why, in one circuit," recorded O'Connell, "during the administration of the cold-hearted and cruel Camden, there were a
hundred individuals tried before *one* judge. Of these ninety-eight
were capitally convicted and ninety-seven hanged. One escaped—
but he was a soldier who murdered a peasant, a thing of a trivial
nature. *Ninety-seven victims in one circuit.*" [14] That judge was

Toler, later Lord Norbury. For years Dublin Castle protected him, and it was not until he was eighty-seven that an end was put to his career. He was trying a murder case, at the conclusion of which he pronounced sentence with his usual relish. But O'Connell discovered that he had been asleep during a large portion of the trial, and was able to present a petition which at last forced the resignation of the most serenely brutal of the Irish judges.

Such was Irish society in the late eighteenth century; such were its administrators. They were ill-prepared for the sudden shock that came to Ireland, as to every other country, the shock of the French Revolution.

Irish Protestants had always believed that Catholics were natural slaves. The spectacle of the first Catholic nation in Europe hurling itself far further forward on the road to freedom than any other country wiped away their centenarian doubts. The Ulster reformers felt that they could now go forward unhesitating, that their previous distrust had been unmanly. They were full of an eager friendliness toward the Catholics, and in 1792 another great bulwark of oppression toppled and crashed when the Irish Parliament found it prudent to repeal the acts forbidding Catholics to keep schools, marry Protestants, act as lawyers, send their children abroad and have more than a certain number of apprentices.

Nor were the Catholics themselves unaffected. Their bishops, indeed, were far from enthusiastic, but they had lost influence since they had allied themselves in 1783 with Lord Kenmare and his Committee. Of those mostly middle-class Catholics who supplanted them, the most important was a rich Dublin merchant named John Keogh.[15] In his faults as much as his virtues Keogh was their natural leader. His heavy-lidded, large, slow-moving face gave an impression of cunning and timidity. He had both these qualities, but in them he truly represented his supporters, whose most frequent emotion was queasy astonishment at their own audacity. At the conferences he held at Mount Jerome, his luxurious house, he always advocated indirect rather than direct methods; he would lapse into long periods of inertia and discourage with the amiable condescension of an experienced old man the enthusiasms of his chief assistant, Richard McCormick, the secretary of the now reconstructed Catholic Committee. But his

public speeches and his pamphlets were always clear and to the
point, and phrased in a carefully moderate manner which appealed to a class at once oppressed and fearful; and when the
crisis came he had so undermined the position of the Catholic
nobles that they found themselves without supporters. Dublin
Castle itself was afraid of him, but was unable at any time to find
grounds on which to proceed against him.

Keogh, moreover, had the essential ability of recognizing men
of talent. In 1792 he induced the Catholic Committee to select as
assistant secretary and agent a twenty-nine-year-old penniless
Protestant named Theobald Wolfe Tone, who was in every characteristic his opposite. Impatient, eloquent, reckless, and boyishly
direct, Tone had an overflowing humor, which embarrassed as
much as it amused the Catholic Committee. He fastened upon
every one of his colleagues' nicknames—Keogh he called "Gog"
and McCormick "Magog"—which delight us in his diary, and
though we may not understand them, in some way carry a flavor of
the bearers' character to this day.[16]

It was at the time of Tone's appointment that Keogh sprang the
surprise that he had for long been preparing. It was announced
that the Catholic Committee would not be contented with the
concessions just made, but would demand the elective franchise
for all Catholics. Furthermore, as it had been described as an
unimportant collection of self-appointed Dubliners, it would appeal to the Catholics of all Ireland to accept or to reject its policy.
It would call a great delegate convention for the end of 1792, and
its own members would go out into the country to explain their
views to Catholic gentlemen. There was an instantaneous uproar.
Lord Kenmare and sixty-eight other Catholic members of the
Catholic gentry issued a vehement attack, intended to destroy the
credit of the Committee. There was a momentary pause, and then
the Catholics in general resumed their activity unperturbed. A
condemnation which once would have paralyzed the whole Catholic community was almost forgotten after a week.

Tone himself went out on what was perhaps the most important mission of all—to Belfast, to secure the friendship and support of the Dissenters. Keogh went down to Munster, "preaching
for three days to six bishops" (whom he converted), and then

joined Tone in the north. Tone had already collected a number of influential Ulster friends. Closest to his heart was Thomas Russell, on whom for some unknown reason he fastened the nickname "P.P., Clerk of this Parish." Russell was a man who would stand out in any company. He was over six feet in height, with a martial bearing acquired through service in India. His face was of an exemplary handsomeness, dark, regular-featured, and with a steady, straight glance. He had what is described as a smile so sweet as to be almost infantile, and a great charm of manner. He had a very fine taste in claret. He turned Tone's sober tour into a series of riotous excursions, which, in the Ireland of that century, were even more successful than Keogh's patient and respectable visits.

The next most important adherent to Tone's mind was probably Robert Simms, part proprietor of a powerful paper called the *Northern Star*. Simms was rich, silent and a little solemn. Tone and Keogh took him at his own valuation, though the former had more pleasure in the society of Sam Neilson, a violent-tempered, short-necked, red-faced Belfast draper, who was the effective editor of the *Northern Star*. Neilson was the most indiscreet and wrongheaded of all the Ulstermen, but he was also a man to whom fear was utterly unknown and who spent his life hurling himself against immovable obstacles.

Tone and Keogh were convinced that only in the middle and upper ranks could real support be found for liberty. They therefore paid little attention to one man whose acquaintance was pressed upon them. Jemmy Hope—no man called him James—was a weaver, after having been an agricultural laborer. He was able to read, but wrote imperfectly. He had an unusual influence over the working class of Ulster, partly owing to his opinions on the subject of class divisions. "The higher ranks of society," he observed, "in which there never was nor never will be a majority of honest-principled men, have usurped the privilege of lawmaking." Such views seemed merely fantastic, but at least the support of the Ulster artisans need not be turned away, and Tone and Keogh returned south with Jemmy Hope's blessing among many others.

Out they went to Connaught, and then back again to Dublin, where Tone continued his same methods of proselytism. "Nov.

1st, 1792," his diary records, "dinner at Warren's. All very pleasant and good. Mr. Hutton [Tone's nickname for himself] being
entre deux vins, tried to delude the gentlemen present into forming a Volunteer company on good principles, civil and military.
A. H. Rowan rises thereat, also Magog [R. McCormick]. Mr.
Hutton a little mad on the subject of volunteering; would be a
great martinet. 'Army, damn me!' Talk a great deal of tactics and
treason. Mr. Hutton grows warm with the subject; very much surprised, on looking down the table, to see two glasses before him;
finds, on looking at Hamilton Rowan, that he has four eyes; various other phenomena in optics equally curious. Mr. Hutton, like
the sun in the centre of the system, fixed, but everything about
him moving in a rapid rotation; perfectly sober, but perceives that
everyone else is getting very drunk; essays to walk across the
room, but finds it impossible to move rectilineally, proceeding entirely from his having taken a sprig of watercress with his bread at
dinner. 'God bless everybody.' Sundry excellent toasts. All em-
brace and depart at 12. Fine doings! Fine doings!

"Nov. 2nd. Sick as Demogorgon, purpose to leave off water-
cresses with my bread." [17]

About the same time Tone brought into the service of the
Catholic Committee a man who became before long second only
to Russell in his esteem—a solid lawyer named Thomas Emmet.
"Emmet introduced to the sub-committee. All say O! to him, and
he richly deserves their admiration. Emmet the best of all friends
to Catholic emancipation, always excepting Mr. Hutton." Emmet
being an old English word for "ant," he christened his new friend
the Pismire, under which grotesque name he henceforward figures
in Tone's diary.

Name after name poured in of delegates to the Catholic Convention. "Wexford returns at last. Rent roll of their delegates
£15,000 per annum. Bravo! This makes eight counties." By December, the date of the meeting, every county was represented.
There had not been such an assembly since the Irish Parliament
of James II. The Convention was the sensation of the day, perhaps more because of the victories of the French armies in Belgium than for the justice of its cause. In any case, the delegates
swept aside half-measures and determined to present a demand

for complete Catholic emancipation, a demand which would in-
volve the repeal of every law in which any distinction was made
between the two religions. They further decided to ignore the
Viceroy and present their petition direct to the King in London.
They picked a delegation of five, but adverse winds prevented its
sailing by the long sea route. The delegation therefore decided to
go north and cross by Belfast. As they left this town, once the
center of Ulster bigotry, a strange scene took place. A great con-
course of men who, many of them, were not long after to be
known as rigid Orangemen, approached the carriages which were
waiting to take them to the quay, took out the horses and, amid
loud cheering, themselves drew the delegates to the waterside.
This, perhaps, perturbed the British government most of all. The
delegates were received in London with exact courtesy, they were
admitted to the immediate presence of the King, and George III
carefully exchanged with each one a courteous remark. On their
return to Dublin they received the news that the government had
decided to accede to their petition. A bill was presented to the
Irish House of Commons covering all the specific points in the
petition, but evading its general prayer—that is to say, every mentioned grievance was righted, but general equality was not
granted. There remained certain positions, of which the most important was member of Parliament, which no Catholic could
hold. However, practically every other disability was removed,
and when the bill received royal assent on April 9, 1793, John
Keogh might have felt his life's work was mostly done.

Both he and Tone, indeed, had for some time not concentrated
the whole of their thoughts upon the Catholic Committee. Tone
was actively, Keogh passively, interested in an organization with
much wider objects. In 1791, in October, Tone, on his first visit
to Belfast, had found a small secret committee among whose
chiefs were Neilson, Russell, and Simms. Tone was able to per-
suade them almost in his first conversation that their secret methods were unwise and their objects too limited. It was swiftly
agreed that their objects must be to secure a fraternal unity of all
Irishmen, irrespective of religious barriers, to remove the tangle
of legal oppressions and restrictions which held down any part of
the Irish nation, and to end the domination of England in Ireland.

These objects it seemed easy to describe in a single phrase; to be united and to be Irish were the aims, and the name "Society of United Irishmen" was easily adopted. Each member was to take an oath:

"I, ... , in the presence of God, do pledge myself to my country that I will use all my abilities and influence in the attainment of an impartial and adequate representation of the Irish nation in Parliament; and as a means of absolute and immediate necessity in the establishment of this chief good of Ireland, I will endeavour, as much as lies in my ability, to forward a brotherhood of affection, an identity of interests, a communion of rights and a union of power among Irishmen of all religious persuasions, without which every reform in Parliament must be partial, not national, inadequate to the wants, delusive to the wishes, and insufficient for the freedom and happiness of this country."

This oath contained all the objects on which the United Irishmen were ever wholly united. They were not all even republican. Tone and the Ulstermen were; but when on his return to Dublin Tone induced Tandy to found a Dublin society, he discovered that its members wanted no more than a reform of Parliament. He was always welcomed and liked in the Dublin society, but his influence was in a short while outweighed by that of older and more cautious men. He often regretted his forthright Ulster friends. But even these were not free from criticism in Belfast. Were they right to assume that with the destruction of religious privilege and a corrupt Parliament the life of Ireland, like a plant forced to grow awry by stones and rocks, would at once right itself and become a natural and luxuriant growth? The voice of Jemmy Hope, the weaver, proclaimed that even after parliamentary reform and the defeat of Dublin Castle the Catholic laborer would remain half starved and landless and the Protestant tenant would still be rackrented into ruin. Few listened; he recorded at the end of his life that only Russell, Neilson, McCracken and the Emmet brothers among the United Irish ever saw the "true cause of social derangement."

The new society, at its beginning, did not have a large membership. Its influence, however, was wide, and throughout 1791, '92, and '93 the United Irish interested every thinking Irishman and annoyed Dublin Castle by a series of addresses on every subject of the day. "Our late revolution," they said, "we declare to be fallacious and ideal—a thing much talked of, but neither felt nor seen. The act of Irish sovereignty has been merely tossed out of the English Houses into the cabinet of the Minister; and nothing remains to the people, who of right are everything, but a servile majesty and a ragged independence." And again, "An unalterable constitution, whatever be its nature, must be despotism. It is not the constitution, but the people, which ought to be inviolable." To the Volunteers they said, "You first took up arms to protect your country from foreign enemies and domestic disturbances. For the same purposes it now becomes necessary that you should resume them. . . . In four words lies all our power—universal emancipation and representative legislature." Early in 1793 they published a brief reform bill, which was widely read throughout the country.

Dublin Castle could not prevent all this; but whenever it could, it struck. The secretary of the Dublin society, Archibald Hamilton Rowan, was a well-to-do gentleman of past middle age and a very peppery temper. He was so irritated by attacks on himself and the United Irishmen made by Lord Clare in Parliament that he conveyed to the Lord Chancellor an invitation to a duel with himself or another champion, with the intention of running him through as a lesson to others. This imprudence and others brought him within reach of the law, and he was compelled to leave Ireland after a case in which observers noticed anxiously the appearance of jury packing—for the first time for some while in the broad light of a Dublin court.[18]

Dublin Castle also discovered that Napper Tandy, of whom it was perennially afraid, had taken an illegal oath at Castle Bellingham, where he was sworn into the Catholic peasant association of "Defenders"; it used this in 1792 to drive him out of the kingdom.[19] Because the agitation of the United Irishmen had caused a revival of the Irish Volunteers, Dublin Castle on the declaration of war with France formally prohibited them, announcing the institution of a militia to take their place. The Castle carried out the Volunteers' extinction with the nicest attention to the methods suitable to each class. Dealing with the Dublin working class, the government "seized the artillery of the Liberty Corps," noted the younger Grattan, adding, "it made a private arrangement by which it got possession of that belonging to the Merchant Corps; they induced the lawyers to give up theirs, just making a public procession before they were surrendered." [20] In general, the Volunteers dispersed without resistance, but in Belfast they made an attempt on March 15, 1793, to resist forcible quartering by the 17th Regiment. After a short scuffle they were defeated, and the Irish Volunteers passed out of history.

But though the Volunteers had vanished, new recruits rapidly joined the United Irish. "A unity among Irishmen" was their objective and wherever the United Irish oath was taken it reconciled Catholic and Protestant. A sudden peace spread over the countryside where it had passed, a peace which the governing clique afterward looked back on with terror. "For some months previous to the late Rebellions," Lord Ashtown, a Galway peer, wrote to the Viceroy ten years later, "when the lower classes were mediately to disturb the publick peace, drunkenness was almost unknown, and private quarrel extremely rare." Miles Byrne, later the most famous leader in Wexford, Carlow and Wicklow, saw that "the Government suspected something extraordinary was going on, finding that disputes, fighting at fairs and other places of public meeting had completely ceased. The man who had the misfortune to drink too much considered himself a lost man as soon as he became sober, fearing that no more confidence would be placed in him." [21] Tone, Neilson, Keogh and others would sometimes go out on actual missions of pacification. In August 1792, they traveled north to a place called Rathfriland, where the Protestant Peep o' Day Boys and the Catholic Defenders had come to blows. Tone's diary reads:

"August 11th. Breakfast at O'Hanlon's, Newry. Hear just now that if we go to Rathfriland we shall be houghed: *'pleasant but wrong.'* What is to be done? This information we have from Mr. O'Neil of Cabra: cowardly enough, but daresay he heard it. Set off for Mr. O'Neil of Banvale on our way to Rathfriland. Arrive at length at that flourishing seat of liberality and public virtue. *'I fear thee, O Rathfriland, lest thy girls with spits and thy boys with stones in fury of battle slay me.'* Stop at Murphy's Inn, six in number, all valiant. Get paper and begin to write to Dr. Tighe,

Mr. Barber and Mr. A. Lowry. Stop short by the intelligence that the landlord will give us no accommodations. Hey! Hey! The fellow absolutely refuses. He has cold beef and lamb chops and will give us neither."

Tone returned to Newry to see the responsible landlords, Lords Downshire and Hillsborough. "It cannot be that the rabble of Rathfriland should stop the growing liberty of Ireland." Tone took Neilson with him to see the two lords. He found Downshire, the same lord whose greed was responsible for the first rack-renting, had fallen into decay. "Lord Downshire's faculties quite gone. Lord Hillsborough's sharp enough; a high aristocrat. Angry at the committee's interference. . . . On the whole his lordship was just civil and no more." But his lordship's anger was to no point. The United Irishmen had already appeased the major portion of the dissensions of Rathfriland, and there was no more to be done by Tone than to reflect on the curious fact that the appointed defenders of the law were so angry at the restoration of order.

The chief cause of exasperation in Dublin Castle was in truth that the activities of the United Irishmen appeared to be wholly legal, and however much individuals could be harassed there were no grounds for proscribing the society itself. Grounds were provided by the folly of the French government, which in 1793 sent over to Dublin as its representative a very unwise clergyman named William Jackson. He picked up in London on his way a lawyer friend named Cockayne, who was in fact instructed by Pitt. Keogh refused to see Jackson, but Tone, Rowan and others accepted his credentials and spoke to him freely; when they disclosed to him their plans for breaking away from Britain and even (it appears) listed names of a probable Irish government, Jackson was arrested and his papers seized.[22] Rowan already was on his way out of the country; Tone on Keogh's advice fled to America, and from there to France. Keogh in a grave conversation with him in his garden told Tone that he himself was too old to bear arms, but that if Tone could return with a French force all the Keogh money and influence would be offered to him, and his son Cornelius would be proud to receive a commission in the army.

That the United Irishmen did not immediately turn themselves into a secret society after this exposure was probably due to a curious interlude in the years 1794 and 1795. Pitt needed the support of the Whig Duke of Portland; part of the Duke's price was the viceroyalty of Ireland for his protégé Lord Fitzwilliam, who had large Irish estates and close links with the reformers. On reaching Ireland Fitzwilliam at once started a program agreed on in London with the Duke, and, tacitly at least, approved by Pitt. Grattan was made the mouthpiece of the government in the House of Commons; a bill was brought in removing the last disabilities of the Catholics, and resolutions were passed requiring both parliamentary reform and a wholesale review of national expenditure that would wipe out sinecures and "places"; Irish parliaments were subservient bodies; only three M.P.'s and one lord voted against proposals which a year ago they had considered intolerable. Even the most skeptical United Irishman was conciliated when Fitzwilliam took the further step of ejecting from power the men who had been the instruments of oppression. Toler was scheduled for dismissal, his place was to be taken by the Whig George Ponsonby. Wolfe would be made a peer; Curran would replace him. Best of all, John Claudius Beresford, the king spider, was deprived of all the six offices which he held under the crown; he left them in silence.

It was a false dawn. Beresford sailed for London; Fitzwilliam stayed innocently in Dublin to complete his near-revolution. He found a sudden lack of support from London—even his dismissal of Toler was not confirmed. He wrote confidently "giving Mr. Pitt his choice between Mr. Beresford and me." Pitt made his choice quickly; the political circumstances which made Fitzwilliam necessary no longer obtained, and a Lord Camden was sent to replace him. Mr. Beresford also returned. The Catholic relief bill was defeated, the reform resolutions forgotten, and the Fitzwilliam appointments reversed.[23] An opportunity for reconciliation and unity, which would never recur, was lost, and a civil war which has not yet ended was made inevitable.

The United Irishmen now drew the natural conclusions from Fitzwilliam's fall; the society became a secret organization. Three Belfast clubs took the initiative, and by May 10, 1795, the conversion was completed for all Ulster.[24] Seventy-two societies then adhered to the new organization. Leinster was soon organized on the same basis. Munster and Connaught were hardly touched. The oath was changed—secrecy and fidelity were now required— and a military organization was established as well as a civilian. Each society consisted of twelve members, bound by oath. Above these societies were "baronial" committees, above them "upper baronial," and then county committees, and above them provincial committees. From the last named was elected the Executive Directory which sat in Dublin. Elaborate recognition tests were devised. One was a sort of catechism, running as follows:

"Are you straight?"

"I am."

"How straight?"

"As straight as a rush."

"Go on, then."

"In truth, in trust, in unity and liberty."

"What have you got in your hand?"

"A green bough."

"Where did it first grow?"

"In America."

"Where did it bud?"

"In France."

"Where are you going to plant it?"

"In the crown of Great Britain."

These precautions put the United Irishmen for the moment out of the reach of Dublin Castle. But the Beresford faction was not thereby to be thwarted. "Means were taken," said Lord Castlereagh later, "to make the United Irish system explode." In other words, an attempt was made to cause such exasperation as would drive the Irish into premature revolt. Horrible events fill the years 1796, '97, and '98, and both sides were deeply implicated. But in this case, as in many others, the old schoolroom test can be applied: "Who began it?" To that there is but one answer: Dublin Castle began it. There were attempts to conceal the Castle's responsibility for direct violence. Pitt, in the British Commons, and, in the Lords, Lord Downshire denied the direct accusations of Fox and the Duke of Bedford.[25] But few nowadays will believe them;

not only is there Castlereagh's boast, but there are such things as the letters from Beresford to London: "The organisation of rebellion goes on and increases daily; if we do not attack them they will us; we have been too long looking on" (February 8), and in July "The rabble did rise, and fortunate it was." [26] There is also the evidence of a man on the spot who can hardly be controverted, Sir John Moore, then only a brigadier sent out late in 1797 to pacify the southwest. "The mode which has been followed has been . . . to let loose the military who were encouraged in acts of violence"; this caused more disaffection but "the gentlemen in general still call aloud for violent measures . . . a complete line seems to be drawn between the upper and lower orders." The officers he found to be "profligate and idle," particularly those in the militia, and at Wexford he warned the yeomanry that if they carried out their intention to "revenge and burn," he would put them in irons. He could not understand why he was not supported in his attempt; his commander in chief, Abercromby, had issued an order stating that the army "was in a state of licentiousness which must render it formidable to every one but the enemy" and that discipline must be restored. But it was not; both he and his chief resigned in despair, and he records in his diary Abercromby's reason: "The Chancellor and his party would never explain exactly what they wished, but it was evident that they wished the commander in chief with the army to take upon themselves to act with a violence . . . for which they would give no public authority." [27]

Abercromby's predecessor, and a soldier on whom a great share of guilt lies, was a man called Lord Carhampton, who is better known by his previous name, Colonel Henry Lawes Luttrell. He had first come into prominence as the only man who dared to oppose in Middlesex the famous democrat John Wilkes. His reputation was worse than that of Wilkes; he was equally licentious with women, but, unlike his rival, he bilked his mistresses. "There is in this young man's conduct," wrote "Junius," "a strain of prostitution which for its singularity I cannot but admire." His appearance was dark and scarred. "These horrid features, a countenance the most repelling I ever beheld," observed a prisoner in 1796. The speaker was lucky to escape unharmed, for another man whom Carhampton visited in prison paid for an intemperate remark with a skinned eye from a blow with a whip.[28]

In Ireland, he knew what was his duty. He instituted the system of "picketings, free quarters, half hangings, floggings and pitchcappings," which quickly drove Irishmen to despair. His most extensive exploits took place in Connaught, that half-wild district of which Englishmen scarcely knew. The figures are disputed, but it is probable that some 1,300 men were illegally deported and forced into the navy. Certainly, an act of indemnity had to be passed to cover him from after proceedings.[29]

Cornwallis, who took over command after the insurrection began, wrote of the yeomanry to the Duke of Portland that they were "totally without discipline, contemptible before the enemy when any serious resistance is made to them, but ferocious and cruel in the extreme when any poor wretches with or without arms came within their power." Since the militia, for the reasons given by Colonel Moore, was useless, commanders were forced to rely on the yeomanry even when they would have preferred not to. And this yeomanry was soon acting independently, and on political grounds, even in the centers of great cities. In Belfast in 1795 they seized Sam Neilson, the editor of the *Northern Star,* and sent him under arrest to Dublin; in 1796 they broke open the building of this famous United Irish newspaper, plundered it of everything of value, and sent the printers to Newgate; in 1797 they broke in again and wrecked the whole plant and building so effectively that the paper could never be printed again.

In Dublin, John Claudius Beresford converted his riding school in Marlborough Street into a flogging arena, into which were dragged day after day men suspected of being Defenders or United Irish, who were whipped with cat-o'-nine-tails until their bones often showed through their flesh. Torture, for the same end of forcing the victims to "discover their conspiracy," was applied in the Royal Exchange at Dublin. Lord Castlereagh, in the popular belief, had the chief responsibility for this, and his name is described as having in history "the faint, sickening smell of hot blood." He denied that the Royal Exchange tortures were with the connivance of the government. "But the Exchange," answers the historian Madden, "immediately adjoins the Castle, and from

it the cries of the sufferers might have been heard in Lord Castlereagh's office, where his personal interposition, where the mere
expression of his will, might have prevented the continuance of
the torture." [30]

Lieutenant Hepenstal, of the Wicklow Militia, in June 1797 led
a party into the house at Gardenstown of an old man named Carroll, promising pardon if all concealed arms were surrendered.
Carroll surrendered three guns, and Hepenstal then shot him and
his two sons, and burned the house, crops, barns and all the property. The wife of one of the sons, with her child, was in the burning house and begged to be allowed to escape. Hepenstal agreed
to spare her life, "but if the bitch makes the least noise," he told
the soldiers, she was to share her husband's fate. He then loaded
the three corpses onto a cart, drove to Moyvore, where he arrested three men, Michael Murray, Henry Smith and John Smith,
who (he said) were United Irishmen, and threw them into the
cart, tying them to the corpses, whose blood poured over them.
When he reached the village green of Ballymore he took them out
and shot them. In the case of Hyland, tried at Athy, Hepenstal
himself recounted in the witness box how he attempted to extract
evidence from a prisoner by repeated pricking with bayonets. On
this failing, he threw a rope around the prisoner's neck, swung the
rope over his shoulder—he was a man of gigantic height—pulled
it, and so hanged the man on himself.

> "Here lie the bones of Hepenstal,
> Judge, jury, gallows, rope and all"

was the epitaph written for him but never inscribed upon his grave.

Irish propaganda frequently referred to "your violated fe-
males"; Castle replies repudiated even indelicacy toward any
woman. With one exception,[31] there appears to be little valid evidence of this particular accusation, but there are other pictures,
repulsive enough to condemn the Castle, drawn in the memoirs of
the period. The Ancient Britons and Newtown-Mount-Kennedy
Cavalry amusing themselves by driving their spurs into the up-
turned face of young Richard Neill, a prisoner whom they tormented till he burst his bonds and fought two dozen of them with
an iron weight; for which crime he was bayoneted and hanged.

Hunter Gowan, a Protestant landlord, riding into Gorey at the head of his yeomanry, with the finger of a dead peasant spiked on the tip of his sword, and using it later in a public house to stir the punch for the officers' mess. The invention of a special form of "wire cat," weighted with scraps of tin and lead, to cause Peter O'Neil, a suspected priest, to "shake the triangle" with his writhings, because the assembled yeomanry expected that sign of agony. "Half-hangings"—a trick by which the prisoner was hanged till he was nearly insensible, let down and cross-examined, hanged again, and so forth, until he said whatever he wished. Judkin Fitzgerald, high sheriff of Tipperary, flogging a teacher of French, for having a scrap of innocuous French writing on his person, until he was nearly dead, and leaving his wounds undressed in the hope that he would die.[32]

There is no need to continue such descriptions; there is, however, one device that must be described. "Pitch-capping" is said to have been the invention of Lord Kingsborough and to have been practiced first in the southeastern corner of Ireland. However that may be, its practice was quickly spread all over the country. Many of the United Irishmen, for reasons unknown, cut their hair short. This marked them out and earned them the name of "croppies." When a "croppy" was caught and brought to the guardhouse, a cap of coarse linen or strong brown paper covered with boiling pitch was produced and forced on his head. There it was held until the pitch so far cooled that it was impossible to remove it without pulling out all the hair, and the victim was then turned loose. Of several of the subordinate leaders in the insurrection of 1798 it was recorded that their heads were still one huge sore from pitch-capping.[33]

Legal remedy against such actions could rarely, if ever, be secured. The case of Orr was the first as it was the most infamous. Orr was a United Irishman of Ferranshane, tried for felony in 1797. The jury which convicted him was drunk. The chief witness against him made an affidavit afterward that he had lied. Four of the jury swore either that they were drunk or that threats had been used to force their verdict. The presiding judge personally intervened to secure a pardon. Nevertheless Lord Camden refused a pardon and Orr was executed.[34]

For a short while Ponsonby, Grattan, Curran and other moderates endeavored to use constitutional means to secure redress. They founded in 1797 a society to obtain "Authentic Information of Outrages Committed on the People." [35] They found that their complaints were received with inattention or ridicule, that the behavior of the government became worse, and on May 15, 1797, they gave up the struggle and ceased to attend in the House of Commons.

Three lords, Camden, Clare and Castlereagh, were chiefly responsible for the reign of terror. Camden, the Viceroy, was a man of weak rather than vicious mind. The records of his private secretary show that his first inclination, in most individual cases, was toward mercy. But he was usually overridden by the more forceful characters of Clare and Castlereagh, and afterward adhered to his decisions with the obstinacy of a weak man who fears to show his weakness. Clare, once John Fitzgibbon the lawyer, was able and not ungenerous, but he had a violent temper and a growing dislike of the Irish people; his abilities and his legal position (he was Lord Chancellor) made him one of the most dangerous opponents of the United Irish. In judging the third of this triumvirate, Lord Castlereagh, we must wipe from our minds what was afterward written about his foreign policy or his later record as an English politician. To the Irish he was always the younger Robert Stewart, the onetime reformer responsible for the provocation which drove the men of 1798 to their ruin. He more than anyone else was held responsible for the organization of the Castle's terror, and popular opinion in both Dublin and London fastened upon him the guilt of the half-hangings, floggings and deaths of '98. When he died, by his own hand, Cobbett, the most influential British journalist, posted outside his Fleet Street office a placard reading PEOPLE OF ENGLAND REJOICE! CASTLEREAGH IS DEAD. When his hearse stopped outside the door of Westminster Abbey, the Duke of Wellington, two princes of the blood, and other noblemen pressed forward to take the pall. As they did so, a tremendous cheer broke out from the assembled audience. The victor of Waterloo, for once unnerved, stopped still, and after a moment's hesitation again gave the signal to proceed. Immediately the same cheer was repeated, and the royal and noble dukes, disconcerted and in ragged formation, carried the coffin to the Abbey door. As they reached the porch, the same cheer broke forth again, this time more like an exultant yell, and accompanied by a general waving of hats and sticks.[36]

What these men did not inspire or do themselves was done for them by voluntary violence. Where the United Irishmen were not powerful, the old antagonism between Catholic and Protestant rose to a new fury. Since 1794, when the vote had been given to Catholics, landlords no longer needed Protestant tenants as voters, and began to lease their farms to the dispossessed and eager Catholics, who worked harder and offered higher prices. The Peep o' Day Boys were early in operation in Ulster, driving out, menacing, and even killing Catholics who took the farms of evicted Protestants. Then the Peep o' Day Boys vanished before a new organization, the Orange lodges. Their origin is uncertain, but it is said that the first Orange lodge was formed on September 21, 1795, at the house of a man named Sloan in the obscure village of Loughgall. Another account (Jemmy Hope's) gives "a person called Atkinson and Philip Johnson, a Low Church clergyman," as the first Orange organizers. However this may be, the Orange societies spread rapidly, and before long had in every town replaced the Peep o' Day Boys and the Hearts of Steel. It is impossible to separate their violences with certainty from those of the military and militia, but in general it may be said that their outrages were distinguished by an immediate economic purpose. They were directed usually to the expulsion of a Catholic tenant, or the protection of a Protestant. They attempted, after 1795, a general expulsion of Catholics from the county of Armagh, as a result of a pitched battle with the Catholics, known as the "Battle of the Diamond," in which the Catholics were defeated. Their chief, and for long sole, opponents were the Defenders, an organization of the Catholic workers and poorest peasantry, which is one of the enigmas of history. Nothing is known of their principles, program or organization. No man not of the working class was ever admitted, with the one exception of the famous Napper Tandy, and he would never at any time disclose anything of their secrets. As time went on the Defenders gradually joined the United Irishmen and, as a separate organization, disappeared.[37]

The United Irishmen were often extraordinarily careless in preserving their new secrecy. It was this laxity which cost them the adhesion of John Keogh and several of the more cautious Catholics. Keogh attended but one meeting, on the urging of a friend. He observed most of those present, and recognized them; the others his friend was able to name to him. Soon there came in some more men. His friend was able to name one, who (he said) had brought two friends with him. And who were the fourth, and the fifth, and the others, he was asked. He enquired, and it appeared that the friends had brought other friends, and so on. Keogh signaled silently to Richard McCormick, his colleague, rose and quietly left the room. "Dick," he said, as he closed the door, "no man's life is safe in the hands of gentlemen who will behave as lightly as this." Such carelessness was common, and its chief cause was drunkenness. "All Ireland was somewhat drunk at this time," noted an observer broadly. The business of country societies was invariably conducted in public houses—in shebeens by the "lower orders," such as the Muddlers' Club in Belfast, and in elegant taverns for the upper class, such as the Eagle in Exchequer Street or Strugglers' Tavern in Cook Street. It was impossible that information should not leak out from such meetings. Quite highly placed officers set the example. Neilson was frequently paralytically drunk, and Bond and Butler, two eminent Dublin leaders, ran up in Newgate in six months a wine bill of £500.[38]

The Leinster Directory, which included Dublin, should have consisted of five members; it had at the beginning but three— Tom Emmet, a gentle and earnest Catholic named Dr. Macneven, and the once-famous Arthur O'Connor. This fantastic person came from the county of Cork, where he boasted of a descent from Ir, son of Milesius, and the line of equally mythical kings who succeeded him. He was, he said, the legitimate representative (with his brother Roger, who was partly crazy, and his brother Robert, who hated him) of the great sept (clan) of O'Connor Kerry; he was also descended from King Feargus and Queen Maeve. There were few who, to Arthur O'Connor's face, would dare remind him that his father's name had been plain Conner and that he had kept an oil shop in London. His whole conversation was disturbing and ferocious: he impeded Directory meetings with inopportune rhetoric, and treated any disagreement as a sign of cowardice. Tom Emmet, who was naturally repelled by him, gradually came to believe he must be either an idiot or a spy. Before long they had a more serious reason for disagreement. All the United Irish now looked to France for aid, and Emmet, inside their Directory, laid it down as an axiom that no revolt could be attempted until French aid was actually at hand. O'Connor replied contemptuously that French aid was no doubt desirable, but that Ireland must and could win her own freedom; he continually endeavored to force the Directory to fix a date for an insurrection, and as continually Emmet and Macneven held him back. It was fortunate for the United Irishmen that their dissensions were overborne and sometimes even silenced by the chief of the military organization, Lord Edward Fitzgerald. As brother of the Duke of Leinster, Ireland's premier peer, Lord Edward imposed respect by his rank; his character reinforced it. His military experience, his intelligence and his winning personality brought him a silent affection which was one of the greatest strengths of the United Irish movement. His aristocratic origin was, in the eighteenth century, almost an essential qualification for leadership; but his wife brought with her a democratic tang which delighted the rank and file. Lady Pamela was the illegitimate daughter by Madame de Genlis of Philippe Egalité, the Duke of Orléans, the only member of the house of Bourbon who had supported the French Revolution. She was not, however, as is usually alleged, the ward of the terrorist Barère.[39] Her character was considered *"légère"* by her husband's relatives—perhaps with some reason—and she was subjected to snubs which only endeared her more to her husband and to the United Irish.

In the year 1796 the strength of the United Irishmen had been suddenly increased. The reason for this was neither the misbehavior of Dublin Castle, nor yet the inherent reasonableness of the Irish cause; it was an event which is generally written down in history as a fiasco. Wolfe Tone, in France, had so worked on the French Directory that he had persuaded it to arrange a serious expedition to free Ireland. He had, moreover, been able to engage in his plan Lazare Hoche, the most disinterested and, after Bonaparte, the ablest of French generals. In 1796 the force was ready and set sail. Storms scattered it, and the fleet which arrived at Bantry Bay was only a portion of the great expedition. This would not have mattered—there were men enough for a big attack—but among the missing ships was that which had General Hoche on board. The responsible authorities who remained were Bompard, the Admiral, and Grouchy, the General. They had no exact and absolutely phrased orders, and spent days of hesitation in sight of the Irish mountains. Grouchy was a man whose physical courage was undoubted, but he had an indecision of mind and a fatal formalism which made him, perhaps, the only general who twice lost an empire. Nineteen years later he was in charge of that detachment of the French army which Napoleon sent off to pursue the Prussians after the victories of Ligny and Quatre Bras. He followed the Prussian detachments opposed to him, and entangled himself in a subordinate conflict at the village of Wavre. The thunder of the guns of Waterloo was clearly heard in his headquarters: his officers begged him to turn around and march to his Emperor's side. But no such orders were written down in his instructions; he refused, and hours later, after the main French army was wrecked and the empire was ruined, he dignifiedly withdrew from his engagement, victorious, and with his troops wholly intact and wholly useless. So, too, in 1796, he could find no peremptory instructions to land in Ireland at all costs. He hesitated for days, decided the weather was too adverse, and returned to France.

But though his inaction, and a strong wind from the land, had saved the British power in Ireland, both Dublin Castle and the rebels realized that if he had landed the reign of George III in Ireland would have ended. There was no power which could have effectively opposed a French landing. The militia and the troops were both contemptible; and now that it was clear that the French were prepared to make a serious effort, everyone believed that the days of British domination were limited. Hope and fear changed sides. Dublin Castle, which had been confident in its power of oppression, was in an agony of alarm. On the rebels' side there was an unconsidered confidence. All manner of men who had hesitated now joined their ranks. The sworn members of the United Irishmen rose to 500,000, and of these nearly 300,000 were capable of bearing arms and were roughly instructed in their use. Whole districts of Ireland fell quietly under their control; at one time the town of Cahir in Tipperary was actually occupied by them, searched for arms, and evacuated. But this inrush of members had its disadvantages, though the Irish Directory was slow to realize it. Jemmy Hope, the Ulster weaver, wrote, "The appearance of the French in Bantry Bay brought the rich farmers and shopkeepers into the societies, and with them all the corruption essential to the objects of the British ministry." He saw the complex hierarchy of local and district committees filled with men who were at the best wealthy and timid, at the worst (he said) corruptible and the agents of the British government.

There was before long confirmation of his fears. On the night of October 8, 1797, the bell rang loudly at the front door of the London house of Lord Downshire, the Ulster peer. After some parley the butler admitted a tall, dark man, whose face was completely muffled in a large neckcloth, and who declined to give his name. He was, he said, a member of the Ulster Directory of the United Irishmen, and was prepared to divulge all their secrets for a sufficient consideration. He dictated a brief account of the members of the Directories of Leinster and Ulster which was sufficient to establish his *bona fides*. Lord Downshire, obeying his instructions, withheld his name for some time from the government, but sent on his reports. He signed "Richardson"—he had a pretty wit in his way, for one of his chief duties was to spy on Lord Edward Fitzgerald, whose wife's name, Pamela, was the title of Samuel Richardson's most famous novel. His real name was Samuel Turner; he was an attorney in Newry.[40]

Turner was soon joined by others. James M'Gucken, an attorney from Belfast, who handled much of the United Irishmen's legal business, regularly passed on his information to the government. Leonard MacNally, the United Irishmen's chief lawyer, was reporting already. John Hughes, a Belfast bookseller, supplied the names of the committeemen in his district. He was, however, imprudent enough to tamper with Jemmy Hope. He came to him with the ingenious argument that Robert Simms, who was the commander of the Ulster forces of the United Irish, and another man whose name is not recorded were ruining the cause by their hesitations. "Let us two," he said (or something to that effect), "go now to the government and lay information against these two men. We shall have removed two probable traitors and have gained the hope of victory." Hope answered by drawing out a pistol from his pocket and telling Hughes that he would shoot him if he ever made such a suggestion again. From that moment Hughes was a marked man, trusted by no one in Ulster. E. J. Newell, a portrait painter, first betrayed the United Irishmen to the government, and then, after a violent quarrel with Secretary Cooke at Dublin Castle, betrayed Dublin Castle to the Irish. After this he again attempted to return to governmental spying, and disappeared. He can be traced, on a day in June 1798, as far as Doagh, a place about ten miles out by road from Belfast. He was never seen again.[41]

There is little doubt that he was killed by the United Irishmen. Assassination was vehemently opposed by the Society: a resolution carried by the unfortunate William Orr declared that "a man who would recommend the killing of another is a coward as well as a murderer." But no resolutions could hold back the rage of United Irishmen when they saw their fellows and relatives shot or flogged to death through the agency of spies who still walked carelessly and safely through the streets. It is astonishing, indeed, that there were so few of such illicit executions of spies. Hope, who knew the working-class United Irishmen as no one else did, recalled only the following men, apart from Newell, who were killed: McBride, of Donegore, shot in a Belfast alley called Saw's Entry; McClure, of Craigbally, who vanished mysteriously; Harper, of County Down, shot on a bridge near Ballygowan; Henry Caghally, of County Derry, stabbed at Templepatrick; and the Reverend Mr. Phillips, of Frenchpark, who swore men in at a shilling a head to the Defenders and then handed their names to the government, and who was found drowned in a paper-mill stream near Belfast, with leaden weights in his pockets.

The most immediately useful of all the government's new acquisitions was a brother-in-law of Mrs. Tone, deep in the United Irish secrets. His name was Thomas Reynolds, and he was a distant relative of Lord Edward, who had even secured for him some financial aid from the Duke of Leinster. He was a silk merchant in the Liberty district of Dublin, and he moved without question or suspicion in the most intimate circles of the United Irishmen. The government realized that in him it had an unusually valuable instrument and decided to use him not to pick up here and there an indiscreet leader, but to capture, if possible, the whole controlling body of the Society.[42]

Such men as Reynolds worked under the direction of Cooke, the Secretary at Dublin Castle, and, through him, of Castlereagh. The others, like Newell, reported to a man whose name looms enormous in the records of Dublin about the turn of the century —Major Sirr. Henry Charles Sirr's title was not military, but civilian; he was "town major," or chief of police. He was not, despite his reputation, noticeably either a cruel or an unjust man; it was, indeed, for his courage, his speed, his incorruptibility and his acuteness that he was hated. He was better than his subordinates; Major Sandys was greedier and Major Swan more brutal. He had, as was the habit of eighteenth-century policemen, a way of appropriating to himself odd valuables, correspondence or curiosities of his victims; but he never allowed himself the wholesale looting or blackmail which Castle agents frequently enough practiced. His face was one of those large-nosed, big, blond and smooth countenances which bear a false appearance of geniality. He endeavored mechanically, by bad jokes delivered in a loud monotone, to hold a reputation of cheeriness. "You were taking pains to take panes," he told a prisoner charged with glass stealing. "Theophilus Molloy O'Regan, why is your name longer than yourself?" he said to an unusually short defendant. But his cold blue eyes gave away his fundamental hardness. When he became a police magistrate no man was more feared than he. "The Major's coming," would be whispered from the court door, as soon as his figure was seen in the distance. Every policeman would spring to attention and remain rigid, anxiously wondering if each button was bright enough and in place, until the Major had passed by with his quick, firm step and rapid glance from side to side, like a predatory bird. He would sit collapsed in his seat with his eyes half shut, in the hope that some man would believe him to be really asleep and commit some irregularity for which he could be instantly punished. He was not tall, but he gave as much impression

as he could of height by holding himself stiffly upright and walking very fast upon the balls of his feet. In 1798 he regularly pa-
trolled the streets of Dublin, with a bodyguard of truculent informers in civilian clothes behind him. "Here comes the Major
and his gang," was the word passed invariably before him, and all
who had any fear of his attentions vanished down alleys and into
doorways until he had passed, fleeing before him like pigeons
from a hawk.[43]

The United Irishmen's Directory was not without its own spies.
It seems likely that not only had it an agent—a friend of Sam
Neilson's—in "Mr. Kemmis's office," where the government's
concoction of informers' evidence was carried on, but that a
member of the Privy Council and a general both gave it information of the government's intentions.[44] It had other agents in official
places, it had no suspicion of the extent to which it was itself
spied upon, it received reports from Tone as to the French intentions which were on the whole encouraging, it was, finally, gradually driven to desperation by the terror. Consequently, early in
1798 it at last decided that a date must be fixed for an insurrection. Eventually May 23 was selected. Lord Edward Fitzgerald
had a full inventory drawn up of the men and money available.
The money was but £1,485 4s. 9d; but, as Tom Emmet pointed
out, there was now "immense property" within the ranks of the
United Irish which could at need be called upon. The registers of
armed men laid before Lord Edward showed the following figures:

Ulster	110,990	Queen's County	11,689
Munster	100,634	King's County	3,600
Kildare	10,863	Carlow	9,414
Wicklow	12,895	Kilkenny	624
Dublin County	3,010	Meath	1,400
Dublin City	2,177		

He thus had, on paper, a force of nearly 280,000 men. Being a
man of experience in military matters, he reduced this estimate to
100,000. With such a force, and with his general officers appointed, he felt that he was certain of victory, even if there was no

French landing. Such a calculation was not unreasonable in itself, but there was a fatal flaw in it. Had there been five other men of his experience, authority, and courage to assist him, his endeavor might have succeeded. But in a few hours he was alone.

As soon as it was known by the government that a date for insurrection had been fixed, it acted with unprecedented speed. In one day, March 12, 1798, it completely shattered the central organization. Tom Emmet and Dr. Macneven were arrested in their homes, so also were two prominent assistants named Jackson and Sweetman. A crucial assembly of fourteen provincial delegates was being held at the house of Oliver Bond. Reynolds, the spy, had informed the government, and everyone present at the meeting was arrested and taken to the Castle. Arthur O'Connor was already under lock and key.

The whole Society was disorganized. What hope remained was centered on Lord Edward, who had, fortunately, been absent from the meeting. But Lord Edward was ill, and a sick man hurried secretly from house to house could not easily direct an insurrection. Assistants he had scarcely any. There were two young men named Sheares, Henry and John, and Sam Neilson, the Ulster draper, whose courage was set off by his extreme imprudence. Moreover, everyone was discomfited by the realization that there must have been treachery in high places. Reynolds, with calm brazenness, continued his usual activities, even calling upon Mrs. Bond to condole with her upon her husband's fate, kissing her baby and dancing it on his knee. Some suspicion must have crossed Neilson's mind: he stopped Reynolds in the street, and, his eyes almost popping out of his head with rage, drew his pistol and said, "What should I do, Reynolds, to a man who inserted himself into our intimacy to betray us?" Reynolds drew himself up and looked at him coldly. "You should shoot him through the heart," he answered, and passed on, leaving Neilson and uncertain and dejected.

As the government continued its efforts to seize the United Irish leaders, it swept into jail even those most distantly connected with the movement. Surgeon-General Stewart, despite his official position, sent private warning of their impending arrest to two fellow members of the College of Surgeons, Mr. Lawless and

Mr. Dease, both men of great eminence. Mr. Lawless, immediately on reading the note, walked straight to the Dublin quayside, stepped aboard a ship, and escaped to the Continent. The same note was delivered to Mr. Dease in the College, where he was lecturing. He read it, paused a moment, and then continued his lecture without any change of tone or color. At the conclusion of his class, he bowed to the students and went home, where he cut his femoral artery, and so died.[45]

But, however wide they cast their net, the officers of the government could not find Lord Edward. Perhaps, indeed, they were not at first anxious to do so. "Will no one urge Lord Edward to fly? I pledge myself that every port in the kingdom shall be left open to him," cried Lord Clare in public.[46] For Lord Edward had powerful friends, and Lord Clare may also have calculated that if he would only remove himself, the rest of the United Irishmen could be dealt with easily.

But Lord Edward was not the man to run away, and the government willy-nilly had to track him down and arrest him. Nor was this easy. To betray O'Connor, Bond or Emmet was one thing, to betray Lord Edward was to incur the hatred and possible vengeance of every patriotic Irishman. There were few informers with the hardihood to do this. From suspicion, or native caution, Lord Edward would not see either Turner or Reynolds. Neilson was a fool, but he was incorruptible. Eventually an informer was found, almost by accident, and for fifty years his identity was unsuspected. The only clue for a long time was a Secret Service money entry:

"June 20. F.H. Discovery of L.E.F. £1,000."

The most fantastic guesses were made as to the identity of "F.H." It was suggested that the initial letter, which is blurred, might be "J.," and that the spy was John Hughes, the Belfast bookseller. It was suggested that the letters could be read as "S.N.," meaning Sam Neilson. It was even argued that the spy was really Thomas Reynolds again, but of that there was no evidence. Nearly all of Lord Edward's personal following—Peter Finnerty, Laurence Tighe, Nick Murphy, Felix Rourke, and even the housemaid—were also suspected of what was universally regarded as the greatest of all such crimes. Half a century later, investigators, of whom the chief was Dr. Madden, were able to establish that "F.H." was Francis Higgins, a broken-down attorney who had earned by an early fraud the nickname "the Sham Squire," and was a regular government agent. But he, it was known, had had no connection with Lord Edward. It was clear that he must have used a "setter." Further research discovered the name of this, the real culprit. Francis Magan was a solicitor of small practice in Dublin, grumpy and undistinguished, but trusted by the United Irish in minor matters. One night Lord Edward was challenged in the street; his followers set upon the police and raised a riot, under cover of which Lord Edward escaped to the nearest friendly house, that of a man named Nicholas Murphy. His hiding place was reported to Magan, Magan carried it to Higgins, and for the rest of his life bore on his conscience the responsibility of Lord Edward's arrest and death. He lived to an advanced age, working obscurely at his profession, unnoticed, sullen; and friendless by choice. He died in 1843 and was buried in the Church of St. Michael and St. John. A century after his betrayal the priest of this church informed an inquirer: "The remains of Francis Magan lie in our vault. There is a perpetual endowment for prayers to be said for the repose of his soul. I have been praying for him, once every year, ever since I was attached to this parish. Neither I nor anyone else here knows who he was or what he did." [47]

The day after Francis Higgins carried Magan's information to the Castle, Samuel Neilson called on Lord Edward at Murphy's house, openly, and had dinner with him at four o'clock in the afternoon. Despite Neilson's presence, there was very little wine taken. Lord Edward was always abstemious, and at the moment was also out of health. Then, as soon as Neilson had left, he went upstairs to his room and lay down. He had been resting but a few minutes when the door was suddenly flung open, and there appeared Major Swan, Sirr's bullock-like assistant. Behind him was a man who is described only as "a person with a sword and a round hat." Lord Edward immediately leaped from his bed and struck at Swan with his dagger, the only weapon he carried. The man in the round hat at once turned tail and ran downstairs. Swan received Lord Edward's blow upon his fingers, and at the sight of his own blood let out a loud scream and followed his assistant down the stairs. He did not stop till he reached the street, where he ran up and down the pavement showing his wounded hand and crying, "Oh, I am killed; oh, I am killed! Ryan! Ryan! See what they have done to me." Captain Thomas Ryan, a yeoman who was approaching with Major Sirr and eight soldiers, responded to this appeal by bounding up the stairs to where Lord Edward stood hesitating at the door of his room. He hurled himself on the slight figure and crushed it down upon the bed, and a short and bloody struggle followed. Ryan was unarmed but for a sword cane; Lord Edward had his dagger, and stabbed him again and again. Though bleeding from nearly a dozen wounds, Ryan, as he fell to the floor, grasped Lord Edward's knees, hoping to prevent his escape long enough for the soldiers to arrive. Major Swan, still running up and down outside the house and bleating like a sheep, was useless, but Sirr, with his usual coolness, ordered his eight soldiers into formation and marched them up the stairs, himself leading. He stopped at the right side of the door, drew his pistol and, aiming very deliberately, shot Lord Edward through the right shoulder. As Lord Edward's dagger dropped and he staggered back to the bed, Sirr motioned his soldiers forward. Lord Edward leaped up again, to make a last resistance. "Cross your muskets," ordered Sirr. His soldiers formed a sort of grill with their guns and forced the struggling man to the floor, pinning him down, as it were, into a cage. They then bound him firmly and sent him to Newgate. Some stayed to sack the house; Sirr turned his attention to Ryan. He secured medical attention for him, but the Captain was obviously dying, and Sirr felt it his duty to write a few words of condolence to his son. He was not an expert correspondent, but his policeman's pen at last found a phrase which seemed to him happy. "Having secured the titled prisoner," he wrote, "my first concern was for your dear father's safety. I viewed his intestines with grief and sorrow." [48]

When Lord Edward, gravely wounded, was taken to Newgate, nobody was allowed to see him. His lawyer, whom he called to draw up his will, was forbidden to enter the prison. He was instructed to stay in his coach, and his messages were conveyed through a warder, who transmitted the prisoner's answers, and in this peculiar manner the will was drawn up. Government officials, indeed, visited him, and among them his old enemy Lord Clare. One of Lord Edward's last recorded utterances is his farewell to Lord Clare. "As I cannot shake hands with you," he said, looking at his bandaged fingers, "I must only shake a toe," which he did. He was rapidly sinking, but retained his senses until, by cruelty or heedlessness, the jail authorities erected outside his window a gallows and hanged upon it a harmless young farmer named John Clinch, a United Irishman. From that moment Lord Edward's reason gave way. He imagined himself to be conducting in reality the insurrection which he would now never see. He held his consultations, cried out his orders in a loud voice, and passed through all the passions and agitations of a campaign. His colleagues in their separate cells could hear his great voice echoing through the corridors. They heard him rallying his imaginary army. "Come on! Damn you! Come on!" He shouted again and again, until gradually his voice became fainter and his words more confused.

The Viceroy, Camden, issued an order that none of his relatives should see the dying man. He remained obstinate to the appeals of both Lord Henry, Lord Edward's brother, and his cousin, Lady Louisa Connolly, leaving the latter abruptly when she fell on her knees before him. Anger as well as despair took her then to her cousin's chief enemy, Lord Clare, whom she interrupted at his dinner. He came out, holding his napkin in his hand, and heard her dignified request for an order to see Lord Edward. "I cannot give it to you; it has been so ordered," he replied, and added with a sudden decision, "but I can take you there myself. Bring Lord Henry." He flung a cloak around him, and, still grasping his napkin, drove with the two to Newgate Jail. There the warders attempted to stop the party, asking him who he was and by what right he came. "I am the Lord Clare; let us pass." He escorted them to Lord Edward's bedside, and left them. Lord Edward for a moment recognized them. "This is very pleasant," he said. But in a few minutes he had returned to his delirium and was calculating the numbers of militia opposed to him. He began to array his men for battle; his voice became harsh and his eyes glared. "My dear, don't talk of these things; it agitates you," said Lady Louisa gently. A cloud of perplexity appeared on his face; he looked at her uncertainly, and said, more quietly, "Very well, I won't," but in a minute or two he was raving again. An hour or so after they had left, he died in a great convulsion, in the early hours of Monday, June 4, 1798.[49]

With Lord Edward in jail, the few remaining United Irish leaders had rapidly involved themselves in disaster. Neilson came to the two Sheares brothers with a proposal to storm Kilmainham Jail and liberate the leaders. The Sheareses answered that this was the project of a fool; John Sheares, the younger, told Neilson that only a spy would propose it. The interview rapidly became a violent quarrel, with the three men shouting insults at one another, and they parted on the worst possible terms. They refused, thenceforward, either to meet or to correspond with each other. The Sheareses withdrew to their own homes, endeavoring to reorganize Lord Edward's forces, with the assistance of a Captain J. W. Armstrong, of the King's County Militia, who had put his military experience at their disposal. They had decided to appoint him to the command of the King's County Regiment, and had taken his advice on the organization of the revolt in Dublin. On Sunday, May 20, he dined at Henry's house, and there was a scene of friendly affection. He played with the elder brother's children, while Mrs. Sheares played for his especial benefit some patriotic airs upon the harp. Immediately after dinner was over he left the house, and went across to Dublin Castle, where he completed the reports he had been making; the next morning the Sheares brothers were both safely lodged in jail.[50]

Neilson, left alone, formed a desperate plan which, if he could but have executed it with ordinary prudence, might have rallied the United Irishmen at the last minute. He assembled in Barley Fields the best force he could find, for an attack on Newgate Jail. He knew his way about that jail well enough to be sure that it was possible to seize it and free the leaders. But he found at the last moment, characteristically enough, that no one had troubled to discover how high were Newgate walls, and what ladder lengths were consequently necessary. Instead of sending a subordinate, he must himself leave Barley Fields and run down to Newgate, where he went up to the walls, peering up and taking measurements. The guard recognized him, and from two directions soldiers rushed upon him. Neilson fought furiously, anger giving him strength, and for a minute the circle of struggling men rolled like a giant football at the foot of the walls. But there were sixteen armed men to one unarmed, and in a short while, covered with cuts and bruises, Neilson was discharged with some violence into Newgate courtyard. With his arrest vanished the last man who could give any general control to the United Irish.[51]

But at least the orders had been sent out to the provincial organizations before Lord Edward's arrest, and Ulster, the pride of the Society, might act upon them. The Irish commander here was Robert Simms, the rich Belfast merchant and onetime newspaper owner whom Tone had enrolled five years before. He received his orders on May 21 for an insurrection on May 23. At once Hope's misgivings over the reliability of wealthy rebels were confirmed. Simms was not a traitor, but he had lived soft too long. The prospect of an insurrection, not in theory and at some future date, but in fact and the day after tomorrow, filled him with sick terror. He thrust the orders into his pocket, dismissed the messenger quietly, and did no more. To Hope and other Ulstermen who pestered him to move he solemnly averred that he had received no instructions. Day after day Hope and his colleagues became more restless. The Ulster organization began to scatter. The county gentlemen abandoned their waiting and returned to their affairs. The townsmen, working-class and middle-class, decided their leaders had failed and there was nothing to be done. At last Hope and another leader, Henry Joy McCracken, called on Simms and cross-examined him. For a while he stood up to them, but at last broke down, produced his papers, and confessed hysterically that his nerves would not allow him to lead a rebellion. McCracken and Hope forced him to resign and to sign a paper appointing his second-in-command, a Dr. Dixon, as general. Leaving the fat Simms sobbing in a chair, they rode hastily out in search of Dr. Dixon, only to find that he had just been arrested. This, they realized, had finally disorganized the Ulster forces, and for some days they hesitated. Finally they felt they could not let this last chance pass without at least making an attempt in defense of Irish freedom. They collected as many as they could of the United Irish and descended on the town of Antrim, which they captured. But

Ulster was heavily garrisoned, and troops were rushed up at once. The ill-armed and undisciplined United Irish carried on for a while a disorderly and scattering fight with the English, but before long the "Battle of Antrim" ended in their defeat and dispersal. McCracken was caught and hanged, Hope escaped.

There were momentary insurrections, easily dispersed, on May 23 in Dublin County, Meath and Kildare. The call of the United Irishmen was fully answered in one county alone, and that a county of which they had had small hopes—Wexford. It was partly accident, but even more the ferocity of the Orangemen in this corner of Ireland, which was responsible. Several landlords, of whom the most famous was Lord Kingsborough, the pitch capper, had distinguished themselves for their malevolence, and the lower ranks of the militia and soldiers appear to have been unusually brutish. "Tom the Devil," a sergeant in the North Cork Regiment, invented the practice of cutting prisoners' hair short, rubbing in damp gunpowder, and lighting it. Particular resentment was caused by a trick, frequently played on Wexford women and considered very humorous by the soldiers. They alleged that any green ribbon, green cap or handkerchief was a sign of "croppy" sympathies, and professed to have instructions to stop any attractive young woman and examine her clothes and underclothes to discover and remove any garment of that color.

For months this had gone on in Wexford, Carlow and Wicklow. The Catholic priests, whose influence was immense, refused to countenance the United Irish societies: they even in church pushed away from their knees United Irishmen who wished to confess to them. They preached peace and resignation, and few were more vehement in this than Father John Murphy of Bonagar and Boleyvogue. One day, hearing of the approach of a raiding party of yeomanry, he called his flock together, warned it to behave peaceably and greet the yeomen as friends. The yeomanry, when they came, sacked the village, burned his chapel and his house, and passed on with their booty. Rage seized Father Murphy; he called out his villagers from the woods into which they had fled, and set them in an ambush on the road by which the yeomen must return. As soon as the raiders appeared, his men, armed with pitchforks, rushed out upon them. The yeomen scarcely resisted; they dropped their loot and fled in terror, leaving several dead.

Once set on his path, Father Murphy continued the fight. He was joined by many United Irishmen and marched on Whitsunday, May 27, 1798, to a place called Oulart Hill, where he made a rough encampment. As he expected, troops were sent in to attack him. He let them discharge their first volley and then sent his ragged force charging down on them with pitchforks, yelling hideously. The troops, ill-disciplined and frightened, broke at once, and were driven away. There was a general slaughter, for the peasants took no prisoners. From there, his army increased to 8,000, Father Murphy marched to Enniscorthy. Here he could not break the line of his opponents, for he had but seven hundred muskets in his force, so with rustic cunning he drove onto them a herd of young cattle, and into the hole thus made poured his troops. Once again the infantry broke and ran, this time as far as Wexford. Father Murphy followed them and camped outside the city. He now found his ranks swollen by an immense number of volunteers, including two men who afterward became famous as guerrilla leaders, Michael Dwyer and Miles Byrne. He himself had no military talent. He distracted himself by ambushing small parties of militia, and did not even occupy the town of Wexford.[52]

Meanwhile the King's troops silently slipped out of the town with their stores. On their disappearance, a number of the chief inhabitants of United Irish sympathies decided it was necessary to appoint a regular leader to take charge, and in particular to come to an arrangement with Father Murphy's irregular and menacing army outside the walls. They selected a Protestant gentleman named Beauchamp Bagenal Harvey, and a deputation of "eight respectable persons" called on him to offer him the post of commander in chief. They secured admission to the jail (where Mr. Harvey, having been once arrested, had decided to remain) with some difficulty, and only after repeated assurances that they meant him no harm. They were then shown into an apparently empty room.

"But we wish to speak to Mr. Harvey," they protested.

"Speak, then," said a voice, which appeared to come from nowhere.

A little startled, they examined the room, turned over the furniture, looked under tables and chairs, and out the windows, but could discover no Mr. Harvey. Perplexed, but perforce accepting the mystery, they then delivered their message. They pointed out that the British forces had fled, while outside the town there was an army which might have the appearance of a United Irish force, but had a great many of the characteristics of a marauding rabble. Mr. Harvey, for his well-known honesty and mildness, would be an admirable emissary to Father Murphy's troops. Would he not consent to take supreme authority, negotiate with the rabble and perhaps admit them peaceably, so that no violence or robbery would occur?

"The insurgents," replied the same disembodied voice, "do not come from my neighborhood, and I could not influence them. Further, I am not even sure that they know I am not an enemy."

"But if you were to show yourself—"

"I am not suited to a command such as this."

"Would you not consent to write to them?"

The voice assented, saying that its owner would gladly write whatever was thought desirable. This decision was immediately followed by a distinct rustling sound, and two crashes. A thick fall of soot and two bricks came down the chimney, followed by two swinging boots. The half-choked voice of Mr. Harvey begged the deputation to pull on his legs, because his clothes had become tucked up and he was lodged in the chimney. Three pulls at his feet, a fresh shower of soot, a rattle of fire irons followed, and the rebel commander in chief was ready to take charge of his forces.[53]

This singular commander could hardly control his troops. Many of them ignored his appointment and followed Father Murphy, who at once set out again wandering about the country; nor did those who remained pay much attention to his orders; they were more interested in seeing that everyone attended mass. But for the moment, so long as they faced only the local militia and yeomanry, the Irish were almost uniformly victorious. They scored victories at Clough on June 4 and Arklow on June 9. On June 5, Harvey led a full-scale assault against regular troops at New Ross: the town was captured, lost, recaptured and lost again. At this, the first grave check, the Irish forces began to disintegrate. In their flight, some of them committed one of the worst atrocities of the campaign. They drove a hundred Protestants into a barn at Scullabogue and burned them alive. On June 21 followed the last important battle, at Vinegar Hill. The Irish were defeated and scattered, Wexford retaken, and Harvey hanged. Father Murphy was able to withdraw with a number of his followers, but he himself, in a skirmish at Scollagh Gap on June 26, disappeared, and was never seen again. The command of his forces devolved on Dwyer and Byrne, who were able to trap and destroy the much-hated Ancient Britons at Bally Ellis. Their last regular conflict with the British forces was the Battle of Ballygullen on July 4.[54]

The Irish had had latterly to face a more formidable antagonist than Lord Camden. That Viceroy had served his purpose in provoking the revolt; once in full swing, it had to be handled by another man. On June 20, 1798, there arrived in Dublin Camden's successor, the Earl of Cornwallis, energetic, merciful, and an able soldier. He was responsible for the direction of overwhelming forces to Wicklow and Wexford, which scattered and overwhelmed the rebels, and for an even more efficacious measure which dried up the source of their recruits. Early in July, just as the crops were ripening, he issued a proclamation of general amnesty to all but the chiefs. The effect was instantaneous; Colonel (now General) Moore wrote to him that the retention of the troops was indeed "perhaps still necessary" but "more to check the yeomen and the Protestants than the people." [55] Only two Irish leaders remained, Dwyer, who refused to leave his native county of Wicklow, kept together a small force in the mountains; Byrne made his way secretly to Dublin.[56]

Cornwallis's anxiety to finish quickly with the rebels was due partly to his fear of what might happen if any French landed while Ireland was still disturbed. Wolfe Tone, on the first news of the insurrection, had been frantically urging the French Directory, and at last an expedition of sorts was arranged. It consisted in the end of only a thousand grenadiers, under General Humbert, which landed in Killala in western Ireland next month, on August 22. The effect of even so small a force was startling. Five days later it was confronted at Castlebar by a greatly superior army, under General Lake. The battle which followed lasted exactly half an hour, and is notable only for the speed at which the governmental forces ran away.

Had Humbert pushed forward instantly into Ulster or toward Dublin, he might perhaps even now have shaken the government. But he spent his time (as he had been ordered by the Directory)[57] in attempting to organize the Connaught peasantry. The recruits he got were worthless; Mr. Edgeworth (the author, with his daughter, of the once-famous *Practical Education* published this year) recorded afterward the contempt with which "the French, both officers and soldiers," spoke of them; "the same rebels frequently returning with different tones and new stories, to obtain double and treble provisions of arms, ammunition and uniforms —selling the arms for whiskey and running away at the first fire in the day of battle." [58] Cornwallis, on his side, moved quickly. He had had experience of Indian campaigning, where a handful of trained English troops would easily cut through the unwarlike hordes of the rajahs. Now he had the reverse problem to solve, but he had no better tactics to use than those of the Indian princes. He assembled so vast an accumulation of his inferior troops that Humbert's army would be swamped by mere numbers. In his case the device succeeded: Humbert was surrounded at a place called Ballinamuck, on September 7. He and the French troops briefly resisted and were well treated, his Irish allies ran away and were slaughtered. A rash man called John Moore who had accepted the position of president of Connaught was hanged in Castlebar.[59] Nine days later Napper Tandy, with a boat's crew, landed on the island of Rutland, off Donegal, but finding all was over, distributed some proclamations[60] and took himself away again.

One final effort was made this year. Wolfe Tone, in Paris, had been driven nearly to despair by the squabbles of the Irish there— Napper Tandy was intriguing against him and Lewins, Quigley making a domain for himself—and he had not much more hope of the United Irishmen still in Ireland. "Keogh, I know, is not fit for a *coup de main;* he has got McCormick latterly into his hands and besides Dick is now past the age of adventure," he noted. He was surprised that Tom Emmet had not shown more energy "because I know he is as brave as Caesar of his person." But his very despair gave him energy enough to force the Directory's hand again. Early in October a fresh expedition, still small, set sail with him on board.[61] It was promptly scattered by bad weather, and only eight ships arrived off Lough Swilly in Ulster in the evening of October 10. No sooner had they anchored than their presence was signaled, and in the morning they saw the whole squadron of Sir Joshua Warren bearing down upon them.

There was just a short while for escape. Their frigates immediately set sail and turned back to France. Of the four largest ships, the fast-sailing *Biche* was so placed that she was almost certain to get away. The *Loire* and *Résolue* would have to fight for it; the *Hoche,* aboard which was Tone, was hopelessly trapped. The *Biche* sent a boat for Tone. "Our lives will be spared," said the French officers, "but you will be shot, for they will not take you as a prisoner of war." Tone answered that he would never have it said that he had fled while Frenchmen stayed to fight Ireland's battles. He went down below and took his station in command of one of the batteries. Soon four British ships of the line and one frigate surrounded the *Hoche,* and a fierce and wild fight followed. The *Hoche* was swept clean of anything that cannon shot could carry away: her rudder was destroyed, her masts and cordage cut down, her ribs yawned and let in the water. She did not strike her flag till her last gun was dismantled, and among the few survivors who lined up as prisoners was Wolfe Tone in his French officer's uniform. It is said that the British naval officers who took charge of them avoided picking him out; however that may be, he was recognized by a onetime friend, Sir George Hill, brother-in-law of Marcus Beresford and a violent opponent of Cornwallis's merciful policies.[62]

He was brought before a court-martial in Dublin on November 10. The trial was technically illegal, for he had never been in the British army and should have had a civil trial. But Tone confined himself to defending his principles and producing documents to show that he was a colonel in the French army. This he did so that he might be shot as a soldier and not hanged. But this grace was denied him, and sentence of death by hanging was pronounced.

Dublin was silent and "in a kind of stupor": Tone might never
have had a friend there. Only one man took any action—John
Philpot Curran, the lawyer. He realized that if he could raise the
money to secure a "bar" on the ground that Tone's trial was irregular, the case would have to be heard over again in a civil
court. The result must be the same, but there would be time for
France to intervene and the life of this gay and gallant young man
might be saved. He went first of all to John Keogh—"Gog" of
happier days—who had written to Tone, "Remember and execute
your garden conversation," and had promised that his son Cornelius would join the invaders.[63] Keogh shut the door in his face. All
that Sunday, November 11, Curran went from door to door of
men who had known Tone. Not a single one would help. At last
he took the money from his own resources and went to the court
of King's Bench, where Wolfe, Lord Kilwarden, was sitting. Curran explained the position—the trial had been held by court-
martial, which was irregular; here was an affidavit proving that
Tone had never held the King's commission, and therefore must
be tried in a civil court; on behalf of Tone's father he applied for
a writ of habeas corpus to get Tone away from the barracks lest
he be executed. Kilwarden bent his head. "Have a writ instantly
prepared," he said. Curran replied, "But my client may die while
the writ is being prepared." "Mr. Sheriff," said the judge, "proceed to the barracks, and acquaint the Provost Marshal that a
writ is preparing to suspend Mr. Tone's execution; and see that he
be not executed."

Kilwarden was by now alarmed. He knew how likely it was that
Tone would be killed out of hand, and illegally. His agitation was
obvious when the Sheriff hurriedly reappeared. "My lord," said
the officer, "I have been to the barracks. The Provost Marshal
says he must obey Major Sandys and Major Sandys says he must
obey Lord Cornwallis." Curran rose before the judge could speak.
Old Mr. Tone, he said, had been to General Craig, who commanded at the barracks, had served on him the writ of habeas
corpus, and the General had merely refused to pay it any attention.

It was at such a moment as this that Kilwarden was at his best.
He half rose from his seat and raised his voice. He spoke impres-

sively, separating each sentence: "Mr. Sheriff. Take the body of Tone into custody. Take the Provost Marshal and Major Sandys into custody. And show the order of the court to General Craig."

The Sheriff immediately left the court, and returned again in a few minutes with another unexpected piece of news. Tone could not be brought to court: he lay on the point of death after an attempt at suicide.

Tone's friends hastily went to the barracks. There was no doubt of the fact. Tone had often said to his colleagues, "You may do as you please, but they shall never have my poor bones to pick." Late on the night of his trial he had cut his throat with a penknife. A surgeon was brought hastily, who sewed up the wound. Tone, he announced, had just missed the carotid artery and might yet survive, though he was in great danger. "I am sorry I have been so bad an anatomist," answered the prisoner.

For seven days his body hesitated between life and death. On November 19 the surgeon noticed symptoms that gave him acute anxiety. He called the nurse aside, and having gone a distance which he judged to be sufficient, spoke in a low voice: "He is in the greatest danger. If he attempts to move or to speak he will expire at once." A voice answered him from behind. The patient had with great difficulty raised his head. "I can yet find words to thank you, sir," he said. "This is the most welcome news you could give. What should I wish to live for?" His head fell back; a yellow and a red stain spread over the bandages and onto the sheets; Theobald Wolfe Tone was dead.[64]

This was the true end of the Irish rebellion of 1798. But the Dublin Corporation, now only a knot of loyal and well-to-do Protestants, had a week or two earlier marked the end in its own fashion. It had by resolution struck Henry Grattan, Hamilton Rowan, Napper Tandy and Arthur Dillon off the list of freemen, and replaced them by Sir Horatio Nelson, Major Sirr, Major Swan "and Mr. Reynolds the informer." [65]

3

THE BLACK REVOLUTIONARY:

TOUSSAINT

THERE were two islands whose
fate seemed to have been settled this year, Ireland and St. Domingo, better known to us as "Haiti," which is really only the western part of it. For Ireland the year was one of disaster; nothing
had happened that was fortunate or even hopeful; the best that
the most zealous supporter of Protestantism and British domination could have said was that a danger had been averted. There
had been misery, civil war, and murder, the nation was irremedi-
ably divided into two, and the future promised nothing but darkness. For St. Domingo the story seemed to be exactly the opposite. An end was at last put to the devastations and civil wars
which had been wrecking the country. The invading armies of
Britain were driven out. The island was reunited. The country
was under the firm control of one of the most noble and ablest

men that his race has ever produced—Toussaint. This phrase is not too strong; his figure has been blurred by melodramatic biographies filled with imaginary conversations,[1] but there is no doubt that he was a man on whom the widest hopes could be founded. The future at least seemed likely to be all sunshine.

Never were anticipations more dramatically unfulfilled. Ireland was to rise again; St. Domingo to slide down to savagery, from the nobility of French republicanism to voodoo, from Toussaint to Trujillo and Duvalier of today.

A comparison of the islands was by no means as absurd then as it seems now. Their area was much the same (30,000 square miles to 32,000); the population of St. Domingo was less, but its resources and riches greater. Haitian power was very considerable; Pickering, the United States Secretary of State, was given an official report on Toussaint's victorious army as consisting of "55,000 men of whom 30,000 are of the line and disciplined; the remainder are militia." Washington had never had more than 20,-000.[2] Before the French Revolution, Haiti had supplied "half Europe" with sugar, cotton, and coffee; Port-au-Prince and Le Cap, the two chief towns, were greatly admired for their buildings and streets. Though the planters who occupied them exaggerated their opulence when they visited France and spent their money wildly, they probably were in fact more elegant than any other town in the West Indies or in the United States. Haiti, the western half of the island, the French-speaking area, was the richer and more fertile; coffee grew wild in it. The Spaniards had allowed the eastern end to decay. Their roads were so bad that there was no wheeled traffic outside the town of Santo Domingo; almost the sole occupation here was cattle breeding, or, rather, cattle owning. A man might possess thousands of beasts which he left roaming about the wilds, and himself live in rags in a decrepit house, where his slaves' chief duty was to swing him in his hammock.

When Columbus discovered the island, the first of all his discoveries, he called it Hispaniola; since then it has had various names and in the twentieth century is divided into the two republics of Haiti (west) and Santo Domingo (east). In 1798 it was generally called St. Domingo and was nominally all French.

Life in the French-speaking part had had an unusual glamour

for the French of Europe. The scenery was grand and the climate delightful. The planters seemed not only to be rich and carefree, but to live lives of singular ease and beauty. Their women were agreeably loose in morals and singularly lovely; "the Creole ladies," wrote Bryan Edwards, a historian as well as a planter and M.P., "have in general the finest eyes in the world, large, languishing, expressive, sometimes beaming with animation and sometimes melting with tenderness." [3] They tended to be dark, with fine olive skins, passionate, beautifully mannered toward their equals, inclining to plumpness because they were greedy and took no exercise; but that was to the taste of the eighteenth century. Color was not a bar to the extent that it was later in the Southern states of the United States, or in South Africa. There were many Haitians of mixed blood, and many alliances between white males and dark women. But color was nevertheless very important, and was noted with great care; there were as many as twelve gradations listed. The main divisions however in 1789 were: whites, 39,000; free people of color, mostly mulattoes, 27,000; slaves, mostly black, 450,000. These were divisions of status, and they were the divisions that mattered. Members of the first two classes had certain rights and could be called "Creoles," even the free blacks (to the great vexation of the mulattoes); members of the last had none. The mulattoes, under the royal regime, could not hold any public office, or enter the professions, or even become skilled workers with their hands. But they could own property, and buy and sell, and some of them became very rich—richer than the whites who looked down on them and were sometimes in their debt. Nor were they habitually treated with personal violence. That was reserved for the slaves, plenty of it. A modern historian who has lived through two world wars is cautious of accepting stories of atrocities, but there seems no reasonable doubt that the Creole aristocracy was exceptionally cruel, and that the Creole women with their languishing eyes were if anything more vicious than the men. "They order and witness with perfect equanimity the most inhuman punishment inflicted upon the slaves and appear completely insensitive to cries for mercy or the pouring out of blood." [4] There were slave owners elsewhere who worked their slaves to death and after five years indifferently bought new substitutes (a million are calculated to have been shipped to St. Domingo), but the Creoles enjoyed tormenting their slaves, thrusting gunpowder up their rectums and making it explode, cutting off their noses, ears or genitals, burying them up to the neck and smearing their heads with sugar to attract insects, forcing them to eat excrement, hanging them upside down—there is no need to list their filthy but apparently authenticated brutalities.[5] In 1786 the King of France, hearing of such horrors, issued an edict forbidding the worst of them; two years later an attempt was made to enforce this decree against a planter called Le Jeune. He had killed four male slaves; he had chained up two women slaves, burned their feet, legs and buttocks and left the burns to fester, and to the neck of one had fastened an iron collar preventing her from swallowing. Both of them had ultimately died. The planters combined to force his acquittal, against the personal intervention of the Governor.

The protection of the King was shown to be ineffectual, nor was the church of more help. The Domingan clergy in general was of the same type as the planter class, with a veneer of hypocrisy added. But there were a few of the lower clergy who took their profession seriously, helped and comforted the slaves, tried to teach them religion and even interceded for them with their masters. A remembrance of these men and of the King's ineffectual effort almost certainly stayed in the mind of the short and almost wizened coachman of Bayou de Libertat, owner of the Breda plantation. His name was Toussaint. He was fairly elderly for a Haitian (he seems to have been born in 1744) and had been well treated; his owner had taken him from the cane fields to drive his horses, given him a small plot for himself, and even lent him books which the parish priest helped him to read. Thereafter his mind was formed by two main influences. The first was the Bible, in which, unlike those of his fellow Haitians who read it at all, he studied and followed the New Testament rather than the Old. He had at times an almost evangelical fervor, not at all common in the eighteenth-century Roman Catholic Church, and his life had the plain piety of a much earlier age. "On the Sabbath we went to church," he recalled later, "my wife, my parents and myself. Returning to our cottage we closed the day in prayer in which all took part." His Christian faith, and the humanity which went with it, he might perhaps have hoped to communicate to his fellows; the other great influence on him he hardly could have shared. He was a disciple of Epictetus, and though that philosoper was an eighteenth-century favorite, there were few indeed on the island who had read, let alone understood, him.

Epictetus was a Stoic who lived in the first century A.D. He had been a slave, and what was his real name is unknown—"Epictetus" means "the purchased man" (from the Greek word *epictaomai,* to buy something extra) and he probably called himself that as a kind of defiance. He had been bought by Epaphroditus, one of the administration secretaries of the Emperor Nero, who set him free; he became a friend of the Emperor Hadrian and Marcus Aurelius was his pupil. Four small volumes of his lectures remain and were read by Toussaint in a French translation; unlike almost any other classical records, it is fairly certain that they are verbatim reports.[6] They are not easy to summarize, partly because they are conversational; but it is abundantly clear to anyone who reads them why they had a powerful influence on Toussaint. His love of freedom, for instance. "The words *free,* adjective and verb, and *freedom,* appear some 130 times in Epictetus; that is, with a relative frequency about six times that in the New Testament and twice that in Marcus Aurelius," writes one of his recent editors.[7] Perhaps the most central point of his doctrine is that man's will, or power of choice (*proairesis*), is the only thing which is truly his own. This is how he opens the subject:

"What does Zeus say? He says 'Epictetus, if it had been possible I would have made your wretched body, and your small property too, free and unhampered. As it is, and don't forget this, it isn't yours; only some cleverly modelled clay. So as I couldn't give you that, we gave you a portion of ourselves, this faculty of choosing and refusing, of desiring or pushing aside, in short of making use of external things. If you pay attention to this and give yourself to it you will not be thwarted, you will not whine, you will not blame other people, and you will suck up to nobody. Well? Does this seem unimportant to you?'

" 'No, indeed not.'

" 'Will you be satisfied with it?'

" 'I hope I may be.' "

"What did Agrippinus say?" (Epictetus said later, mentioning an aristocrat whom he greatly admired). "He said: 'I don't stand in my own way.' He was told 'Your case is now being tried in the Senate.' 'Wish me luck; but it's ten o'clock' (he used to take his exercise and a cold swim then) 'so let's go to the gymnasium.' He was in the gymnasium when a man came to say 'They've given the verdict.'

" 'Banishment or death?' he asked.

" 'Banishment.'

" 'And my estate?'

" 'Not confiscated.'

" 'Then we'll have lunch in Aricia.' " (Aricia was a morning's drive out of Rome.)

"That," continued Epictetus, "is an example of having given thought to what you should, of having your desire and aversion free and prepared for everything. So I have to die. If it is now, then I die now. If not yet, then I will lunch because it is lunch-time, and die later. Die how? As a man should who is giving back what was someone else's." [8]

He told several stories in his first two lectures to the same effect, and broke off with a sudden adjuration: "One thing, do consider what you sell your freedom of choice for. If you can't do anything else, man, at least don't sell it cheap." [9] A man with freedom of choice would accept what was rational—even at times punishment and beating—but not what was unreasonable; and this it was which distinguished man from beasts and was divine in him. But "the irrational and rational are different for different persons, as are good and evil too; and this is the real reason why we need education, so as to apply our preconceived idea of what is rational, or not, to nature," that is, to the world around us.[10] (These, again, could have been Toussaint's words.)

For all his love of liberty, and his loyalty to the people of St. Domingo, there was a streak of aristocracy in Toussaint's thought, and this too was Epictetan. Epictetus used examples drawn from a slave's life (such as holding out the chamber pot for a master) but his most famous instance is the almost arrogant advice by the same Agrippinus to a man who thought he should put a play on in one of Nero's festivals to ingratiate himself. *You should* (he said in effect), but I would not even think of it. "For you look on yourself as one thread of all those which go into the making of a toga; so, you ought to be thinking of how to be exactly like other men, just as a single thread should not stand out from the rest. But I wish to be the purple thread, that small and brilliant edging which makes the whole garment bright and lovely. Then why say to me 'be like everyone else'? If I was, how could I be the purple?"

"Helvidius Priscus" (continued Epictetus) "saw this too and acted on it. When Vespasian sent him an instruction not to come to the Senate he replied: 'You have the authority to stop me being a Senator, but so long as I am one I must attend.'

" 'Very well,' said Vespasian, 'but you are not to speak.'

" 'Then do not call on me, and I will not.'

" 'But I have to call you' (as he had, by Senate rules).

" 'And I have to say what seems right to me.'

" 'If you do speak, I will execute you.'

" 'And when did I ever tell you I was immortal? You will do your job, I will do mine. Yours is to kill, mine to die without fear. Yours is to banish, mine to go away without complaining.'

"So, you say, what good did Priscus do, he being only one man? Well, what good does the purple do to the toga? It stands out, conspicuous in itself, purple, displayed as a fine example to all others."

Epictetus called man's purposefulness, *proairesis,* divine for an almost mystical reason—because through it he was part of an ideal community which was in a sense more real than the city which he lived in. "Socrates, asked what his country was, would never say 'I am *Athenaios* or *Corinthios,*' but always, 'I am *cosmios*' "—not Athenian nor Corinthian but Universalian. Just as an Acharnian or Marathonian had learned to call himself "Athenian" (or a Virginian an "American") so naturally an Athenian must learn to call himself a citizen of "the most comprehensive and authoritative of all communities, which is a republic" (organization, *systema*) "of men and god."

How could a man like Toussaint apply Epictetan principles to resisting tyranny?

"Diogenes wrote to the King of Persia 'You cannot enslave the city of Athens any more than you can fish.'

" 'Why? Can't I capture it?'

" 'If you do take it, they will at once slip away and disappear like fish. Fish also if you capture them, die; and if they too die when you capture them, what is the good of your enormous armament?' " [11]

Two words, a contemporary said, Epictetus used to call the most important in the language, *anechou* and *apechou*, meaning roughly "bear" and "abstain." [12] Toussaint, as a slave, had to learn to do both these, and also what any slave who survived had had to learn—evasiveness and subtlety as well as patience. His favorite motto was *Patience bat la force* (Patience defeats force). At home he spoke and probably thought in Creole, a French patois mixed with Spanish and African words, but he could and did use classic and sometimes even elegant French. He also knew a few Latin phrases, mostly legal or ecclesiastical, and used them to impress his fellow Negroes. "You don't understand?" he would say in mock surprise, and tell them they would never amount to anything while they stayed ignorant.

No doubt he was respected locally but it is improbable that he was at all well known generally to his fellow slaves before the revolution; nor yet for a year or two afterward. Indeed the revolution itself at first passed by them unnoticed. The planters to begin with welcomed it; it seemed an opportunity to break free of the strict royal ordinances which forbade them to trade with any country but France. Immediate profits were possible if they could sell their sugar, rum and coffee directly to England and the English-speaking colonies or ex-colonies; their representatives in Paris lobbied for this vigorously. They were enraged and astounded when on May 15, 1791, the National Assembly, so far from deferring to them, passed a decree granting the vote and civic rights to the mulattoes.[13] They reacted as might be expected; they simply prevented the decree being applied. They drove the unhappy Governor, whose name was Blanchelande, out of Port-au-Prince by violence; he retired to Le Cap in the north. Seeing his authority disappear, he or his officials took in August one of those apparently clever steps which can never be undone. It meant the end of a society, though one which was not worth preserving. He decided to remind the colonists of their dangerous position, and their need for the support of France and the King, by staging a walkout of slaves. It was, of course, to be a small one, without any violence and well under control. The slaves would be told that the King had granted them one free day a week and the abolition of flogging, and was sending an army to force the planters to obey. A good man to organize this was needed; Bayou de Libertat of the Breda estate recommended his intelligent coachman.[14]

The operation started late in the evening of August 22; the Negroes in the Turpin & Flaville plantation poured out of their huts, chased the manager into his house, and marched on en bloc to the Clement plantation, where they scooped up the forewarned slaves who were waiting for them. Then they went on to Tremes, where the same thing occurred. There was no violence; all was peace and gaiety, but the excitement was mounting as each contingent joined up. It was at the Noé plantation that disaster came. The manager and another white were either particularly hated or perhaps attempted to resist; anyway, they were killed. Some of the slaves then broke into the big house to search for firearms; they began to loot what they found there. One set fire to an outhouse; next the house itself was fired; then the wide fields of dry sugar cane; they burned with a great flash and whoosh of flame. This was the end, or the beginning; the slaves went mad. Whatever control Toussaint had had, it vanished. Almost the whole of the northern province was wrecked and burned in the next few weeks; there was savage fighting, murder, torture and rape. It was calculated that 100,000 slaves were in revolt.[15] One hundred and eighty sugar plantations and nine hundred coffee or indigo estates were destroyed, according to Edwards's estimate; 2,000 whites and 10,000 blacks died.[16] From then on there was a continuous running war; great armed Negro bands were roaming the country commanded by men who had none of the merits of Toussaint, except bravery. They, like their followers, were little better than savages; they were as cruel as their ex-masters, they dressed themselves up in fancy uniforms and gave themselves high titles, usually "in the King's name," and their ambitions were commonly merely to become slave owners themselves. They had names like Biassou, Jeannot, and Jean-François, which history has gladly forgotten. Only Toussaint among them was able to assemble an organized force; lack of ferocity made his rise slow.

About this time Toussaint added to his name the surname "L'Ouverture," around which there has been much unnecessary speculation, one patronizing authority even trying to find in it a voodoo word. "L'Ouverture" means "the opening" (in Greek, *anoixis*), as of a door; Toussaint's intention was not to be the master of his fellow slaves, but to provide and indeed to be the opening through which they could view a new life of liberty, and if they made the effort could enter upon it.

The three-sided race war—whites, mulattoes, Negroes—which was gradually devastating St. Domingo was not allowed to be fought out within the island. The minds of the deputies in Paris were rarely on Domingan problems; nevertheless the republic did intervene, unpredictably and—partly because of the British navy —with too-small forces. In September 1792 three commissioners arrived with 6,000 troops, not enough to pacify the country but enough to overawe any one section. The most active and in the end the only commissioner had the unusual name of Sonthonax; some months were passed by him in complex negotiations, but in August 1793, overruling his colleagues, he proclaimed what most of his advisers had insisted was unthinkable—the freeing of all slaves. He was, indeed, only anticipating orders; in April of 1794 Victor Hugues sailed to Guadeloupe nearby as governor and published the decree "of the 16th Pluviose Year II" that "all men domiciled in the colonies are declared to be French citizens without distinction of race and with an absolute equality of rights." [17] He also started the Terror just when it was about to end in France. Sonthonax did not, and probably could not, do likewise; there is indeed a story that he once proposed to Toussaint to exterminate the whites and was indignantly rebuked, but it is unproved. He was not naturally a terrorist, and his general, Laveaux, on whom he ultimately depended, was a man of great probity, to whom Toussaint once wrote "my affection for you is that of a son to his father." "Next to God, Laveaux," he said in public.

Neither Toussaint nor the other Negro generals accepted Sonthonax's proclamation at its face value. They did not trust the French republicans; Toussaint was still signing himself "General of the Armies of the King." They doubted if the support of the French was worth having—France was now at war with both Spain and Britain; the garrison in St. Domingo was cut off and might be annihilated at any time. The Spaniards courted Toussaint, awarding him a decoration, and for a while he co-operated with them; but when they and the British joined in an invasion his mind cleared. The Spaniards were as they always had been, slave traders; the British were putting down rebellions and re-enslaving Negroes in all their colonies.[18] He broke away with his army from the Spaniards after a brief struggle, wrote to General Laveaux, and placed himself under his orders. "It is true, General, that I have been deceived by enemies of the Republic, but what man can escape every trap?" he said.

Laveaux accepted with delight and gratitude, for his own position was nearly desperate. The planters had surrendered town after town to the British, not unexpectedly; even the languid Spanish soldiers were a danger. What Toussaint's fellow rebels despised in him, Laveaux could see were fiercely needed virtues. Toussaint was a small gray man of late middle age among big young shiny-black bucks, a quiet man among swaggerers, a civilized man among brutes, a cautious maneuverer among rash blunderers, a man of Christian morality among torturers and lechers, a democrat among gang leaders, an admirer of order and discipline among lovers of anarchy. No person could have been of greater use to Laveaux; in the next few months his confidence was wholly justified. The one likely source of disagreement, Toussaint's piety, Laveaux was sensible enough to ignore. He was not an atheist himself, anyway, and even Robespierre worshiped the Supreme Being. As time went on, he invested Toussaint with the titles of general and even of lieutenant governor.

Toussaint's army had grown in a few months from a band of 600 to 5,000; now it rapidly increased. It was not the numbers that mattered, however, it was the quality. The other Negro armies were little more than armed mobs, who won their successes largely by tumult and yelling. They appalled their antagonists by

their numbers and their shrieking and threatening, making wild
dashes and retreating, and eventually overwhelming the defense in
a torrent of raging, shooting and slicing madmen. Toussaint's
men, even if they were half-clothed and half-armed, were disciplined. Noise meant nothing to them; they drove the yelling mobs
the other way. Before long the two other chief generals, Biassou
and Jean-François, found their armies scattered (Jeannot was
killed) and fled into the Spanish half of the island; then, in 1795
Spain made peace, handing over its section of St. Domingo to
France. The Spanish Governor remained there only until Laveaux
should have enough troops to take possession. The British, indeed,
Toussaint could not dislodge from the towns, mostly coastal,
which they held; but by 1797 he was able to present Laveaux and
Sonthonax with a mainland which, if not wholly pacified, was
generally subordinate to the French Republic. There was only one
threat to his authority; in the south a mulatto general, Rigaud,
was at the head of a mulatto army, and his loyalty was doubtful.
The mulattoes, to Toussaint's rather simple astonishment, had
shown themselves more dangerous and arrogant to the Negroes
than the whites.

Toussaint had not gained his successes by military skill alone,
but by mercy. All races were brothers, he continually proclaimed,
and he had prevented the massacres of white prisoners which had
become habitual. The only instance in which he is reasonably suspected of killing a prisoner was when one of his officers, Blanc
Cazenave, shot forty white prisoners.[19] He had him arrested; in a
few days he was found dead in his cell. It was said he had been
strangled; Toussaint reported to Laveaux that he had died of
apoplexy, and added, in Latin, "let him rest in peace." He was
criticized, not only by the mulattoes, of too great kindness to the
whites. He forgave them again and again for treacheries; he even
welcomed back the royalist *émigrés* when they surrendered. He
needed their intelligence and capacity, and knew that he could
restore Domingan prosperity only with their help; probably he
also thought that they were by now frightened enough to be no
danger. His Negro soldiers followed his orders without understanding, because they revered him; one commander, however,
Henri Christophe, already resented that he was "partial" to the

whites "instead of those of his own colour." Sonthonax (as has
been said) is believed to have argued to him that it would be
better to exterminate the whites.

But Sonthonax's opinions soon no longer mattered. The Directory was in power and delegates to the two Assemblies were required from St. Domingo. Who better, said Toussaint, than General Laveaux for the Elders and Commissioner Sonthonax for the
Council of Five Hundred? A specially convened electoral assembly agreed with him unanimously. Laveaux accepted with good
grace; he may well have thought the decision right, for all his life
he kept a great respect for Toussaint. But Sonthonax saw through
the trick; he was enraged and refused to go; he even tried to col-
lect troops to arrest Toussaint. Then patience came to an end.
Sonthonax found himself surrounded by black troops in Le Cap,
and a frigate waiting in the harbor. There appeared to be no
choice. He dictated a letter for Toussaint to sign, couched in
terms of effusive admiration and humility; Toussaint signed it,
and Sonthonax replied that his emotion in reading it was such that
he would agree to represent St. Domingo in Paris. Nevertheless he
began to move some artillery into the town; Toussaint's chief of
staff entered his palace early in the morning, lit candles, and told
him he must go on board by eight o'clock. "I don't wish it to be
known," was Toussaint's message, "that I am forcing you to
leave. You are my superior in rank. It might be bad for discipline."

Sonthonax rode to the ship between two lines of dragoons
standing at attention, and the guns of the fortress fired a salute;
every formality was observed. But he went, and at the beginning
of 1798 Toussaint L'Ouverture, Commander in Chief, was the
only man with a claim to authority over St. Domingo, except in
those places occupied by the British.

The British army was deployed in accordance with accepted
eighteenth-century practice; to understand its position one must
have a rough picture of the island. St. Domingo is, in shape,
rather like the blade of a two-pronged fork. The narrow end is the
Spanish part; the western part widens and ends in two long thin
promontories, the southern longer than the northern, separated by
a large, almost square bay. The British occupied in force two

places on the promontories—Mole St. Nicolas, "as srong as Gibraltar," at the end of the northern one, and Jérémie, a well-protected harbor on the south—and with rather less force held the coastal or near-coastal towns and villages connecting them. Of these the most important were Port-au-Prince (the capital), L'Arcahaye, St. Marc and Mirebalais. They were joined together by a line of forts making a sort of primitive Maginot Line and one in which the defenders had similar confidence. It was true that the British had found it impossible to destroy Toussaint and his troops. They could never be caught; they were as slippery as fish. "He disappears—he has flown—as if by magic. Now he reappears again where he is least expected. One never knows where his army is, what it substists on, in what mountain fastness he has hidden his supplies and his treasury." [20] Fortunately (since yellow fever was decimating the British) this was of no importance. No ragged Negro militia could take the forts, even if it would stand and fight at all—which was probably too much to hope for.

On February 3, 1798, confounding all the experts, Toussaint attacked the British. He had some 16,000 men, trained by himself; the British had just over 20,000, largely regulars and led by an experienced general named Whyte. Toussaint's tactics were simple, quick and Nelsonic. Moving swiftly, and ignoring any threats to his flank, he concentrated his forces in mass against particular parts of the thinly held line, and broke through each time by a combination of local superiority and enthusiasm.

"Do not disappoint me" ran his proclamation to the army. "Prove yourselves men who know how to value liberty, and how to defend it. Do not allow the desire for booty to turn you aside. . . . We are fighting in order that liberty, the most precious of all booty, may not perish." And to the commanding officers: "I call your attention to the strict orders given by me not to burn plantations, to treat all prisoners humanely, and to receive deserters from the enemy as friends and brothers. I will hold you personally responsible for any act contrary to these orders which remains unpunished."

A British officer, Captain Marcus Rainsford, a little later watched the training which had wrecked his army: "Each general officer had a demi-brigade, which went through the normal exercises with a degree of expertness I had seldom before witnessed. They performed, excellently well, several manoeuvres applicable to their method of fighting. At a whistle, a whole brigade ran three or four hundred yards, and then, separating, threw themselves flat on the ground, changing to their backs and sides, and all the time keeping up a strong fire; after this they formed in an instant again with their wonted regularity." [21]

In little more than a month, the line had been broken in so many places that Port-au-Prince, L'Arcahaye, St. Marc and the rest were no longer strong points in an organized defense. They were cut-off outposts, whose garrisons it might not even be possible to rescue. The position of the British was humiliating as well as dangerous; for an example take this letter from Toussaint to General Whyte about an order issued by a mulatto commander under him:

"You have disgraced yourself in the eyes of this and future generations in allowing one of your commanders (the cowardly Lepointe) to issue this order, which could not have been done without your knowledge:—'No quarter for the brigands. Take no prisoners.' And that in spite of the fact that I have given instructions to my commanders to treat all prisoners with humanity.

"I am only a black man. I have not had the advantage of the fine education the officers of His Britannic Majesty are said to receive. But were I to be guilty of so infamous an act I should feel I had sullied the honour of my country." [22]

Not long after this letter, and as soon as the War Office had grasped the military position, Whyte was replaced by a new general, Maitland, who immediately wrote to Toussaint asking for an armistice and offering to evacuate every place except the Mole and Jérémie, provided that the inhabitants, of any color, who had sided with the British were granted an amnesty.[23] "If you had not made that demand I myself would have insisted that it be included in the terms," replied Toussaint, scoring again as he accepted the offer, and puzzling his followers, who thought he should not have allowed the British to escape at all. He had his own reasons for this, not unconnected with the fact that a new French commissioner, a "Special Agent" with three ships, some staff and no troops, had just arrived at Santo Domingo City.

His name was Hédouville (ex-count), he had held long conversations with Sonthonax before leaving Paris, and he soon decided that the best way to restore French control over the island, since he had no army, would be to set the mulattoes against the blacks, in particular Rigaud against Toussaint. He was particularly exasperated by an order of the day issued at this time by Toussaint and communicated to him: "The heads of regiments are required to see that the troops join in prayer morning and evening, as far as the service will permit." [24] The upstart general, he may well have thought, was not merely an ignorant black; he was a religious bigot and no real republican. Toussaint cannot have known what was in his mind; but he treated Hédouville with the greatest caution, almost indeed with offhandedness.

Toussaint's relations with the French were strange and complex. He was, and still is, charged with duplicity, lying and disloyalty. Even to others than Frenchmen his behavior at first sight often seemed inexplicable. On the one hand, he had sent his son and stepson, on the invitation of the Directory, to be educated in France; "hostages," as even the least cynical said. On the other, he was negotiating on his own authority with the British, who were at war with France, and was in fact contemplating a treaty with them, while protesting his "unshakable loyalty to France, respect and obedience to her laws," and was also systematically getting all the power and authority in the island he could into his own hands. Had they known his mind, or even Epictetus's, the French would have been less puzzled, though probably equally displeased. He sent his boys to France because education was what was needed above everything else for his ignorant country. Where else at that date could they be given a republican education of any value but in France? If there was a risk, it was one to be taken. They were needed for the future of St. Domingo. As for his loyalty to France, certainly his language was deliberately misleading. But it was not, to him, dishonest. His loyalty was indeed "unshakable," but it was not loyalty to the French Republic, it was loyalty to The Republic, the *systema* of which both God and men were a part. So long as the French state was even an imperfect image of this, so long as French armies defended liberty, equality and fraternity for all men of all colors, he would be loyal to them. If they failed, he would follow the greater loyalty. Meanwhile, as an ex-slave, he knew when to be silent, or evasive, or untruthful, as circumstances required. At the moment they required a certain amount of ceremonial, and of delay, which would enable both Hédouville to realize the importance and power of his commander in chief, and General Maitland to realize how singularly uncomfortable was the position of his remaining troops, perched separately at the ends of two long promontories separated by over eighty miles of ocean. He therefore moved very slowly and formally into the various towns which the British had evacuated, giving an account of his progress to Hédouville ("What has given me the greatest satisfaction is that I have not found it necessary in St. Marc to punish a single person") but not reporting in person to him. He did not reach Port-au-Prince, the capital, until April 14, when the population was in a state of the highest tension. They had been expecting some sort of brutal revenge for their treachery; their fears had gradually lifted as one by one the smaller towns had been reoccupied without a house robbed or a man executed; when Toussaint approached, almost the whole population went out to meet their apparent savior. The procession was headed by a cross and flag, choirboys and the clergy; then there were the Mayor and the chief citizens; swooningly elegant Creole ladies in carriages; a guard of honor on horseback; finally the mass of the population, whites, mulattoes and Negroes for once marching together. Girls of good family stood by the roadside and threw flowers to the General and his soldiers.

When Toussaint saw the cross, he knelt to it (which was probably reported to Hédouville); when he rose, the Mayor read an address of welcome, and four of the richest planters advanced holding a baldaquin, which they tried to raise over Toussaint's head, while the choirboys swung censers full of incense. He refused with a scowl: "Such things are only for God," he said, and walked uncovered into the palace. The next day, there was a *Te Deum* in the cathedral, after which the Mayor and twelve eminent planters presented him with a gold medal with the inscription "Next to God—Him," an adaptation of words Toussaint had used about Laveaux. Toussaint replied in a dry speech calling the attention of the planters to the miserable condition of their estates cultivated by slave labor, and informing them that only now when all men were free was there a chance of prosperity returning. He spent the next few days reorganizing the government of the province, appointing officials without reference to Hédouville. He named more whites than Negroes or mulattoes because so few blacks were literate and because he knew the mulattoes could not be trusted. Only thereafter did he give way to his "burning desire" to meet Hédouville; he traveled in May to Le Cap, where the Special Agent had been for nearly two months. They exchanged insincere compliments, and parted false friends, Toussaint to negotiate with the British, Hédouville to link up with Rigaud.

Toussaint met General Maitland at the end of August, just outside Mole St. Nicolas. The General offered him very attractive terms. The British would evacuate St. Domingo altogether, handing Jérémie and the Mole over to him. They would recognize him as king of Haiti. They would protect him against a French naval attack. And they would sign a commercial treaty. The discussions did not take long. Toussaint rejected the title of king, and did not accept the British offer of protection; he preferred momentarily to pose as a French patriot. But he accepted the rest of the proposals. The British surrendered the Mole and Jérémie and the Domingan ports were opened to trade; the blockade which had been strangling St. Domingo's prosperity was over. A secret and permanent treaty of commerce (to apply also to the United States) was drafted, signed and sent across to London for confirmation. The London government, with typical ineptitude, announced its confirmation and so alerted the Directory. Meanwhile Toussaint made a victorious entry into the Mole in October. It was a triumphal moment; only the historian notes with a shudder among his generals the names of Dessalines and Henri Christophe.

How much of this Hédouville knew is uncertain; all of it was highly illegal. But what he thought did not matter. He tried to annul Toussaint's appointments of reconciled planters and to enforce the French laws against *émigrés;* failed; and took ship again to France from Le Cap to denounce him to the Directory. Toussaint sent an aide-de-camp after him immediately, calling him a cowardly deserter, announcing a complete victory over the British, and declaring his fervent loyalty to France. The dispatches were eloquent and convincing; the Directory might even have believed them, if they had not been informed of the treaty.[25]

The way before Toussaint was now clear. He knew that he would probably have before long to fight Rigaud and his mulattoes, and that, after no doubt a sharp struggle, he would destroy him. (This he did, using as general commanding Dessalines, who perpetrated an appalling massacre which Toussaint neither prevented nor condemned adequately.) Then he would take over the Spanish end of the island which was waiting for him, and be the ruler of all St. Domingo.

Despite his refusal of the title of king, his rule would be more monarchical, or at least aristocratic, than democratic. He was not a Jefferson. He knew well that the average Negro was not his equal, nor was the mulatto, nor yet the degraded if repentant planter. He intended to be the purple edge on the toga, not just another white thread. He would rule by a combination of personal virtue, of education of others, and of military force. The constitution which was proposed by him to the General Assembly when he had one elected (and which was naturally accepted) shows his ideas clearly. It might have been written for the Emperor Antoninus or Marcus Aurelius. The Assembly would make the laws (as the Roman Senate had) but he, as governor for life, would execute them and, like an Antonine emperor, could name his successor (whose term, however, would only be five years). All citizens, no matter what their color, were free and eligible for any office. After the constitution was passed, his demeanor was appropriate. Though he dressed fairly simply himself, he had a brilliantly uniformed bodyguard; he lived in a palace which was dignified without being flamboyant and only criticized for the number of pictures of women, not always adequately clothed, and too often white. He held a regular reception, called the *Grand Cercle;* but every citizen, however poor and ignorant, could attend it and would be listened to by him; no invitation was needed. Schools were built and education was free for the poor; roads were constructed and the Spanish end of the island restored to cultivation. He tried the experiment of dividing estates and giving small holdings to the cultivators; production fell catastrophically, the Negroes seeing no reason to work when they could live off a few chickens and fruit; he replaced this by contract labor on the plantations. The cultivators received one quarter of the revenues, and the Administrator, a man called Idlinger, who checked the payments in detail, became the official most disliked by the planters (who also had to pay a twenty-five per cent tax to the state). The ending of the blockade restored prosperity, and Haitian production, in 1798 almost at rock bottom, rose to two-thirds of the prerevolution figure.

Some of this Toussaint may well have foreseen, or planned, in 1798. But the purple edging of a toga is not made of one thread alone. There was no other man at all, white, mulatto or black, who could take Toussaint's place in St. Domingo if he disappeared. A sequence of five exceptional emperors—Nerva, Trajan, Hadrian, Antoninus and Marcus Aurelius—and a senatorial circle from which such men could be drawn were needed for the golden age of the Antonine emperors; Toussaint was alone. If he had held power for the natural term of his life, or the term he would possibly (in the ancient manner) have set for himself, then it is conceivable that he might have educated by training and example men fit to succeed him. But though he may have realized this danger, there were two others that he did not foresee; they were the treachery of his assistants and the craftiness of Bonaparte. His two most important generals were named Dessalines and Henri Christophe. Dessalines was a clever Congo Negro, whose cruelty had already troubled Toussaint and who was treating the cultivators on his estate as if they were still slaves; Christophe was in all probability already mad. In the future, Bonaparte, now wholly a Jonathan Wild, was to send to St. Domingo a seasoned army under his sister Pauline's husband, Leclerc, to restore slavery; by this artfulness he would, he thought, both found a French empire in America and rid himself of thousands of steady republican soldiers who might prevent his destruction of the republic in France. For the moment, he was to succeed; Dessalines and Christophe betrayed Toussaint, who was trapped and died in a French prison.

It can have been small consolation to Toussaint, if he ever

knew of it, that Leclerc and his army perished of yellow fever; that Dessalines proclaimed himself emperor and enforced his rule by murdering everyone in the island who was not black; and that he was in his turn murdered by Christophe's followers. Christophe proclaimed himself King Henry I, instituted an order of nobility including the Duke of Marmalade and the Count of Lemonade,[26] and, before he blew his brains out, built himself the fortress and palace of La Ferrière to terrify the populace; it is "a huge mass of masonry perched on the highest and most inaccessible peak" [27] near Le Cap, and it is the sole monument or building of architectural or historical interest left today in the whole of the island.

4

THE UNITED STATES
IS DRAWN IN

THE PRESENT generation claims
to have lived through the first world-wide wars in history; it even
labels them "World War I" and "World War II." It is a melancholy boast, and it is not even true. The war that was in progress
in 1798 was a world war as truly as either of the later wars. Pretty
nearly all the known world, with the exception of the closed societies of China and Japan, was, or had been, or would be drawn in.
Latin America was involved because of Spain and Portugal, internal Africa was unknown (but it too was almost certainly mostly
at war), Russia was about to re-enter the war, Turkey had been
plunged into it by Bonaparte, and the warfare in India had
reached out nearly as far as the Philippines. As the year went on,
the last remaining area of peace, the recently formed United
States of America, was drawn in.

The belt of settled territory along the Atlantic coast, from the border of Canada southward, seemed to be in a very fortunate position, internationally. Throughout its short history its inhabitants had lived under the shadow of two incessant enemies—the French and the Red Indians. The wars of the 1760's had broken the French militarily, and the War of Independence had turned them into allies. The Indians were still a plague, but victory over them was by now certain in any conflicts. The great expanse of the Atlantic ought (they could reasonably think) to insulate them from European quarrels. A European ambassador attending a conference could reach his capital, seeking instructions and bringing peace or war, in a matter of days; to reach Philadelphia he would require weeks or even months. What troubles the Americans had must surely be of their own making.

But they were not so insulated in geographical fact; they were even less insulated in spirit. Later history distorts our view of America in 1798; perhaps the most important thing to remember about it is that there was no adult man or woman there at all—none over twenty-two anyway—who had not started life as a subject of the king still ruling England, George III. The habits and thoughts of colonial days were deeply impressed on them. They were still emotionally involved in British and to a less extent in French politics and thought. Their state assemblies were still mostly led by the same men as led them before independence, and had the same ways of behaving. For years their chief problem had been the handling of the representative of central authority, the governor, flattering or flouting him as the interests of the province required, and considering nothing else. Very often they behaved the same way still, so much so that in the eighties there had been observers who thought the union would break up and some of the states at least return to their old allegiance. Nor was this "separatism" mere perversity. It was a fact that quite often the assemblies of, say, Virginia or Massachusetts contained men of better caliber than Congress and their debates were weightier and more individual. Even their constitutions varied enormously, especially in the vital areas of the separation or amalgamation of the executive, legislative and judicial powers, which were discussed with some discomfort by observers like Madison.[1]

Nevertheless, though American civilization was derivative and the American nation only beginning to form, there was already a national philosophy, expressed in the Declaration of Independence, and there did exist a central government. Its first head, Washington, and therefore to some extent its creator, had become a national figure in the true sense of those two words. He incarnated or seemed to incarnate not what the Americans were but what they wished they were. It was not modern French, but ancient Roman, republicanism which formed the American political mind; Washington in his life and even his appearance might have been one of the marble heroes of Cato's day. Half a century later Daniel Webster concluded a eulogy of him in Latin (and very good Latin at that). His high nose, his close-pressed lips, his upright military carriage, his straight glance, his rigid morality and his formal and unemotional courtesy were what the eighteenth century believed to be characteristic of a Roman senator. He could be generous to those who deserved it; to the undeserving he could be harsh. One, whom he eventually decided to be undeserving, Tom Paine, wrote (about a proposed statue to him):

> Take from the mine the coldest, hardest stone
> It needs no fashion: it is Washington.[2]

One of his most percipient biographers, Cunliffe, has analyzed how he did in fact possess three of the chief qualities of a noble Roman.[3] *Gravitas:* a serious demeanor and a concentration upon the important things of life. *Pietas:* an urgent sense of family and civic duty. *Simplicitas:* a dislike and avoidance of luxury, ostentation and softness of life.

Even this marmoreal figure had not been free from insult, backbiting and denigration. To succeed him was bound to be a task of enormous difficulty; for a man who did not possess his qualities or appearance it might be impossible. The man who occupied his office in 1798 was John Adams.

A charm that leaps a century and three-quarters makes us indulgent to Lord Nelson, despite his many faults. A lack of charm makes us unfair to the second President of the United States, despite his many virtues. John Adams in his lifetime complained ceaselessly of men's injustice to him; historians try, and fail, to remedy it. One of the latest, Gilbert Chinard, entitles his biography *Honest John Adams,* a wholly justified adjective. He reminds us of Adams's hard and blameless early years, and describes vividly life in Braintree, the little New England town of his origin;[4] it was slow, bleak and laborious. There were no slaves and no servants in its houses; the climate was such that for at least five months no work was possible in the fields. The women then would tend house, cook and spin; the men would make shoes, furniture and farm implements, or repair harnesses, the house and the outbuildings. They had to be butchers, smiths, carpenters and bricklayers, and these, says the Professor defiantly, are still "true American traits." When John Adams rebelled at learning Latin grammar his father said, "Very well; you may try ditching"; the work was so hard that after two days the boy went back to Latin. Later he was sent to Harvard, which meant something very different from what it does today. The life was still hard and the education was narrow and poor; until 1766 every tutor was supposed to teach everything; there was no specialization. Theology was vastly the preponderant subject, and it was mostly Calvinist. What Adams learned (and he learned a great deal) was due to his own energy, not to his teachers. He decided to become a lawyer instead of a minister; in the atmosphere of Boston of that day, this seemed a decline, almost a disgrace; but he was already a man of independent mind.[5] He was also a brave man, and not merely physically brave. In 1770 there was a small but bloody scuffle which was elevated by propaganda into "the Boston Massacre" and the patriots, urged on by his distant relative Samuel Adams, determined to make an example of the British soldiers concerned. Adams, considering that injustice was being done, took up the defense of Captain Preston when no one else dared to, and saved him and the other accused. He often asserted that he was never forgiven for this; that is far from certain, but it is quite certain that he risked his whole career for a few men with whom he had no sympathy. His life was pure, even puritanical, and without vices—for to "drink madeira at a great rate" [6] is not a vice but an unwisdom, and anyway like all the founders of the American Republic bar one he could carry his wine.[7] Throughout the War of Independence he had been a rock of firmness and wisdom; he was widely read and well informed; he had traveled; he was a clear and sometimes even vivid speaker and writer; he was utterly and profoundly honest; he was the choice of his countrymen to succeed Washington.

Yet with all these merits he had one, or perhaps two, disadvantages that denied him the affection of his countrymen or the respect of posterity, both of which he deserved. Tom Paine, who in Paris was rather out of touch with American political possibilities, wrote to Jefferson asking him as Vice-President to control him, "for John Adams has such a talent for blundering and offending, it will be necessary to keep an eye over him." [8] Benjamin Franklin, shrewder and nearer, had already said "he is always an honest man, often a wise one, but sometimes and in some things absolutely out of his senses." [9]

This fault was not simple egoism, nor vanity, nor venom; it was a combination of all three, a recurrent boiling up of jealousy and anger, which distorted his judgment, made him ridiculous and offended his friends. He may have thought—for though he was clever he lacked common sense—that the furious words he wrote in his diaries, his book margins and his private letters, or spoke in private conversation, remained private; if so, he was very innocent. Philadelphia was a small town, New York was a small town, indeed the United States was wholly a small-town country and nothing is more active and swift in small towns than malicious gossip. Adams's vitriol was spread around quickly and widely. His favorite theme was that he was underestimated, ignored and even hated, and that credit for his own achievements was regularly given to others. "From the year 1761, now more than fifty years," he wrote at the end of his life, "I have constantly lived in an enemies' country." Franklin's and Washington's reputations particularly provoked him: "the history of our Revolution will be one continued lie from one end to the other," he wrote to Dr. Rush. "The essence of the whole will be that Dr Franklin's electric rod smote the earth and out sprang General Washington." [10] His arrival in France in 1778 as American ambassador instead of soothing his vanity inflamed it; he was enraged because he was mistaken for *"le fameux Adams,"* his cousin Sam,[11] and when the error was corrected he was thought to be "a man who did not

understand a word of French, awkward in his figure, awkward in
his dress; no abilities; a perfect bigot and a fanatic." The French
he discovered to be immoral and corrupt; it was some consolation
to him to be able to return their contempt, and in this year to
exercise it. But he was equally venomous toward his own countrymen. Alexander Hamilton was "the Creole bastard";[12] Jefferson, the Vice-President (whom he respected and even loved as
much as he did any man; they died many years later on the same
day after a long period of aged harmonious correspondence), was
consumed with "thirst of popularity, inordinate ambition and
want of sincerity";[13] and as for a minor character who crossed
him, Peter Oliver, "I have him in the utmost contempt. I have the
utmost contempt of him, I had as lief say it to him as not. I have
the utmost contempt for him."

The immense deposit of papers which he left behind him has
not yet been thoroughly analyzed, but his annotations on the margins of his books, collected by the devoted Dr. Haraszti, are illuminating. "Thou louse, flea, tick, ant, wasp or whatever vermin thou
art," he writes against the name of the gentle d'Alembert; half of
his comments are intelligent, half are the splenetic abuse that one
finds scribbled by fanatics in the margins of books from public
libraries, stained by thumbmarks and smears of fat. "This is most
obvious," "Superficial dogmatist!," "True," "Not at all"; and on
the books of the Abbé Mably "Poor Abby!" or (where the text
says "we can find happiness only in the common ownership of
goods") "Stark mad."

His second disability was no fault of his; it was his appearance.
He was an unhappy contrast to the man who became, against
both their wishes, his chief antagonist this year, Thomas Jefferson. Jefferson had a broad head and a face rather closed between
the eyes and lower lip, whose expression in his best-known portrait gives some color to Adams's accusation of his "indirection,"
but otherwise he was an attractive figure of an upcountry squire
from Virginia, upright among the city slickers—loose-jointed,
over six feet high, gangly, with reddish hair and blue eyes, large-
mouthed, with a mild expression and carelessly dressed. His
clothes were usually rather too small for him.[14] Adams was bald,
was short, was fat and fidgety, with a round plump face, and dully

but always correctly dressed.[15] Maclay of Pennsylvania watched him as he presided over the Senate when he was Vice-President: "instead of the sedate easy manner I would have him possess he will look on one side, then on the other, then down on the knees of his breeches, then dimple his visage with the most silly kind of half-smile." Representative Izard, "describing his air, manner, deportment and personal figure in the chair," called him "His Rotundity";[16] another unforgivable insult. It was not only out of personal vanity that Adams insisted on protocol and pomposity; it was on principle. He had worried himself almost sick at the inauguration of Washington in case he did not welcome him properly: "How shall I behave? How shall we receive him? Shall it be standing or sitting?" [17] He insisted that if Washington was not given some title like "His Highness" he would be "despised *to all eternity*" by common people, soldiers and sailors." [18] He called himself in later years "the Duke of Braintree"—playfully, no doubt, but he would not have welcomed laughter.[19]

These foibles fitted in with his political philosophy, for though he was a republican Adams was not a democrat, and with typical honesty never concealed this. Late in life he wrote, "Remember, there never was a democracy that did not commit suicide," and "If you give more than a share in the sovereignty to the Democrats, that is, if you give them the command or preponderance . . . they will vote all property out of the hands of you aristocrats and if they let you escape with your lives it will be more humanity, consideration and generosity than any triumphant democracy ever displayed since the creation." [20] Early in the French Revolution he repudiated dramatically the most famous formulation in the English language of its principles. Laying his hand on his breast he said gravely: "I detest that book, *The Rights of Man,* and its tendency from the bottom of my heart." [21] Three classes of human beings, he believed, must be excluded from participating in governing the country; they were children, women and men of no property. He had phrased this more concretely when discussing the British constitution with Alexander Hamilton at dinner in Jefferson's house; this was in an earlier year (April 1791) when party hatreds and personal malice had not become rampant. "Purge that constitution," he had said, "of its corruption, and give to its popular branch equality of representation, and it would be the most perfect constitution ever devised by the wit of man." He disagreed with Hamilton's reply that the changes he asked would make the constitution "impracticable" and that the British constitution was already "the most perfect government which ever existed"; but he was not scandalized as his host Jefferson was.[22]

Since then the three men had drifted, or perhaps deliberately traveled, apart. Hamilton had originally accepted and even pressed through the existing Constitution of the United States, but his heart had stayed with his own project, which was for a lifetime president, who would appoint the governors of the separate states also for life, and for senators elected by men of property only, for life or "good behaviour" like English judges.[23] He was, in short, in favor of the most dominant central government possible, and his concern for liberty, either of citizens or the states, was very small. Since the central government was federal, those who agreed with him were naturally called Federalists; it was equally natural that they disliked the French and admired the English, to the point of absurdity. Jefferson called them "Anglo-men"; his own followers, to the confusion of modern readers, were indifferently called "Republicans" and "Democrats," and they defended against the center both individual liberty and the rights of the states, which at the time seemed indivisibly connected. Indeed, Jefferson carried this principle so far that Hamilton's accusations of encouraging "anarchy" did not seem baseless. He argued, for example, that the government should be forbidden to raise a loan at all. "I know that to pay all proper expenses within the year would in the case of war be hard on us— But wars would be reduced in proportion," [24] an argument so simple-minded that Adams could well have thought it dishonest.

The operation of the Constitution at this date meant that the vice-president was likely to be an opponent of the president; Adams therefore had Jefferson as his vice-president, he having received seventy-one electoral votes against Jefferson's sixty-eight. It cannot have been easy, but he made real efforts to collaborate with him in the early days of his presidency. They came to nothing; as things were, they probably would have done so anyway. But the failure was none of Adams's wish. He insisted all his life that he was not a party man; and he believed it.[25] He looked back still longingly to the days, only seven years back, when senior statesmen, veterans of the Revolution, could sit over their madeira long hours into the night, discussing benevolently the first principles of politics, and part friends—still confident in each other's integrity and wisdom, and with a warm certainty about the future of the state. He was rebuffed by Jefferson and meanly tricked (though he did not yet know it) by Hamilton, and he was personally least of all men qualified to secure such a high-minded unity; but there is both pathos and dignity in the way the splenetic and sometimes absurd little man clung to his hope.

Such then was the President who headed the United States government when the French Directory took an action which was certain to give his country offense. It may have considered, and the world may have considered, that the two republics were natural allies against the British, and that it could afford to behave cavalierly. Moreover, the history of the past few years had put it out of temper. The French exaggerated, as is not unusual in such cases, the quality of the aid they had given to the American rebels; they felt that they had saved them from imminent defeat, had liberated them, and since then had received little but ingratitude and impudence. When France too had become a republic and was at war with the English oppressors in 1793, Washington had deliberately failed to operate the alliance treaty of 1788.[26] Avarice had since been added to treachery; John Jay, a close supporter of Adams, had in 1795 actually concluded for financial reasons a commercial treaty with Great Britain, on terms which even some of his countrymen thought ignoble; from that date the life of the American envoy in Paris, Monroe, had been made a misery.[27]

But neither he nor anyone else expected what happened on the fourth day of 1798. On that day the Directory informed the envoy that it had decided that any vessel, no matter what flag it sailed under, would be stopped by French warships and if it contained any cargo of British origin would be seized as a prize.[28] The message took some little while to reach America but its implication to a maritime nation like the United States was immediate; it was nothing less than an act of war. Perhaps the New England traders

felt it more sharply than the Southern estate owners, but there
were very few who were not infuriated. Very well, then, if the
French wanted war, they should have it; Adams, who was no fire-
eater, at first took the halfway measure which in similar circumstances recommended itself to his successor in the twentieth century, Woodrow Wilson; he decided to arm the ships which might
be attacked. "The principle on which orders were issued to restrain vessels of the United States from sailing in an armed condition has ceased to exist" he wrote in his message of March 19. "I
therefore deem it proper to inform Congress that I no longer conceive myself justifiable in continuing them." [29] But like his successor he found this was not enough, and his Cabinet was quick to
provide him with proposals for more vigorous action. James Mc-
Henry, the Secretary of War, in particular, proposed the building
of twenty ships of the line, the cancellation of existing treaties
with France, and the raising of an army immediately of 16,000
men which should be expanded to 35,000 later—very large figures for the place and time.[30]

McHenry, like other Cabinet members, was not Adams's own
choice. His Cabinet had been bequeathed him by Washington.
The General had left the presidency in a rage. On the very last
day of his tenure, February 28, all the acts of the entire session,
bar two or three trivialities, had been presented to him in a lump
for signature "although the constitution" (he protested) "allows
the President ten days to deliberate on each bill." [31] This last exasperation was unbearable; he did not so much hand over his
office to Adams as turn his back and walk away. Even his behavior on Inauguration Day (March 3, 1797) was peculiar. "He
seemed to enjoy a triumph over me," Adams wrote to his wife.
"Methought I heard him say 'Ay! I am fairly out, and you fairly
in. See which of us will be happiest.' " [32] He left, wittingly or un-
wittingly, an unsuspected legacy to his successor. The three most
important Cabinet officers were not loyal to the new President,
but were the creatures of an outsider. Oliver Wolcott, Secretary of
the Treasury, Timothy Pickering, Secretary of State (that is, foreign affairs), and McHenry, the Secretary of War, were Alexander Hamilton's men; his was the pen which drafted the orders
Adams signed, and his the will which carried out, or prevented,

the acts of policy, which appeared to be Adams's. When he discovered this, Adams's resentment was intense; most of his angers blew away in time, but Hamilton is said to have been the only man whom he really hated. However, as yet he had no suspicions.

Jefferson was horrified by the approach of war with France; he inspired what was called the Sprigg resolution at the end of March ("under existing conditions it is not expedient for the United States to resort to war against the French Republic") but what chances of success this policy might have had were destroyed by the publication of what are called the XYZ letters. The shock these caused still sometimes surprises historians; after all, accusations of corruption, dishonesty, venality and lying were flying to and fro weekly in the American press. But these charges were in fact merely conventional abuse, not really believed in, even by the writers or speakers; small-town manners they were no doubt, but behind them was small-town morality. The letters now published showed that there was a country where these gross accusations were true. French officials, headed by the Foreign Secretary, Talleyrand, had crudely demanded to be bribed by the Americans to change their policy. Talleyrand's price was £50,000—say, half a million dollars in present values.³³ That a thing like this should happen seemed an unspeakable indecency; the names in the documents were left out and X, Y and Z substituted, as one used asterisks to replace a filthy word. The American public was not merely annoyed; it was revolted. Two politicians, Griswold the Federalist and Lyon the Democrat actually fought each other in the House of Representatives with a stick and a pair of tongs (the furniture of the House was more homely in those days).³⁴ The press became uncontrollable, the most venomous writer being a recent English immigrant, William Cobbett, who wrote as "Peter Porcupine." "Take care, take care, you sleepy Southern fools," he said to the Democrats. "Your negroes will probably be your masters this day twelve months." And since they still would not see the danger of their Jacobinical principles he added threats: "When the occasion requires the Yankees will show themselves as ready at stringing up insurgents as in stringing onions." ³⁵ Vice-President Jefferson himself was discouraged. "Men cross the street to avoid meeting me, and turn their heads another way lest they be obliged to touch their hat." More significant still was the enthusiasm with which the warlike program was carried out; batteries constructed and ships built. $430,000 were voted by Congress for batteries; three frigates were reported completed by July (the *United States* of forty-four guns, the *Constitution* of forty-four guns and the *Constellation* of thirty-six guns), and "found no difficulty in procuring their full complement of men although the monthly pay is much inferior to the wages given at present." The merchants of Philadelphia undertook to construct another frigate of forty-four guns; Boston and Baltimore each raised a hundred thousand dollars for the same purpose, and "New York, Alexandria, Norfolk, Richmond, Charleston and almost all considerable towns of the union" raised "proportionate" sums, or at least promises.[36] Many smaller ships were constructed; the sloop *Delaware* was the first to capture a French privateer and its crew was rewarded by the Court of Admiralty.

The act under whose authority the *Delaware* had attacked the Frenchman had been passed in May; it was a sign of how Adams's and Hamilton's policy was sweeping all before it. It put America in a state of war, but nevertheless was less serious than two which succeeded it. It is strange, in the late twentieth century, to record that two world powers were in mortal conflict and the fact that the United States went to war with one was of no importance; but this was so. The two more serious acts were the Alien Act and the Sedition Act, passed in June and July respectively. They were intended to hasten the prosecution of the war, and were followed at once by the almost forcible recall of Washington as commander in chief of the armies to be raised. But they had but little military effect; the appointment of Washington's staff was delayed by Hamilton's determination to become not only a major general but the senior major general, and it was not till November that the commander even met his three major generals and staff, which he did with dissatisfaction.[37] Their effect was far greater upon internal United States history; they split wide open a division which dominated politics for a century and has not vanished yet. It was considered as involving the question of states' rights on the one side, and on the other as involving the very existence of the union. The Alien Act empowered the President to expel from the United States any foreigner whom he considered dangerous, and to punish him by fines and imprisonment if he disobeyed. It was fairly dramatically autocratic, and Volney the historian and others fled at once; but it was less far-reaching in its effects than the Sedition Act, which punished with fines and imprisonment anyone who should combine or conspire to oppose government measures or utter any false, scandalous or malicious writing against the government, Congress or the President.[38] Here indeed was the overweening power that Hamilton wanted for the central government, and the state of public opinion was such that it would certainly be used, despite the First Amendment to the Constitution (which forbade the passing of any law "abridging the freedom of speech, or of the press"). Democrats were, for the moment at least, routed and despairing; John Taylor, a respected republican writer, urged Jefferson "to estimate the separate mass of Virginia and North Carolina, with a view to their separate existence"; Jefferson advised holding back, though Massachusetts and Connecticut, he said, were in the saddle, "and they ride us very hard, cruelly insulting our feelings." But, he thought, "a little patience and we shall see the reign of witches pass over." [39] All the same, he inspired or condoned actions which went some way along the road he did not wish to travel. First Kentucky and then Virginia passed resolutions defying the central authority and annulling its actions. They declared the two acts unconstitutional, and enunciated as a principle that when the government assumed undelegated powers its acts were "unauthorised, void and of no force." [40] This was not indeed separation, for they appealed to other states to join them, but it was an attempt at a shattering blow to the federal power.

Adams was less fevered than his supporters. He was sensible enough to realize that the half-declared war was not likely to be serious; the distances were too great, communications too slow, and the available French ships too few. The angry American reaction would be enough to teach the rascally Directory a lesson; when they realized that instead of a bribe they would be more likely to get their ships sunk they would change their tune. He told Congress that he would make sure that no United States minister ever received that particular insult again, and that while continuing all the warlike preparations he would send a special "embassy" to France. This, he hoped and thought, would end the nonsense; he made all the arrangements for it and then retired to his farm at Quincy, where he stayed for months reading the works of King Frederick of Prussia. He had no doubt that he could govern the United States from his farm: "the Secretaries of State, Treasury, War, Navy and the Attorney General transmit to me by post all the business of consequence," he wrote happily. "Nothing is done without my advice and direction." [41]

But in fact Hamilton, who did not want to check the wave on whose crest he was riding, simply prevented the embassy from sailing—a piece of arrogance for which he was to pay later.

The story must not end there. The whole account given above of these excitements, though true in itself, gives an untrue picture of America in the year 1798. Americans were neither deeply nor widely moved by politics. Passionate though the words used were, the passion was confined to small circles. The disputes were almost family quarrels, in a rather large family, it is true, conducted almost exclusively in Philadelphia, Boston, New York, Baltimore and Richmond. Even these towns were so small that the distinctions and dissensions to be found in England were absent—there seem, for example, to have been no workers' organizations at all except possibly of some shoemakers and carpenters in Philadelphia.[42] Citizens from the countryside would drive in, not in great numbers, to watch the disputes of the politicians in the towns as much as to take part in them. The great majority of Americans lived lives as isolated as John Adams's had been in his youth, and had neither interest in nor even knowledge of events which were supposed to stir the whole country.

These Americans were observed by an intelligent traveler whose comments were published in English this year,[43] the French Duke de La Rochefoucauld-Liancourt. "The traits of character common to all Americans," he wrote, "are ardour for enterprise, courage, greediness, and an advantageous opinion of themselves." Their commonest crimes, he reported, were drunkenness and forgery of banknotes. Their most noticeable virtues were their capacity for hard and continuous work, and their profuse and instinctive hospitality. Penniless French refugees were welcomed by

American families and supported for years. A traveler would be taken in ("particularly in Connecticut") if he were stranded "and put to bed with the family—with the boys if there were any, and with the girls if there were no boys," all in the purest innocence, as he explains at length and convincingly.

But rural isolation does not inevitably, as the eighteenth century liked to believe, produce industry, chastity, simplicity and native kindness. Out of stagnation there come strange swollen growths, sometimes fantastically beautiful, sometimes merely fantastic. There was already visible a peculiarly American proliferation, that of eccentric religions. The Duke described an example, a settlement of Shakers, in New York State.[44] The sect was then about twenty years old, and its headquarters were "at Nisqueunia a few miles above Albany," which seems to be what is now called Watervliet; it held all its goods in common and was "a despotic republic," governed absolutely by an elected elder in each settlement, who worked through inspectors. Sexual intercourse was strictly forbidden and in the rare cases "where flesh will have its way, severe and exemplary punishment" was applied to the guilty behinds, and even if the sinners escaped and married they were (says the Duke) "apprehended" and spanked nevertheless. There were no separate houses, only four long hostels, the other buildings being shops and stores, where the Shakers sold the "cloth, gauze, shoes, saddles, whips, furniture, and vegetables" which they produced far better than their neighbors. The Duke and his friends attended a service in their large hall, seventy feet by forty-five, with eighteen windows; it had white walls, light-blue wooden carvings and window frames, and red benches. The men Shakers wore blue coats, black waistcoats and blue-and-white-spotted pantaloons; the women a long white gown, a blue petticoat beneath, a blue-and-white-spotted apron, and a headdress rather like a nun's, but smaller. Everybody looked down at the floor and was completely silent. At a signal from the elder, who stood in the center, the men took off their coats, and they and the women formed themselves into separate rows in the shape of a fan, centered on him. They took quite a time to find their correct places; then, on a signal from the elder, they began to tremble. Their knees and legs shook, their hands twisted, and their faces were "convulsed"; at another signal from him they fell on their knees. They rose when the chief "commenced a chant in which the nose and throat bore an equal share and which was confined within the compass of four deep notes; no words could be distinguished." The service went on for three hours, during which the congregation formed itself into other patterns, and at one time executed what was very like a formal dance. The curious chanting or bellowing, or braying, was resumed at intervals, on different notes, sometimes by the elder alone, sometimes by some or all of the Shakers. Once what might have been words were heard, but they were incomprehensible. The Duke and his friends hoped to have some explanations after service; but the members immediately left the hall, still without speaking, and "we could only view their garden over the railings; it was large, beautiful and kept in good order."

However, apart from such eccentricities, and the unending alternation of sowing and reaping, there was one thing this year which absorbed and indeed alarmed the average American. President Adams, in his message to Congress on December 8, spoke of it at the beginning, before he made any reference to France. It was yellow fever. He urged the members, vainly, to enact health laws to prevent a recurrence of the "malignant pestilence." [45] In September an English visitor to Philadelphia "could hear nothing but the groans of the dying, the lamentations of the living, the hammers of the coffin makers, the dismal howling of deserted dogs." By October 1 only 7,000 people were left in the town, and on the same date 1,400 persons had died of the fever in New York alone.[46] The numbers had risen to 3,000 by the time the *Westmorland* packet sailed in mid-November, because the inhabitants had rashly returned to their homes without having them fumigated. But about that time the pestilence suddenly ended, killed by cold weather. Life was resumed as before; no precautions were taken against the fever's return; the politicians took up their exhilarating squabbles again.

WINTER

III

I

INTERLUDE IN NAPLES

AFTER his victory at Aboukir, Nelson sailed north, leaving three ships of the line and three frigates to blockade Alexandria and patrol the coasts of Egypt and Syria; his enemy was in a cage and these six would be sufficient as its bars.[1] He was now a baron, Lord Nelson of the Nile, and a hero. But he was also an ill man. A modern doctor would probably have recognized immediately after Aboukir that he was suffering from concussion, and treated him accordingly. He was confused, fretful and in almost continuous pain. His recurrent morbid depression was at its worst; during the battle he had believed he was dying, and he now had placed behind his chair each night when he dined a coffin made of the mast of *L'Orient*. A little later a German visitor found him almost a skeleton: "his weight cannot be more than seventy pounds, and a more miserable col-

lection of bones and wizened frame I have never yet come
across"; next spring the Admiralty ordered him home because of
his health.[2] Meanwhile, his judgment was impaired, and he was
about to give the worst possible advice to the court of Naples, to
which he was heading.

In moments of clarity he knew this kingdom, which was also
called the Two Sicilies, for what it was—"a country of fiddlers
and poets, whores and scoundrels."[3] "All are plundering who
can get at Public money or stores. In my own line I can speak,"
he wrote to Lord Spencer. "A Neapolitan Ship of the Line would
cost more than ten English ships fitting out. Five Sail of the Line
must ruin the Country. Everything else is, I have no doubt, going
on in the same system of thieving. I could give your Lordship so
many instances of the greatest mal-conduct of persons in office
and of these very persons being rewarded." "Naples is a dangerous place, and we must keep clear of it," he wrote to Sir James
Saumarez.[4] But he did not. His eyes, as the world soon knew,
were blinded; he fell hopelessly and suddenly in love with Emma,
the wife of the British Ambassador, Sir William Hamilton. And
Emma was in everything but affairs of the heart no more than the
mouthpiece of the Queen of Naples.

Lady Hamilton was a warmhearted, restless, foolish woman,
still unusually beautiful if rather plump and coarse, and she
adored Nelson. But she had no political sense; or, rather, her political views were as reactionary as might be expected in one who
had started her life as a rather pitiable harlot and risen to be the
wife of an ambassador and the confidante and support of a reign-
ing queen—and that queen a Bourbon, and more of a real ruler
than her husband. Now, the court over which Queen Maria Carolina and King Ferdinand presided was one of the most despicable
in Europe; the country was one of the most degraded. Its ruin
dated from long before the current monarchs. It consisted of
southern Italy and Sicily, the area which in ancient times had
been known as Magna Graecia, Greater Greece, and had been a
byword for prosperity. Sybaris, one of the cities which was now a
ruin, had given the world a new word for luxury. The long,
relentless decline had been begun by the Romans who expropri-
ated the working farmers in favor of huge slave-run estates ("*lati-*

fundia perdidere Italiam," great estates destroyed Italy, was their own verdict), and since then nothing politically and socially good or even live had come out of southern Italy except perhaps Masaniello's revolt of 1647.[5] The peasants who formed the greater part of the population were abjectly poor and in everything except phrase were the slaves of the landowners. The law and the social structure were feudal; the lords had monopolies, dungeons, oubliettes and taxes of their own. They were absolute masters in their own localities, sometimes having their own troops, and royal decrees did not necessarily run; they had, however, no political independence, or any thought of overturning the monarch. Like their peasants, they were bigoted Roman Catholics; death they thought the proper fate for anyone showing any sympathy for the French Revolution.[6]

The town workers were mostly concentrated in Naples, a city with the surprisingly large population of 437,000. Out of about 100,000 adult males some thirty thousand were *lazzari* or *lazzaroni,* a class of men peculiar to Naples. The *lazzaroni* had no regular homes, and no regular occupation. They lived by thieving, begging and violence. They were illiterate and savage; they were, in short, hooligans, but hooligans recognizable as a separate class, with their own dialect and a semi-instinctive organization.

To a hooligan people there corresponded a hooligan king. Ferdinand had succeeded to the throne after his eldest brother had gone mad. He had been on the throne since 1759, when he was eight years old, and educating him had been almost impossible. Endeavors had been made to teach him Latin, French and German, but he spoke only the Neapolitan dialect. Until his marriage all but courtiers were forbidden to attend him at meals, because he was so rowdy then. His only skill was in killing mountains of game, and even that was not great—beaters had to chase his prey almost to the muzzle of his gun. He was a practical joker with a predictable sense of humor; when his fiancée, the Archduchess Josepha, died of smallpox and he had to stay indoors for a day "to mourn," he staged a mock of her funeral, in which a sodomitical chamberlain represented the corpse, and chocolate drops were placed on his face and hands as the pustules. He behaved particularly disagreeably at stool, forcing his courtiers to look at his excretions. The Austrian Emperor Joseph II wrote of him, rather kindly, "although an ugly prince, he is not absolutely repulsive . . . at least he does not stink." He behaved like a child: "he distributes blows and smacks the ladies' behinds without distinction." [7] The Emperor was searching for reasons to speak well of him; for he had married his sister Maria Carolina to him. "She sleeps as if she'd been poleaxed and sweats like a pig," announced Ferdinand the morning after the marriage. But before long the pig had the upper hand; like many hooligans Ferdinand was afraid of his wife. If anything about him could be pathetic, it would be his correspondence with his father, Charles III of Spain, complaining of how she bullied him.[8] Most of the official acts of his later life, indeed, were those of the Queen; she was a woman of powerful resolution, no mercy, and narrow clearness of thought, who disliked and despised most people around her, including her daughter-in-law, the Crown Prince's Austrian wife. "Her husband is her husband two or three times in twenty four hours, a matter which interests her. In spite of this there is sadness, a boredom, an invincible disgust. . . . I hope she will have at least one child a year for twelve years running, and rather difficult pregnancies." [9]

Between these two strata of hooliganism there lay a film of civilization. It had always been thin; at the height of the French Revolution, in 1793, there had been just two small republican clubs, curiously called "Romo" and "Lomo"; the numbers of the latter are known—they were just under two hundred, almost all rather young. It was made up of some younger sons of the nobility, a few professional men, and one or two intelligent and reckless women. There were Mario Pagano, the professor of criminal jurisprudence, Pasquale Baffi, the best Greek scholar of his day, Vincente Russo, who gave even his clothes to the poor, Eleonora Pimentel, the poetess. Many of them were imprisoned in the forstress of St. Elmo, fed on bread and water, lying on the ground each in his narrow cell appropriately called the *fossa,* the grave.[10] That they lived at all was probably due only to the court's fear of the French Republic. They had little influence, less even than they imagined. For there was a communion between the two strata of hooligans, fostered by the innumerable clergy, regular or monkish, who thought that in so doing they were defending their religion. A foreign observer was particularly disquieted by "a kind of religious chants (*des espèces de cantiques*) which used to be sung in the streets, inciting men to murder and assassination." [11]

The court gave Nelson and his fleet a delirious welcome. Ferdinand, who fancied himself as a sailor, was rowed out three miles in his barge to welcome him. Lady Hamilton embraced him fervently, and at once fainted away. Balls, illuminations, cockades, speeches, and a banquet by the Hamiltons to eighteen hundred guests followed. In the excitement over Nelson's victory common sense was utterly forgotten. The court—that is, the Queen—decided that now was the time to attack the French. Naples was at peace with France, nor had the Directory any wish for war. It knew that any forces sent down to the foot of Italy would be out on a limb, and could be cut off as soon as an Austrian attack (which looked only too probable) was launched in north Italy. The Emperor of Austria, Ferdinand's brother-in-law and protector, was in no way anxious for a Neapolitan attack on France just then; he would be ready for war at the end of the year, not before. But the Queen observed only that the Pope's ancient domains were occupied by a very small force of atheist troops, and she had no fewer than forty thousand soldiers and a newly fitted navy, both of which she believed to be excellent. She saw before her a pious duty and an easy triumph. Nelson encouraged Ferdinand to "advance, trusting to God for his blessing to a good cause," and gave detailed advice and instructions which were not carried out.[12] The Emperor, once the decision was taken, sent an experienced general, Mack, to lead the troops; unfortunately, he could not speak Italian. At last, late in November, the army invaded the Roman Republic in five columns. They met only a handful of French soldiers, led by a republican general of the old strict guard, Championnet; he withdrew to the north, leaving a garrison in the Castle of St. Angelo, and calling for reinforcements. Ferdinand entered Rome with great pomp on November 29; he did not, though, proclaim the restoration of the Pope. But within the week Championnet's reinforcements started to come up, and some serious fighting began. Ferdinand issued a proclamation to his people: "Let the people arm, let them succour the Faith, let them defend their King and Father, who risked his life, ready to sacrifice it to preserve the altars, possessions, domestic honour, and freedom of his subjects." He dated it "from Rome," but it was a lie; he was already riding south to Naples as fast as his horse would carry him.[13] *"Venne, vide e fuggì"* (he came, he saw, he ran away), the Italian satirist Cantù wrote of him.

The French were still outnumbered four to one but the army followed his example; it ran. Mack was a muddleheaded general of the old formal regime, with an immense personal train; he did the only thing he could; he asked Championnet for an armistice, pointing to the dreadful weather and the badness of the roads. Championnet thanked him for his thoughtfulness but said the French troops had been able to face these hardships, and would continue to march straight on to Naples. He offered Mack a passport to Milan, which Mack accepted, but which the Directory did not honor, and arrested him. (He escaped to Germany, however, writes Madame Giglioli, "with an improper female.") The Neapolitan officers were even more frightened than the soldiers. "They did not lose much honour," said Nelson, "for God knows they had not much to lose—but they lost all they had." The only fighting spirit was shown by the peasants and the *lazzaroni,* who were encouraged by the court to a general massacre, rapine and murder. "The monsters, whose number was immense, fulfilled their commission with horrid joy," recorded the English *Annual Register*.[14] King Ferdinand, hidden in his palace and refusing even to see the people of Naples who implored him to stay, begged Nelson to take him and his family on board and sail away. On December 21 the royal family and about two and a half millions in gold were embarked on the *Vanguard.* But the wind was unfavorable; it could not move from Naples Harbor, despite their prayers. On the 23rd the wind veered north, and the ships could sail; the King's thoughts immediately returned to normal. "We shall have plenty of woodcock, Cavaliere," he said to Hamilton, "this wind will bring them—we shall have rare sport." He landed quite gaily at Palermo in Sicily on the 26th.

Meanwhile, Naples was in the hands of the *lazzaroni,* who were killing any man with short hair (as being a "Jacobin") and robbing any house that seemed worth it; it is estimated that the crowds engaged in this numbered 40,000. Championnet's army only arrived just in time to prevent total destruction; the struggle was severe and he lost more men fighting the *lazzaroni* than in all the rest of the campaign. Their last act, it is pleasant to record, was to strip Ferdinand's palace of everything in it worth stealing, even the doors. Championnet quickly installed a provisional government of what republicans he could find surviving, or bring in from exile. Unlike the previous governors, they were all men of the highest probity and intelligence, but they were not men of the world nor were all his choices happy. The president was Laubert, a fervent republican, unconciliatory, a lapsed monk who had married—an offense to every Roman Catholic—who in addition appeared in French uniform, being chemist-in-chief to Championnet's army. Baffi, the Greek scholar, who "never did anything that was not noble and generous," thought up a name for the new republic. Parthenope was a siren in Greek mythology, who drowned herself for love of Ulysses, and her corpse was cast up in the Bay of Naples; Vergil and Ovid used her name (because it scans more easily) as a synonym for Naples city. Consequently, the new republic was called the Parthenopean Republic; what the peasants and the *lazzaroni* made of that name, no one can guess. Mario Pagano, who had escaped from Naples to Milan, was brought back and set down to write a new constitution; since the publication of his *Saggi Politici* in 1783 he had had a European reputation as a lawyer and his draft was excellent. In his first public speech he showed an untypical knowledge of the weakness of the republic's weakness. "Young men burning for liberty," he cried, "who betray yourselves by the joy shining in your eyes, fly to arms, and under arms be obedient to your commanders. Republics are adorned by all virtues, but the most splendid is seen in the camp." But no adequate and shining-eyed republican army was raised; instead, the whole of the existing army (some units of which were capable and patriotic) was dismissed as being royalist and servile, and dispersed over the countryside, unemployed, angry and trained to violence. Eleanora Pimentel, the poetess, could not be made in this century a member of the government, even in a republic, but she was appointed editor of the official *Monitore,* where she opposed a proposal to raise a republican cavalry regiment, each citizen to bring his own horse. This, she said, would introduce a class distinction into the army; the cavalry would be an aristocratic force. More sensibly, in her second issue, she pleaded for "civic allocutions" to be made in the Neapolitan dialect, or at least that the priests should translate the classical Italian of the decrees and exhortations to their flocks. A vain hope: the priests hated the new regime. They were in no way placated by the appointment of Francesco Conforti, professor of ecclesiastical law, as minister of the interior; Catholic he might be, but he had argued for more independence of the Neapolitan church from the See of Rome, a heresy. The ex-Professor of Medicine (Naples University had once had a brilliant faculty) Domenico Cirillo was a Fellow of the British Royal Society and his papers were printed in its *Philosophical Transactions;* he drew a vivid picture of the damage done to the hospitals by the universal peculation under the Bourbons—the attendants and nurses were "a troop of insensible persons, the vilest on earth, chained to the service of the miserable by the most wretched pay and indifferent to the tears and sufferings of others," the food would be refused by beggars, the medicines were remnants of old and useless drugs, and there was neither ventilation nor cleanliness. But he was unable—perhaps he had not time—to reform them.

All titles of nobility were abolished, legal equality was established, personal and religious liberty decreed, education reformed, and plans drawn up for the dividing of the great estates. But these plans were debated too long, and not consistently carried out. Some communes in the countryside began to distribute the nobles' properties. Some did not. The republicans, if they had been wiser, would have seen the need for haste. They knew nothing of the peasants, those blackly ignorant and half-savage men whose only tutors were the priests; the *democratizzatori* whom they sent out to the provinces to explain liberty, equality, and fraternity and to plant "trees of liberty" were met with incomprehension or hostility.

It would carry this narrative too far into 1799 to detail the rest of their programs. They had but few months to live. From the beginning it could have been seen that they were unlikely to survive once the French army withdrew; in fact every person named in this chapter was to be murdered in the slaughter with which

Maria Carolina and Ferdinand celebrated their return. They were vilified with unusual skill and persistence after their deaths, for the Neapolitan Bourbons excelled in venom; sneering indeed has not stopped and has been repeated in a recent history. Their fate recalls Kipling's lines:

> Valour and innocence
> Have latterly gone hence
> To certain death, by certain shame attended.

The events of 1798 claimed many victims, but few braver and more innocent than the founders of the momentary Parthenopean Republic.

2

THE STAGE IS SET
IN MYSORE

THERE is a Greek word, *peripeteia,* "turnaround," which in Aristotle's opinion described the essence of a drama. The year 1798 was a *peripeteia,* indeed, a series of them, but the turnarounds were not complete; history does not fit so conveniently into dramatic conventions. In India, perhaps the most distant country involved, everything was set for the denouement on the last day of the year, but the actual crash was not to come till 1799.

The opening of the year 1798 had been as discouraging for the enemies of France in India as elsewhere. The British forces were scattered imprudently about the Indian Ocean, complacently occupying colonies which had been taken without difficulty from the Dutch;[1] an expedition had even started out across hundreds of miles of sea to seize the Philippines from Spain; Colonel Arthur

Wesley, one of the most promising officers in the Indian service, had made during its progress a very practical survey of Penang's possibilities as a permanent base. But a slow realization of the British difficulties elsewhere had forced a hurried abandonment of such aspirations. The Governor of Fort St. George (that is, Madras) called the expedition back before it reached Manila; the Governor General of India, Sir John Shore, honest, able, but pedestrian,[2] sent serious warnings to the Court of Directors of the East India Company, the rulers of British India. Their Secret Committee in due course replied that a vast French expedition had left Toulon, quite probably for India, and added the rather meager promise of themselves sending "not less than four thousand seasoned troops."

The danger was, of course, from the French, but not mainly from Frenchmen. The Nizam of Hyderabad had an army of 14,000 men, and he had imported French officers who were rapidly making it into a disciplined force. The Nizam, however, was old and vague; a much more serious enemy was Tippoo, the Sultan of Mysore, his near neighbor in the south. The English may not have known that Tippoo's favorite toy was a clockwork machine showing an Englishman being torn to pieces by a tiger (it is, or was till recently, on show in the Victoria and Albert Museum in London);[3] but they can have had little doubts about his sentiments, and they knew his army to be powerful and ferocious. At the beginning of the year he entered into an alliance with the French. All the required forms were gone through; a "Jacobin Club" was even opened in his capital, Seringapatam, any ill effects on the natives being prevented by its Director, who was naturally *"le citoyen Tippou."* [4] An official embassy was sent out to the nearest French authority, Citizen Malartic on the island of Mauritius, governor of all the remaining French establishments east of the Cape, who had already issued an appeal for volunteers for Tippoo's army.[5] But before long there were clouds on Tippoo's horizon. The report of his ambassadors to Mauritius survives; it is a distressing document. They were treated with an indifference amounting to unkindness. Captain Ripaud, commanding the French vessel which took them to Mauritius, "gave us no more water than Lascars. It is impossible to describe the discomforts we suffered from the rain and the motion of the waves," they complained to Tippoo, ". . . Cherisher of the World, Health!" And what did they bring back? Colonel Wesley reported with his usual cold accuracy: "The consequence of the alliance has been an addition to the forces of Tippoo of 150 men at most and a certainty that he can receive no more assistance from the island of Mauritius." [6]

The Colonel's authority, and his opportunities, were suddenly increased in May; his elder brother, Richard, arrived as Governor General of India, with another brother (Henry) as secretary. Richard was an Irish peer, his title being Lord Mornington, and more than a little pompous. Almost his first act was to inform his brother that "Wesley" was a vulgar spelling, and the family would be henceforward known as "Wellesley." [7] The young man (he was twenty-nine) naturally obeyed at once, and his letters were henceforward signed "Arthur Wellesley" (until later in life they were signed "Wellington"). But although Mornington was, in the words of one of the most intelligent of recent writers on Indian history, "humourless and arrogant," he was a man of incessant energy, high competence, and inflexible resolution. His court, which suffered most from his defects, nevertheless thought of him as "the glorious little man" [8] and within a few weeks he had transformed the prospects of the British; Philip Woodruff, the historian just quoted, goes so far as to mark 1798, the first year of his reign, as the beginning of "the Golden Age" in India. Mornington (better known by his later title of Marquess Wellesley) saw before him a war-torn semicontinent steadily declining into misery and savagery; he may well have compared himself to Caesar conquering and uniting Gaul, or William doing the same for England. The Wellesleys were peculiarly qualified for such a task. They were Irish, indeed, but only (as Wellington himself said later) if being born in a stable made a man a horse; their Irish birth merely gave them a certain aloofness from the details of English aristocratic intrigue, and a greater resolution and clarity in pursuing their personal or family advancement. They were members of the British ruling class, and were the more effective as proconsuls for having had to struggle more than others to arrive at power.

Mornington's first important decision was to send his young brother as a sort of chief of staff down south to Madras, near to the most serious threat to the pacification (as he saw it) of India —Tippoo. Arthur's task was not to make war on Tippoo; orders from home were peremptory against any aggression. "The Act of Parliament says that war is not to be declared nor hostilities to be commenced against any native Prince or State, excepting where preparations [for war] are made against the British nation or against one of their dependents, or against one whose territories the Company have guaranteed." The penalties for defying this included the removal of governors and all lesser officials and sending them to England for punishment.[9] Nor did Arthur himself believe at first that war was inevitable; he hoped that if Tippoo could be convinced that the British were "not bent on annihilating him" he would abandon his hostility. What he had to do was to revitalize civil administration and strengthen the military forces so that victory would be certain in any conflict, and that, with or without one, the Company's authority would be supreme. He had the full co-operation of the local general, Harris, in military affairs; but his task was more difficult with the civilian head, the second Baron Clive, who bore the weight of a great name without the intelligence or energy of its founder, and whose province had only recently come under the control of the Governor General at all. In Calcutta, Lord Clive seemed no better than a nuisance, but Wellesley was confident he could manage him. "My dear Mornington," he wrote in September, "I think that some pains had been taken to mislead Lord Clive, and to frighten him. He is a mild moderate man, remarkably reserved, having a bad delivery and apparently a heavy understanding. He certainly has been unaccustomed to consider questions of the magnitude of that now before him, but I doubt whether he is so dull as he appears, or as people here imagine he is." Next month he successfully appealed to brother Henry to stop Mornington sending Clive what would nowadays be called a rocket. "The truth is, he does not want talents, but he is very diffident of himself; and now he has begun to find out that there is no conjuration" (that is, magic) "in transacting the business of Government he improves daily and takes more upon himself. . . . A violent or harsh letter from

Fort William would spoil all." [10] Soon he had Clive's complete co-operation; a little later even the command of the troops in the field at Arnee near Arcot reverted to him when the previous colonel, Aston, was removed by a duel.

He suggested to Mornington that the Nizam of Hyderabad should be induced to change sides by an offer of British soldiers on loan, without any demand for territory as a pledge for their wages;[11] in August Mornington sent him to Hyderabad to achieve this, and then go on to Seringapatam to bring Tippoo to reason.[12] By October he had done the first, bloodlessly though at a considerable cost (2,000,000 rupees' subsidy to the Nizam instead of 54,000);[13] the French had gone and the Hyderabad army was wholly British-officered. But he could not get to see Tippoo in Seringapatam. The Cherisher of the World made excuses which were almost insulting in their triviality. He was still confident of his superiority in arms and the power of his French allies. Had he not received, dated "the 7th Pluviose Year VII," a letter from General Bonaparte saying, "You have already been informed of my arrival on the borders of the Red Sea with an innumerable and invincible army full of the desire of delivering you from the yoke of England"? [14] In November, it is true, news arrived of a British victory at the mouth of the Nile; however, naval engagements meant but little to an almost landlocked sovereign, and he felt it unnecessary to do more than to send a typical letter to placate Mornington. The news, he said, had given him "more pleasure than writing can possibly convey. Indeed I most firmly hope that the leaders of the English and the Company Bahadur, who ever adhere to the paths of sincerity, friendship and good faith and are the well-wishers of mankind, will at all times be successful and victorious, and the French who are of a crooked disposition, faithless and the enemies of mankind, may be ever depressed and ruined." It was not wise to send a letter as blatant as this to Mornington, already provoked as he was; the Governor General sent yet one more dispatch to Tippoo, a detailed and coldly angry indictment of his hostile behavior ever since his alliance with France, an enemy actually at war with Britain. Tippoo was unashamed and wholly bland: "Continue to rejoice me with happy letters!" he replied.[15]

Enough was enough. Lord Mornington arrived in Madras on the 31st of December, 1798, and took charge. The nutcrackers were about to close; only the victim was unaware of what would result.

What happened during the next year is, strictly speaking, outside the scope of this book; but perhaps it is permissible to summarize it. Under the command of General Harris, Wellesley advanced on Seringapatam with an English regiment, "six excellent battalions of the Company's sepoys, four rapscallion battalions of the Nizam's which however behaved well" and 10,000 cavalry. Tippoo was totally defeated, dying in the defense of Seringapatam. Wellesley occupied the city and restored order, somewhat impeded by the release of Tippoo's collection of live tigers;[16] his brother distributed the Mysore domains. The last but one of the great marauding rulers was destroyed. There remained the even more dangerous Mahrattas, with whom Mornington was shortly to deal, having been made a Marquess (but only in the Irish peerage, which made him call the title "a double-gilt potato"). Any possibility of French rule vanished forever; a century and a half of British rule of India began.

3

THE PEACE CONFERENCE
ENDS

Those who lived through the
months of the Conference of Versailles after the First World War,
and those who have examined the records of the Congress of Vienna after the defeat of Napoleon, have a vivid memory of slowness, boredom, bickering and triviality. But neither of these was
as tedious as the Congress of Rastatt. There were times when it
seemed not to move at all. The thirty-eighth sitting had taken
place on April 2, and no progress had been made; if things moved
a little faster after that, this was due only to an external event a
fortnight later. The French Ambassador in Vienna, Bernadotte,
was insulted, the Embassy attacked, and the republican flag torn
down. Refusing any apology, he took coach to Rastatt and arrived at the congress with his report; the anger of the French commissioners was so loud that the behavior of the other delegates

became at least for the while more obliging.[1] So indeed it should have, for they considered, and had let it be seen that they considered, the French delegates as personally disgusting.[2] The young Metternich (his father was chief imperial representative—that is, representative both of Austria and of what was still called the German Empire) had been found a place as delegate of some nobodies called "the Westphalian counts"; he wrote to his wife: "All these fellows have coarse muddy shoes, great blue pantaloons, a vest of blue or of all colours, peasants' handkerchiefs of either silk or cotton round the neck, the hair long black and dirty, and the hideous head crowned by an enormous hat with a great red feather." All delegates on his side, of course, were exquisite in silk knee breeches.

The points debated seem trivial now, as in 1919 did the questions of Teschen, Danzig and Fiume, but like those latter they might not have been so had the conference ended in a treaty. However there was another reason besides their complexity for the dilatoriness of the debates. The anxiety of the older states for peace was diminishing; something new had happened which the French delegates did not know of, or at least did not understand. There had been a change in the mind of the Tsar of Russia.

It is not at any time easy to say with certainty what was in his mind, for the Tsar Paul was a lunatic, so mad that before long he was murdered by his entourage. But he was a madman of a recognizable type in Russian rulers, exemplified before him in Ivan, and after him in Stalin: egoist, cruel and insensately vain. "There is only one other person of importance in Russia," he said, "and that is the person who is talking with me. And he is only of importance so long as I am talking to him." So far as a consistent motive could be found for his actions, it was hatred of his mother, Catherine the Great. Whatever she had done, he would do the opposite. Since she had disapproved of the French Revolution, he had allowed negotiations for peace to be started the year after his accession (1796). Since she had made the serfs liable to work for their owners every day of the week, he limited their workdays to three, with Sundays off too. Since she had given great administrative power to the gentry, he took it away and set up the first beginnings of a Russian bureaucracy. He also reintroduced flogging for them. Since Suvarov had been Catherine's most successful and trusted general, he insulted him, dismissed him, and put him under police surveillance on his estate. But by 1798 he had completed his immediate revenges on his dead mother, and two other ideas seem to have entered his head. The first was that the principles of the French Revolution were hostile to people like himself, the second was a belief that the Directory was about to restore Poland and put on its throne a Brandenburg prince.[3]

He provided the exiled French Prince of Condé with quarters in southwest Russia for a force of some 10,000 French *émigrés;* by the middle of the year he was deep in negotiations with Britain and Austria for an alliance against France. Both of his new allies asked of him one thing in particular: to appoint General Suvarov as commander of the Russian armies. Suvarov had crushed Kosciuszko's last revolt in Poland. Suvarov had defeated the Turks again and again in Catherine's campaigns, adding more lands to the Russian Empire than any one general had done before. Suvarov, in short, was the only living commander who could match the new dynamic French leaders. When Paul suddenly acceded to his allies' demand, reinstated Suvarov and covered him with honors once more, they knew that the balance of military power had changed.

Paul had an unexpected ally, the Sultan of Turkey. The Sublime Porte, as the court of Constantinople was called, had reacted to Bonaparte's invasion of Egypt with a formal declaration of war. It had invaded and captured Corfu and the other Adriatic islands he had taken away from Venice by the Treaty of Campoformio, thereby isolating him even more effectively from home. The coalition which was now almost visibly forming itself against France had thus already four major members—Great Britain, Austria, Russia and Turkey.

The behavior of the imperial delegation at Rastatt showed no knowledge of this. Indeed, it may well be the fact that the members did not know of it; Count von Metternich and his colleagues discussed every detail with passionate pertinacity, making small advances here, granting small concessions there, as if every word were important, and being apparently genuinely disquieted at any French threat to break off negotiations and restart the war.

The chief French commissioners, after several changes, had been since the end of June two men, named Debry and Bonnier; they were no more conciliatory than their predecessors. During the summer, Count von Metternich rallied his nominal supporters sufficiently to insist that the French evacuate the fortified towns of Kehl and Cassel, well across the Rhine; and at the beginning of October they agreed to do so, provided other problems were settled. But some of these other problems remained very tiresome. There was for example the fortress of Ehrenbreitstein, occupied by German troops, which the French continued to blockade. There was also the island of Buderich in the Rhine opposite the Prussian town of Wesel, which the King of Prussia demanded. The French made an unnecessary enemy by refusing to evacuate it. They also demanded the right to build bridges across the Rhine "for commercial purposes" and the suppression of tolls on the River Weser, so that their commerce could go right through to Bremen (which the British could hardly blockade); trade on the Rhine should be free, they said, but they would not speak about Ehrenbreitstein.

By November things had progressed to the extent that the imperial delegation had countered with a demand that navigation on the whole of the Rhine should be absolutely free, right through republican territory down to the sea in Holland, which was now in French hands; the French now officially lost their tempers and replied tempestuously, with a memorandum fifty-seven pages long. The deputies of the empire in answer resolved unanimously on November 4 to make no further concessions, and Metternich again demanded that the French leave Ehrenbreitstein alone. The French became even angrier, especially at the repetition of an earlier demand that their laws against *émigrés* should not apply to the newly annexed departments in Brabant, Flanders, Alsace and Lorraine.[4] On November 23 they sent an even more bellicose note than usual; on December 6 they sent an ultimatum to expire on the 14th. If their demands were not accepted, it said, they would restart the war.

The reaction appeared to be all that they could wish. The combined imperial delegation (that is, the delegates of the chief members of the vestigial German Empire, including Prussia and

Austria) discussed the ultimatum anxiously and swiftly. On December 10, by a majority of eight to two, it accepted the ultimatum, Saxony and Hanover voting against and Austria abstaining. The French commissioners took no note of the last name, and believed they had finally won all that they wanted. An innocent English editor, going to press too soon, thought the same: "by this measure, the foundation of a peace between the French Republic and the German Empire was laid." [5]

It can only have been a few days before the delegates discovered what (as a less simple-minded editor wrote[6]) "had been known to all Europe six months before." That was an exaggeration; it was scarcely two months since the Russian army had arrived at Brunn in Austria and been reviewed by the Austrian Emperor in person. It had now reached the Bavarian frontier and was marching westward. On the last day of the year the French delegation reacted violently. It sent to the imperial minister a note saying unqualifiedly that unless the Russian advance was stopped forthwith and the army sent back, the Congress of Rastatt would be broken up and the war would be resumed. The imperial delegation received the note with a sudden calm, and made no reply. It merely forwarded it on in two copies, one to Vienna and one to Ratisbon (Regensburg), which was the seat of the Diet which had a shadowy authority over the whole empire.

Possibly the French delegates had not yet finally quitted their fool's paradise; no one can say. But the Directory understood. It cannot have foreseen that two out of three of its commissioners would shortly be waylaid and murdered by Austrian cavalrymen,[7] but it knew what the answer, if any, to the note would be.

Its best army and its cleverest general were far away, caught in a trap in Egypt. Its other armies had wasted away steadily in the months of peace, as armies do; its new conscripts were too few, and were untrained. It had no allies, except the Spanish King, whose heart could not be with them. It did the only thing it could. It sent out a warning to its generals to expect war on all fronts in the coming year.

AUTHORITIES QUOTED

What follows is not a bibliography; a full bibliography for the year 1798 would be enormous. It is a list of the books which are the authorities for statements in the text. The word (or words) preceding the titles of the books is the shortened form used in the reference. It seemed to me preferable to use such a form than to follow the older custom of giving the full title in one footnote, and thereafter using the words *"Ibid."* or *"Op. cit.,"* which I have always found infuriating when I have needed to check on a statement. One has to turn over as many as fifty pages, and then may well miss the original citation.

Acton	Harold Acton, *The Bourbons of Naples*
Adams	C. F. Adams, *Works of John Adams*
Al Jabarti	Abderrahman al Jabarti, *Journal pendant l'occupation française en Egypte*, tr. A. Cardier
Annual Register	*Annual Register*, 1798 or 1799
Army and Navy	Army and Navy Stores, Victoria Street, London S.W.1, Catalogue
Aulard	A. Aulard, *The French Revolution*, tr. B. Miall
Barère	L. Gershoys, *Bertrand Barère*
Beard	Rev. John Beard, Member of the Historico-Theological Society of Leipzig, *Life of Toussaint L'Ouverture*
Beatson	Lt. Col. Alexander Beatson, *War with Tippoo Sultaun*
Beresford	John Beresford, *Correspondence of the Rt. Hon. John Beresford Selected by His Grandson*
Bland, Brown & Tawney	A. E. Bland, P. E. Brown and R. H. Tawney, *English Economic History: Select Documents*
Bourrienne	L.A.F. de Bourrienne, *Mémoires sur Napoléon*
Bowers	C. G. Bowers, *Jefferson and Hamilton*

British Critic	*The British Critic,* year 1798
Bronowski	J. Bronowski, *William Blake*
Bryant	Sir Arthur Bryant, *The Years of Endurance 1793–1802*
Buer	M. C. Buer, *Health, Wealth and Population 1760–1815*
Byrne	Miles Byrne, *Memoirs of Miles Byrne*
Cabet	E. Cabet, *Histoire Populaire de la Révolution Française*
Chinard	Gilbert Chinard, *Honest John Adams*
Cobban	Alfred Cobban, *History of Modern France* (1965 edition)
Cobbett	*Cobbett's Parliamentary History*
Cole	H. Cole, *Christophe, King of Haiti*
Cole & Postgate	G.D.H. Cole and Raymond Postgate, *The British People 1746–1946*
Collis	Maurice Collis, *The Great Within*
Committee of Secrecy	*Report* of the Committee of Secrecy of the House of Commons, 1799
Commons	J. R. Commons & others, *History of Labour in the United States*
Connolly	James Connolly, *Labour in Irish History*
Conway	M. D. Conway, *Life of Thomas Paine*
Cooper	Duff Cooper, *Talleyrand*
Croce	Benedetto Croce, *Studii Storici sulla Rivoluzione Napoletana del 1799*
Cunliffe	Marcus Cunliffe, *George Washington*
Cunnington	C. W. and P. Cunnington, *History of Underclothes*
Curran	W. H. Curran, *Life of J. P. Curran*
Dejoint	G. Dejoint, *La Politique économique du Directoire*
Denon	*Egypt Delineated,* selected engravings from Vivant Denon
Dommanget	M. Dommanget, *Histoire du Drapeau Rouge*
Douglas	*English Historical Documents,* ed. D. C. Douglas
Duval	Amaury Duval, Notes to the *Memoirs* of Count Orloff
Eden	F. Eden, *The State of the Poor, 1797*

Edgeworth	R. L. Edgeworth, *Memoirs*
Emmet Family	Dr. T. A. Emmet, *The Emmet Family*
T. A. & R. Emmet	Dr. T. A. Emmet, *Thomas Addis and Robert Emmet*
Encyclopaedia Britannica, 3 ed.	Encyclopaedia Britannica, completed 1797
Encyclopaedia Britannica, 14 ed.	Encyclopaedia Britannica, 1929
Epictetus	Arrian's *Lectures of Epictetus* in 4 books
European Magazine	*European Magazine and London Review,* 1798
Federalist	*The Federalist Papers,* ed. C. Rossiter
Gardner	J. A. Gardner, *Recollections 1775–1814*
Gastine	L. Gastine, *La Belle Tallien*
Gellius	Aulus Gellius, *Noctes Atticae*
Gentleman's Magazine	*Gentleman's Magazine* by Sylvanus Urban, Gent. 1798, Vol. I
George	Dorothy George, *London Life in the 18th Century*
Geyl	P. Geyl, *Debates with Historians*
Geyl, *Encounters*	P. Geyl, *Encounters in History* (1961 printing)
Giglioli	Constance Giglioli, *Naples in 1799*
Glasgow	"Southport," a study by Eric Glasgow in *Lancashire Life,* March 1967
Guedalla	Philip Guedalla, *The Duke* (of Wellington)
Hale	Leslie Hale, *John Philpot Curran*
Hammond	J. L. and Barbara Hammond, *The Village Labourer*
Haraszti	Z. Haraszti, *John Adams*
Herold	J. C. Herold, *Bonaparte in Egypt*
Hirst	F. W. Hirst, *Life and Letters of Thomas Jefferson*
Hobhouse	Christopher Hobhouse, *Fox*
Holcroft	W. Hazlitt's *Memoirs of Thomas Holcroft*
Hollande	*La Révolution Française en Hollande,* anonymous, (1894)
Hofstadter	Richard Hofstadter, *The American Political Tradition*

Howard	J. E. Howard, *Letters and Documents of Napoleon I*, Vol. I
Howe	P. P. Howe, *Life of William Hazlitt*
Inglis	Brian Inglis, *Freedom of the Press in Ireland*
Jacob	Rosamund Jacob, *Rise of the United Irishmen*
Jaeger	Muriel Jaeger, *Before Victoria*
Jones	Kathleen Jones, *Lunacy, Law and Conscience, 1744–1845*
Keynes	*Poetry & Prose of William Blake,* ed. G. Keynes, 1927
Korngold	Ralph Korngold, *Citizen Toussaint* (1944 edition)
Laborie	L. de Lanzac de Laborie, *La Domination Française en Belgique*
Lady's Magazine	*The Lady's Magazine or Entertaining Companion for the Fair Sex appropriated solely to their Use and Amusement,* Vol. XXIX, 1798
Las Cases	Marquis de Las Cases, *Mémorial de Ste. Hélène*
Lefebvre	G. Lefebvre, *Le Directoire* (1946 edition)
Letters of Napoleon	*Letters of Napoleon to Josephine,* ed. L. Cerf
Little	Shelby Little, *George Washington*
Littledale	H. J. Littledale's introduction to "World's Classics" edition of *Lyrical Ballads*
London Chronicle	*The London Chronicle,* published biweekly, 1798
Lyrical Ballads	*Lyrical Ballads,* quoted from Littledale's facsimile of the original 1798 printing
MacDermot	Frank MacDermot, *Theobald Wolfe Tone*
Madden	R. R. Madden, *Memoirs of the United Irishmen,* 2nd edition
Mahan	Captain A. T. Mahan, *Life of Nelson* (abridged version)
Midon	F. Midon, Jr. *The History of Masaniello*
Moore	Major General J. F. Maurice, *Diary of Sir John Moore*, Vol. I

Moorehead	Alan Moorehead, *The Blue Nile* (1964 edition)
Moorman	Mary Moorman, *William Wordsworth*
Newgate Calendar	*The Newgate Calendar* (1962 reprint)
Nicolson	Harold Nicolson, *The Desire to Please,* a life of Hamilton Rowan
Oldfather	Oldfather (William), Introduction to *Epictetus,* in the Loeb Library edition
Pares	Sir Bernard Pares, *History of Russia* (1944 edition)
Parry & Sherlock	J. H. Parry and P. M. Sherlock, *A Short History of the West Indies* (1963 edition)
Plumb	J. H. Plumb, *The First Four Georges*
Pokrovsky	N. Pokrovsky, *Brief History of Russia,* Vol. I
Postgate	R. Postgate, *Revolution, 1789–1906*
The Press	Reprint of *The Press, 1798*
Proceedings	*Proceedings of the African Association, 1798:* "Observations" by James Rennel, F.R.S., reprinted in *Annual Register,* 125 sqq.
Quellen	*Quellen* zur Schweizer Geschichte IX: E. Dunant (Documents on Franco-Swiss diplomatic relations)
Rose	J. Holland Rose, *Life of Napoleon*
Rudé	George Rudé, *Revolutionary Europe 1783–1815*
Rudkin	Olive Rudkin, *Thomas Spence*
Sandeman	G.A.C. Sandeman, *Metternich*
Secret Service	W. J. Fitzgerald, *Secret Service under Pitt*
Sham Squire	W. J. Fitzgerald, *The Sham Squire*
Sirr	*The Pedigree of Major Sirr,* a scrapbook in the British Museum
Sloane	W. M. Sloane, *Napoleon Bonaparte, a History*
Smith	*Memoir* of the Reverend Sidney Smith, by Lady Holland
Society of Arts	*Transactions* of the Society for the Encouragement of Arts, Manufactures and Commerce

Staunton   Sir George Staunton, *Authentic account
                              of the Voyage and Embassy of Lord
                              Macartney,* serialized in *The Lady's
                              Magazine*

Supplementary Despatches   Duke of Wellington, *Supplementary
                              Despatches*

Thompson   E. P. Thompson, *The Making of the
                              English Working Class*

Tone   T. Wolfe Tone, *Autobiography* (1893
                              edition)

Trafalgar   *The authentic narrative of the proceed-
                              ings of His Majesty's squadron under the
                              command of Rear-Admiral Sir Horatio
                              Nelson . . . drawn up from the minutes
                              of an officer of rank in the squadron,*
                              contemporary ms. mounted in frames on
                              the wall of the London public house
                              "Trafalgar" in St. Martin's Lane. This is
                              probably a version of Captain Berry's
                              account of the battle of Aboukir which
                              was originally circulated in manuscript
                              and published later. The signature (if
                              any) is torn away.

Trevelyan   G. M. Trevelyan, *Illustrated English
                              Social History* (1966 edition)

Vaucaire   Michel Vaucaire, *L'Étrange Destin de
                              Toussaint Louverture*

Walpole   Horace Walpole, *Memoirs and Portraits,*
                              ed. M. Hodgart

Warner   O. Warner, *A Portrait of Lord Nelson*

Warner, *Battle*   O. Warner, *The Battle of the Nile*

Waugh   Alec Waugh, *A Family of Islands: A
                              History of the West Indies*

Whitley   W. T. Whitley, *Artists and Their Friends
                              1700–1799*

Wickwar   W. H. Wickwar, *The Struggle for the
                              Freedom of the Press*

Wilenski   R. H. Wilenski, *Flemish Painters,* Vol. I

Woodruff   Philip Woodruff, *The Men Who Gov-
                              erned India*

Woolf   Leonard Woolf, *After the Deluge*

REFERENCES

PART I, CHAPTER 1

1. Waugh, 95
2. *Proceedings*
3. See Staunton, *passim*
4. Collis, 288–89
5. Rudé, 23, 25
6. *Gentleman's Magazine*, 257
7. Cf. *Lady's Magazine*, 186, 42, 90
8. *Annual Register*, 1799, 259
9. Sloane, II, 52

PART I, CHAPTER 2

1. Warner, 125
2. *London Chronicle*, July 12–14
3. Bryant, 222, 231
4. Buer, 22; Bryant, 42; but see Cobban, I, 48, who estimates the French in 1789 as 26,000,000
5. Cf. Bryant, *passim*
6. Bland, Brown & Tawney, 681–82
7. Douglas, xi, 582; Bland, Brown & Tawney, 683–89. Figures in *European Magazine*, 410
8. *Annual Register*, 1798, 75
9. Moore, I, 261
10. *Annual Register*, "Public Papers," 225; Herold, 36
11. *Annual Register*, "Occurrences," Feb. 11, May 22, July 21; *Lady's Magazine*, 94
12. Bryant, 246
13. Committee of Secrecy, appendixes, 27 sqq.
14. Smith, I, 28
15. Bryant, 9; cf. Plumb, 24
16. Bryant, 10
17. Buer, 38; Trevelyan, III, 260

18. Cf. Hammond, 143
19. Bland, Brown & Tawney, 531, from the Commons' *Journals* of July 19, 1797
20. P. 52, quoted in Bland, Brown & Tawney, 532
21. See Hammond, 34, for their methods and origins
22. Eden, II, 168
23. Committee of Secrecy, xxii, Appendix No. 17 sqq.
24. Postgate, 74
25. Bryant, 212 sqq.
26. Postgate, 72
27. Gardner, 16, 17
28. Gardner, 20
29. *Parliamentary History*, XXXIII, 700–15, reprinted in Bland, Brown & Tawney, 554 sqq.
30. Perceval in Bland, Brown & Tawney, 496; Bronowski, 12; Plumb, 21
31. Cobbett, XXIX, 409
32. Wyvill Papers, III, App. 189 sqq., quoted in Douglas, XI
33. Douglas, XI, 224 sqq.
34. See *European Magazine*, April; *Annual Register*, "Occurrences," January
35. *European Magazine*, April
36. *Annual Register*, 95 sqq.; *European Magazine*, April
37. Parry & Sherlock, 160
38. Bronowski, 74
39. Jaeger, 28 sqq.
40. Thompson, 119
41. Bronowski, 163
42. Thompson, Ch. XI
43. Thompson, Ch. XI
44. Cole & Postgate, 162; Wickwar (who considers the last act "harmless"), 30; Douglas, XI, 319; Keynes, 949

45. Thompson, 137 sqq.
46. Rudkin, 99; Committee of
    Secrecy, xxviii, xxx, 25, 30
47. Thompson, 172
48. *Holcroft*, diary entry Nov. 20,
    1798
49. *European Magazine*, April
50. *Lady's Magazine*, 238; Hob-
    house, 32
51. *European Magazine*, January
52. Thompson, 83
53. *Gentleman's Magazine*, 464
54. Cf. George, 270 sqq.
55. George, 274
56. *Gentleman's Magazine*, April
57. *Lady's Magazine*, April; *Euro-
    pean Magazine*, April; Plumb,
    16
58. *Newgate Calendar*, "Jeremiah
    Lewis Avershaw"
59. Buer, 82 sqq.
60. Encyclopaedia Britannica,
    3 ed., "London"
61. Buer, 83, 104, 256
62. *Holcroft* diary, June 24,
    Oct. 28
63. *Lady's Magazine*, Aug. 2
64. Glasgow
65. Society of Arts, XVI
66. Buer, 162
67. Douglas, 631; *Annual Register*,
    1798, "Anecdotes," 254; Buer,
    Ch. XIV
68. *British Critic*, 311, 450
69. Quoted in Buer, 182
70. Jones, 5
71. Jones, 55
72. Jones, 62
73. Whitley, II, 219
74. *Holcroft*, 246
75. Whitley, II, 219 sqq.
76. Keynes, 980
77. Bronowski, 146
78. Encyclopaedia Britannica,
    14 ed., "Wordsworth"
79. *Lyrical Ballads,* i
80. Littledale, xv
81. Coleridge, *Biographia Liter-
    aria*, II, xiv; cf. Moorman, I,
    374
82. See notes in Littledale

83. Howe, 65; cf. Moorman, I,
    397
84. Howe, 60
85. Howe, 62

PART I, CHAPTER 3

1. Army and Navy, 1966
2. Cunnington, 215
3. *Lady's Magazine*, 212 sqq.;
   Moorman, I, 60. Wordsworth
   signed himself "Axiologus,"
   a Greek translation of his
   name; the poem was published
   in the *European Magazine*,
   March 1787.
4. Cunnington, 100
5. *Lady's Magazine*, 285
6. Cabet, IV, 375; but compare
   Geyl, *Encounters*, II, 2
7. For what follows, see Lefebvre,
   21–22, 101; Aulard, IV, 123;
   Sloane, I, 339
8. Lefebvre, 141
9. See *Quellen, passim*
10. Lefebvre, 49 sqq.
11. Conway, 267
12. Lefebvre, 7, 15
13. Lefebvre, 125, 129
14. Cobban, I, 262 sqq.
15. Cobban, II, 10
16. Lefebvre, 12
17. Woolf, I, 151–52. "Go and do
    your mess on history" is the
    nearest translation of Louis
    XV's epitaph.
18. Cobban, I, 235; Sloane, I,
    276
19. Warner, *Battle*, 103; Lefebvre,
    Ch. VI
20. Dejoint, Annexe 3
21. *Annual Register*, 1799, 231
    sqq.
22. Cobban, I, 180
23. Wilenski, 409, 424
24. Wilenski, 411
25. Aulard, IV, 87 sqq.; Lefebvre,
    96–101
26. Dommanget, 37; Postgate, 54–
    60

PART I, CHAPTER 4

1. Dejoint, 233
2. Howard, 273
3. Lefebvre, 130
4. *Hollande,* 136
5. *Hollande,* 114 and *passim*
6. *Hollande,* 76 sqq.
7. *Hollande,* 152–76; *Annual Register,* 1799, 228; *European Magazine,* 115–17
8. *Hollande,* 204
9. Wilenski, I, 421, 422
10. Wilenski, 409, 429, 574, 775
11. Wilenski, 405
12. Laborie, I, 174
13. Laborie, I, 161–70
14. Laborie, I, 194–200
15. Laborie, I, 237
16. *Annual Register,* 1799, 177 sqq.
17. Lefebvre, 118
18. *Quellen,* xx sqq.; Lefebvre, 118; *Annual Register,* 1798, 311
19. *Quellen,* xxvii; Lefebvre, 118
20. *Quellen,* xxviii–xxxi, Docs. 109, 291; *Annual Register,* 1799, 191 sqq.
21. *Quellen,* Doc. 122
22. Rudé, 193
23. Aulard, IV, 60
24. *Annual Register,* 1798, 308
25. Cabet, IV, 376; Lefebvre, 117
26. *Annual Register,* 1798, 305

PART II, CHAPTER 1

1. Herold, 1
2. Warner, 97
3. Warner, *Battle,* 28
4. Herold, 22, 47
5. The *Times,* and also Pitt, cited in Herold, 35
6. Howard, decrees, 300 sqq.
7. Quoted in Guedalla, 215
8. Bourrienne, II, 231–33
9. Sloane, I, 48, 63
10. Sloane, I, 63 sqq., 39
11. Cf. Walpole, 214
12. Sloane, I, 155

13. Sloane, I, 224
14. Cf. Rudé, 171
15. Geyl, 252
16. *Letters of Napoleon,* II, under dates
17. D'Antraigues, quoted in Sloane, II, 29
18. See Howard, Doc. 75, note
19. Gastine, 291
20. Rose, I, 196
21. *Annual Register,* 1799, 222
22. Las Cases, I, 504
23. *Annual Register,* Sept. 1
24. *Annual Register,* 1798, Oct., 132
25. *Lady's Magazine,* 425
26. Moorehead, 81
27. Herold, 91
28. See Bonaparte's dispatch to the Directory, captured by the British, in *European Magazine,* November, 337
29. Bourrienne, I, 261
30. *European Magazine,* November
31. Herold, 99
32. Herold, 136
33. Howard, decree, 364
34. Al Jabarti, VI, 36
35. Howard, decree, 357
36. Howard, decree, 333
37. Herold, 175
38. See Denon, particularly "Portique de Latopolis" and the two "Temples de l'Apollinopolis"
39. Quoted in Moorehead, 125
40. Mahan, 80
41. Mahan, 106, 109
42. Warner, 68
43. Warner, 64
44. James Harrison, quoted in Warner, 97
45. Warner, 32
46. Buer, 163
47. Lady Hughes, quoted in Warner, 55. She used the verb "rehearse," which in her day had the meaning "repeat."
48. Mahan, 99
49. Trafalgar

50. Mahan, 93
51. Warner, 306 (speaking of the *Victory,* but there is no reason to believe the *Vanguard* was different)
52. Mahan, 102 and map facing
53. Mahan, 107
54. Trafalgar, 5
55. By Mahan, for example, 110
56. *European Magazine,* 336
57. Herold, 218
58. Howard, xvii; cf. Herold, 206
59. Herold, 101; Rose, I, 198

PART II, CHAPTER 2

1. Madden, IV, 429
2. Tone, I, 42
3. Tone, I, 43
4. Madden, I, 14
5. Curran, 65. See also an example of Curran's cross-examination in Hale, 165
6. Madden, I, 16, 24 sqq.
7. Madden, I, 90 sqq.
8. Madden, I, 127
9. Curran, 319
10. Madden, I, 140–48
11. Jacob, 48
12. Madden, IV, 228
13. Curran, 347. In 1803, during Robert Emmet's revolt, the thousandth chance of ill luck caused Shannon's brother to stop Kilwarden's carriage. "You are the man I want," he said, and killed him.
14. *Emmet Family,* 165 sqq.
15. Tone, I, 46 sqq.
16. Tone, I, 72
17. Tone, I, 150
18. Madden, II, 190; Nicolson, 91 sqq.
19. Madden, III, 35
20. Quoted in Connolly, 57
21. Byrne, I, 13
22. Nicolson, 120
23. Madden, I, 156
24. T. A. & R. Emmet, I, 118; Madden, I, 263

25. *Annual Register,* 1798, 83, 115–34, 151–52; "Public Papers," 184
26. Beresford, under dates mentioned
27. Moore, I, 271, 283, 287, 303
28. Madden, IV, 26
29. *Sham Squire,* 47; Madden, II, 178; Nicolson, 78
30. Madden, I, 302
31. *The Press,* 82; Madden, I, 311
32. Madden, I, 332 sqq.; Moore, 295
33. Byrne, I, 35, 279; Madden, I, 318
34. Madden, II, 254
35. Madden, II, 250
36. Madden, I, 354. "I was very near to the Duke of Wellington and observed him closely . . . my impression was that this occurrence shook his faith in the permanence of the regime of Toryism."
37. Madden, I, 100 sqq.
38. Madden, IV, 160
39. *Barère,* 101
40. *Secret Service,* 7
41. Madden, I, 531
42. Madden, I, 372; *Secret Service:* accounts showing an impressive sequence of £1,000 checks to Reynolds in 1798 and '99
43. *Sham Squire,* 317
44. Madden, IV, 45
45. Madden, II, 448
46. *Secret Service,* 120
47. *Sham Squire,* 113; *Secret Service,* 149; Madden, I, 393, II, 438–47, IV, 572; Inglis, 55, 56
48. *Secret Service,* 132; Madden, II, 412–20, 433–37
49. Madden, II, 447–50, 456–59
50. Madden, IV, 251 sqq., 344, 372
51. Madden, IV, 58
52. Byrne, I, 49–64
53. Madden, IV, 427 sqq.

54. Byrne, I, 76, 87, 137, 180, 229, 265, 273
55. Moore, 311
56. Byrne, I, 311; Madden, IV, 143–47
57. Committee of Secrecy, document, 28
58. Edgeworth, 381
59. MacDermot, 287; *European Magazine*, September, October, 212, 277; *London Chronicle*, September
60. Text in *European Magazine*, September, 284
61. MacDermot, 274, 263
62. MacDermot, 292–93
63. Madden, II, 170
64. Curran, 315; Madden, II, 124, 137–39; MacDermot, 299; Moore, 328
65. *European Magazine*, September

PART II, CHAPTER 3

1. For example, Vaucaire
2. Korngold, ix
3. Waugh, 127
4. Descourtilz, quoted in Korngold, 17
5. See references in Korngold, Ch. 3
6. See Oldfather, xiii; for the name see p. i (*doulos epiktetos genomen*)
7. Oldfather, xvii
8. *Epictetus*, I, i, 10–13 and 28–32
9. *Epictetus*, I, ii, 33
10. *Epictetus*, I, ii, 12–23
11. *Epictetus*, IV, i, 30–32
12. Gellius, XVII,19, quoting Favorinus
13. Parry & Sherlock, 163
14. This account is based on that of Celigny-Ardouin, quoted in Korngold, 66 sqq. Other accounts (*e.g.*, Parry & Sherlock, 166; Cole, 39) give Toussaint a far less important role.
15. Korngold, 72

16. Parry & Sherlock, 184
17. Waugh, 171
18. Bryant, 139
19. Korngold, 113
20. A. M. Métral, in Korngold, 111
21. Quoted in Korngold, 85, and Cole, 59
22. Quoted in Korngold, 144
23. *European Magazine*, July, 64
24. Beard, 98
25. *Annual Register*, 1799, 254
26. Cole, 192–93. The names are those of villages which actually existed.
27. Encyclopaedia Britannica, 14 ed., XI, 82

PART II, CHAPTER 4

1. *E.g.*, in *Federalist*, No. 47
2. Conway, 228
3. Cunliffe, 155
4. Chinard, 8 sqq.
5. Chinard, 13
6. Bowers, 326
7. The exception is Tom Paine. MacDermot, 238.
8. Haraszti, 4
9. Conway, 268
10. Haraszti, 2–3
11. Adams, III, 189
12. Haraszti, 5
13. Chinard, 321
14. Bowers, 92; Stuart portrait
15. Bowers, 316
16. Haraszti, 38
17. Little, 357
18. Chinard, 227
19. Chinard, 304
20. Hofstadter, 13
21. Bowers, 322, 84
22. Hirst, 289
23. Bowers, 30
24. Hirst, 354 sqq.
25. Haraszti, 5
26. Cunliffe, 142
27. Hirst, 327
28. Chinard, 272
29. *Annual Register,* 1798, 244
30. Bowers, 362

31. Little, 438
32. Cunliffe, 145
33. *European Magazine,* May, prints a convenient summary. Cf. Cooper, 89
34. Bowers, 360
35. Bowers, 370
36. *Annual Register,* 1798, 131
37. Little, 447, 451
38. Hirst, 348
39. Hirst, 351, 352
40. Hirst, 353
41. Chinard, 285
42. Commons, I, 109–10
43. *Annual Register,* 1799, 81 sqq.
44. *Annual Register,* 1799, 79
45. *Annual Register,* 1798, 244
46. Bowers, 380

PART III, CHAPTER 1

1. Mahan, 112
2. Mahan, 105; Warner, 169, 179, 219
3. Giglioli, 72
4. Giglioli, 72, 74
5. Cf. Midon, *passim,* a most interesting parallel
6. Giglioli, 24 sqq.
7. Acton, 123, 138, 141
8. Acton, 131, 178
9. Acton, 294
10. Giglioli, 49; Croce, 238
11. Duval, quoted in Giglioli, 58
12. Warner, 181
13. Acton, 313
14. *Annual Register,* 1799, 273

PART III, CHAPTER 2

1. Beatson, 2 sqq.
2. Woodruff, I, Ch. V
3. Warner, *Battle,* 41
4. Beatson, App. III
5. Text in Beatson, App. I
6. *Supplementary Despatches,* I, 53
7. *Supplementary Despatches,* I, 52
8. Woodruff, 200, 206
9. *Supplementary Despatches,* I, 68
10. *Supplementary Despatches,* I, 86, 87, 109
11. *Supplementary Despatches,* I, 73
12. *Supplementary Despatches,* I, 90
13. Beatson, 21
14. Beatson, App. VII
15. Beatson, Apps. X and XII
16. Guedalla, 90

PART III, CHAPTER 3

1. *Lady's Magazine,* 233
2. Sandeman, 30–31
3. Pares, 279, 289; Pokrovsky, I, 124
4. *London Chronicle,* November-December; *Annual Register,* 1799, 260 sqq.
5. *Lady's Magazine,* December
6. *Annual Register,* 1799, 268
7. Sandeman, 31

INDEX

237